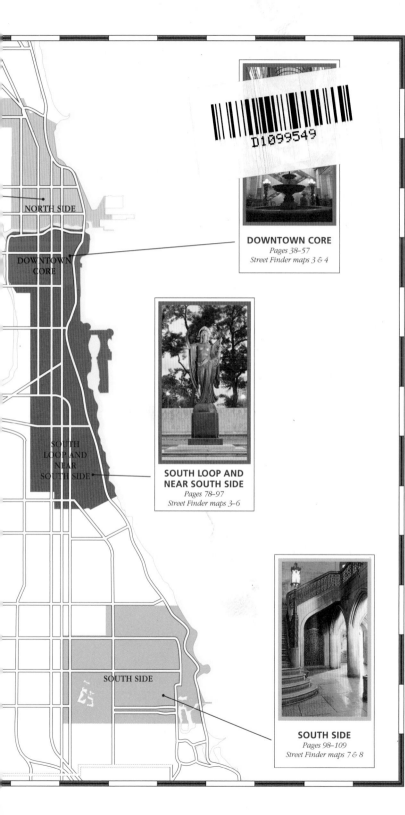

NORTH SIDE

DOWNTOWN
CORE

SOUTH
LOOP AND
NEAR
SOUTH SIDE

SOUTH SIDE

DOWNTOWN CORE
Pages 38–57
Street Finder maps 3 & 4

**SOUTH LOOP AND
NEAR SOUTH SIDE**
Pages 78–97
Street Finder maps 3–6

SOUTH SIDE
Pages 98–109
Street Finder maps 7 & 8

D1099549

EYEWITNESS TRAVEL
CHICAGO

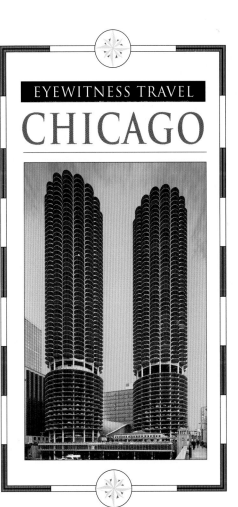

EYEWITNESS TRAVEL

CHICAGO

MAIN CONTRIBUTORS:
LORRAINE JOHNSON AND JOHN RYAN

DK

LONDON, NEW YORK,
MELBOURNE, MUNICH AND DELHI
www.dk.com

PRODUCED BY International Book Productions,
Part of Denise Schon Books Inc.
Toronto, Canada

PROJECT EDITOR AND ART DIRECTOR Barbara Hopkinson
EDITOR Judy Phillips
DESIGNERS Dietmar Kokemohr, Stella Powelczyk
EDITORIAL AND MAP ASSISTANCE Terri Rothman

PICTURE RESEARCH
Karen Taylor Permissions and Photo Research

MAIN CONTRIBUTORS
Lorraine Johnson, John Ryan

PHOTOGRAPHER
Andrew Leyerle

ILLUSTRATOR
William Band

Reproduced by Colourscan, Singapore
Printed and bound by South China Printing Co. Ltd., China

First published in Great Britain in 2001
by Dorling Kindersley Limited
80 Strand, London WC2R 0RL

Reprinted with revisions 2003, 2004, 2006, 2008, 2010

Copyright 2001, 2010 © Dorling Kindersley Limited, London
A Penguin Company

MIX
Paper from
responsible sources
FSC™ C018179
www.fsc.org

Nuclear Energy by Henry Moore at
University of Chicago *(see p100)*

CONTENTS

HOW TO USE THIS GUIDE 6

INTRODUCING CHICAGO

Twisted Columns by Ricardo Bofill,
R.R. Donnelley Building *(see p55)*

◁ Previous pages: *Sundial Sculpture* by Henry Moore outside the Adler Planetarium and Astronomy Museum

The ornate lobby of the Palmer House Hilton (see p140)

Raptor perched on a tree branch in
Washington Park (see p104)

Painted-glass window in St. James
Episcopal Cathedral (see p67)

Street-by-street map of South Loop (see pp80–81)

HOW TO USE THIS GUIDE

This DK Eyewitness travel guide helps you get the most from your stay in Chicago. *Introducing Chicago* locates the city geographically, sets modern Chicago in its historical context, and describes events through the entire year. *Chicago at a Glance* highlights the city's top attractions. The main sightseeing section of the book is *Chicago Area by Area*. It describes the city sights, with photographs, maps, and drawings. It also offers suggestions for

day trips outside the city center. *Beyond Chicago* delves into destinations in the region ideal for either day trips or longer sojourns, such as weekend getaways. Restaurant and hotel recommendations, as well as specially selected information about shops and entertainment, are found in *Travelers' Needs*. The *Survival Guide* gives practical information on everyday needs, from using Chicago's medical system and public transportation to the telephone system.

FINDING YOUR WAY AROUND THE SIGHTSEEING SECTION

Each of the sightseeing areas in Chicago is color-coded for easy reference. Each chapter opens with a description of the area and a list of sights to be covered, located by numbers on an area map. This is followed

by a Street-by-Street map, illustrating an interesting part of the area. Finding your way around the chapter is made simple by the numbering system used throughout. Sights outside Chicago have a regional map.

Each area has color-coded thumb tabs.

1 Area Map
For easy reference, the sights in each area are numbered and plotted on a map of the area. The map also shows CTA and Metra stations and major parking areas, as well as indicating the area covered by the Street-by-Street map. The sights are also shown on the Chicago Street Finder on pages 192–205.

Locator map

A locator map shows where you are in relation to other areas in the city center.

A suggested route takes in some of the most interesting streets in the area.

2 Street-by-Street Map
This gives a bird's-eye view of the most important part of each sightseeing area. The numbering of the sights ties in with the area map and the fuller descriptions on the pages that follow.

The list of star sights recommends the places that no visitor should miss.

CHICAGO AREA MAP

The colored areas shown on this map *(see inside front cover)* are the four main sightseeing areas – each covered by a full chapter in *Chicago Area by Area (see pp36–109)*. The four areas are highlighted on other maps throughout the book. In *Chicago at a Glance (see pp20–31)*, for example, they help locate the top sights.

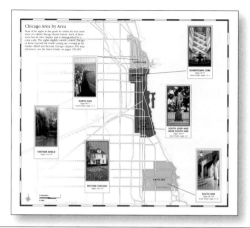

Numbers refer to each sight's position on the area map and its place in the chapter.

Practical information provides all you need to know to visit each sight, including a map reference to the *Chicago Street Finder (see pp192–205)*.

3 Detailed information
All the important sights in Chicago are described individually. They are listed in order, following the numbering on the area map. Practical information such as address, telephone number, and opening hours is provided for each sight. The key to the symbols used is on the back flap.

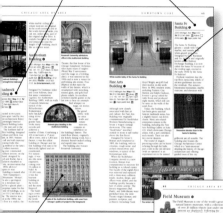

The visitors' checklist provides all the practical information needed to plan your visit.

Façades of important buildings are often shown to illustrate their architectural style, and to help you recognize them quickly.

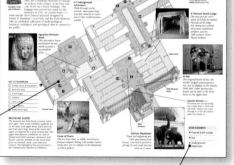

4 Chicago's major sights
These are given two or more full pages in the sightseeing area where they are found. Museums and galleries have color-coded floor plans to help you find important exhibits.

Stars indicate the features no visitor should miss.

INTRODUCING CHICAGO

FOUR GREAT DAYS IN CHICAGO

Chicago is a city full of things to see and do, and is well-known for its excellent shopping, influential architecture, renowned museums, and many cultural institutions. The four itineraries suggested below include a variety of sights and activities, and make for a great introduction to the city's

Shedd Aquarium fish sculpture

history and major landmarks. You can follow the itineraries, or sample something from each. The sights and entertainments are cross-referenced to detailed entries in the guide, and are easily accessible by foot or public transportation. The price guides cover transport, lunch, and admission fees.

Chicago skyline with John Hancock Center and lakeside

CITY OF SKYSCRAPERS

- Breakfast at Lou Mitchell's
- See stunning Willis Tower
- Gaze at historic architecture
- Enjoy the views at the top of John Hancock Center

TWO ADULTS allow at least $50

Morning
Start your day with pancakes at the legendary diner **Lou Mitchell's**, 565 W. Jackson Blvd. Two blocks east, the glass-and-steel **Willis Tower** (see p42) is the tallest building in the West at 1,450 ft (442 m) tall; visit the 103rd-floor Skydeck and The Ledge for views of four states on clear days. The **Monadnock Building** (see p44), a few blocks west, is a lesson in 19th-century architectural history. Finished in 1891, its north half is a traditional structure with 6-ft-(1.85-m) thick walls; the south half, finished in 1893, has a more contemporary steel-frame construction. A five-minute walk north, the

1895 **Reliance Building** (see p50), is an airy, terra cotta-clad gem – forerunner of the modern skyscraper. North on State St. toward the river you'll see more modern architecture. Built in 1964, the two towers of **Marina City** (see p66) rise like twin corn cobs, and to the east is Mies van der Rohe's stark **IBM Building** (see p66). Facing each other are the more Classical **Wrigley Building** (see p62), clad in white terra cotta and **Tribune Tower** (see p62), a Neo-Gothic structure.

Afternoon
After a quick bite on N. Michigan Ave., stroll up to the **Water Tower** (see p63), a Gothic limestone survivor of the Great Chicago Fire of 1871. The interior showcases Chicago-themed photographs. Ahead one block looms the **John Hancock Center** (see p64), for now the city's fourth tallest at 1,127 ft (343 m). Try the screened skywalk, or enjoy the views for the price of a drink in the Signature lounge.

FUN FOR THE FAMILY

- Funfair fun at Navy Pier
- Animal adventures at Lincoln Park Zoo
- Butterfly heaven at Peggy Notebaert Nature Museum

FAMILY OF FOUR allow at least $100

Morning
Jutting out into Lake Michigan just east of downtown, **Navy Pier** (see p65) is the city's most popular attraction and a great place to start a day out with the kids. From interactive exhibits at the Chicago Children's Museum to IMAX movies, boat cruises and a 15-story-high Ferris wheel, there's enough at this 50-acre (20-hectare) park to keep the family busy for the morning. Stop for lunch at the food court or check out the scene in Joe's Be-Bop Café and Jazz Emporium where there's live music daily.

Landing point for Navy Pier, in front of the Ferris wheel

Afternoon

For an animal-themed afternoon, take the bus to the free **Lincoln Park Zoo** *(see pp112–13)*, which teems with rhinos, giraffes, gorillas, snakes, polar bears, and more than 1,000 other animals from the world over. Be sure to visit the Pritzker Family Children's Zoo, which simulates a walk in the woods with exhibits of wolves, bears, beavers, otters and other woodland creatures.

If you still have the energy, pay a visit to the **John G. Shedd Aquarium** *(see pp96–7)*, thronging with sea otters, dolphins, whales, and over two dozen sharks. The Underwater Viewing gallery of the Oceanarium will captivate the kids.

The impressive tyrannosaurus rex skeleton at the Field Museum

MUSEUMS & CULTURE

- **A morning at the Art Institute of Chicago**
- **T. rex at the Field Museum**
- **An interactive Planetarium**

TWO ADULTS allow at least $80

Morning

Spend the morning at the **Art Institute of Chicago** *(see pp46–49)*, one of the world's finest museums, just south of Millennium Park on the east side of Michigan Ave. It has some exquisite works of American art such as Grant Wood's *American Gothic*, Edward Hopper's *Nighthawks*, and several iconic pieces by Georgia O'Keeffe. Admire its French Impressionist collection, the centerpiece

of which is Seurat's *A Sunday on La Grande Jatte–1884*. Also worth checking out is the new Modern Wing, opened in 2009 and designed by Pritzker Prize-winning architect Renzo Piano. For lunch, grab a bite in the lower-level café or pop out to an eaterie on Michigan Avenue nearby.

Afternoon

Catch the No. 146 bus from State St. to the Museum Campus and head for the **Field Museum** *(see pp86–9)*. Inside, you'll come face-to-face with the largest and best-preserved T. rex skeleton ever discovered. Stroll through "Evolving Planet," a look at Earth's 4 billion-year history. Head to the adjacent lakeside **Adler Planetarium** *(see pp86–9)* and try out its interactive exhibit of America's space program.

SHOP TILL YOU DROP

- **Wonderful stores on Michigan Avenue**
- **Boutiques on Oak Street**
- **Upscale elegance on Armitage Avenue**

TWO ADULTS allow at least $30 (cost of transport and food)

Morning

Start your day on Michigan Avenue, one of the world's greatest retail areas, where names such as Crate & Barrel, Gap, and Banana Republic compete with department stores and

Walkers and shoppers on busy Michigan Avenue

shopping centers such as the famous **Water Tower Place** *(see p61)*, the nation's first vertical mall. An all-white interior packed with iPods and iMacs makes the Apple Store a stylish must-stop for the high-tech set. Farther north, Niketown shows off the latest in shoes and sports wear. Or take in the elegant scene of **Oak Street** *(see p64)*, where upscale boutiques such as Hermès, Prada, Kate Spade, and Tod's reside. Lunch in style (Italian-American cuisine) around the corner at Fred's (15 E. Oak St., 312-596-1111) within Barneys department store.

Afternoon

Take the El to the Armitage Brown Line stop for the boutiques of Armitage Avenue district where it's all top-quality, from truffles at Vosges Haut-Chocolat (951 W. Armitage Ave.) to hand-made stationery at Paper Source (No. 919). Or catch the No. 73 bus west to Damen Ave. and stroll south to trendy **Wicker Park** *(see p114)* for some great shopping as well as interesting galleries and cafés.

Exciting and interactive exhibits at the Adler Planetarium

Putting Chicago on the Map

Chicago, a city of almost 3 million people, covers
228 sq miles (591 sq km) of the US's Midwest.
Situated at the southwest edge of Lake Michigan, the
world's fifth-largest freshwater body, Chicago claims
29 miles (47 km) of lakefront. Two airports handle
international and internal flights. There are also
interstate highways and rail links serving both the
East and West Coasts and other parts of the country,
and Canada.

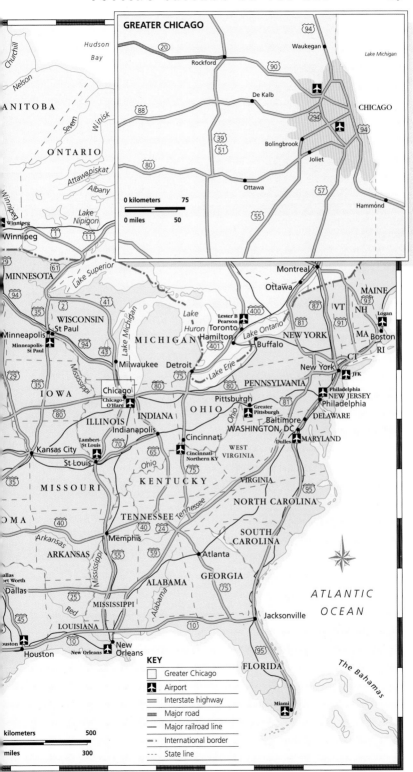

GREATER CHICAGO

Waukegan

Lake Michigan

Rockford

De Kalb

CHICAGO

Bolingbrook

Joliet

Ottawa

Hammond

0 kilometers   75

0 miles   50

Churchill

Nelson

Hudson Bay

MANITOBA

Seem

ONTARIO

Winisk

Attawapiskat

Albany

Lake Nipigon

Winnipeg

Winnipeg

Lake Superior

MINNESOTA

WISCONSIN

St Paul

Minneapolis

Minneapolis-St Paul

Milwaukee

Lake Michigan

MICHIGAN

Lake Huron

Detroit

Lake Erie

Toronto

Hamilton

Lester B Pearson

Lake Ontario

Buffalo

NEW YORK

Montreal

Ottawa

VT

NH

MAINE

Logan

MA   Boston

RI

CT

New York

JFK

Chicago

Chicago O'Hare

IOWA

ILLINOIS

INDIANA

OHIO

Pittsburgh

Greater Pittsburgh

PENNSYLVANIA

Philadelphia

NEW JERSEY

Philadelphia

DELAWARE

Indianapolis

Lambert-St Louis

Kansas City

St Louis

MISSOURI

KENTUCKY

Ohio

Cincinnati

Cincinnati-Northern KY

WEST VIRGINIA

Baltimore

WASHINGTON, DC

Dulles

MARYLAND

VIRGINIA

NORTH CAROLINA

OMA

TENNESSEE

Tennessee

Memphis

Arkansas

ARKANSAS

Mississippi

SOUTH CAROLINA

Atlanta

ALABAMA

GEORGIA

ATLANTIC OCEAN

Dallas

Fort Worth

MISSISSIPPI

Alabama

Red

LOUISIANA

Houston

New Orleans

New Orleans

Jacksonville

FLORIDA

The Bahamas

Miami

KEY

Greater Chicago

Airport

Interstate highway

Major road

Major railroad line

International border

State line

kilometers   500

miles   300

THE HISTORY OF CHICAGO

The third largest city in the US is world famous for magnificent and innovative architecture, its colorful and turbulent political history and significance as a national transportation hub, the now-vanished stockyards, as well as its educational institutes and vibrant cultural venues.

The French missionary Jacques Marquette and French-Canadian explorer Louis Jolliet were the first Europeans to record a visit to this spot at the foot of Lake Michigan, in 1673. The peaceful, friendly local Potawatomi Indians called the low-lying swampy area "Checaugou," which likely means "wild onion" or "skunk cabbage." Jolliet and Marquette used this Indian name on the maps they drew, which were then used by later explorers.

French-Canadian explorer Louis Jolliet

More than 100 years passed before the first permanent settlement was established in 1779 by Jean Baptiste Point du Sable, an African-American trader from the Caribbean. Du Sable and his Indian wife built a house on the north bank near the mouth of the Chicago River.

A treaty negotiated with local Indian tribes in 1795 gave US citizens access to most of Ohio and a 6-sq-mile (15.5-sq-km) area of land where the Chicago River emptied into Lake Michigan – now the heart of Chicago's downtown.

In 1803, the US Army built Fort Dearborn along the river to protect settlers from the Indians, the British, and the French. Fort Dearborn was destroyed during the War of 1812 between the US and Britain; soldiers and their families were slaughtered by the Indians, allies of the British, as they fled the fort. Although the fort was rebuilt in 1816 and Illinois became a state in 1818, the area remained Indian territory until it was ceded in 1833 and the Indians were relocated to reservations by the federal government. That year, Chicago became a town.

EARLY CHICAGO

With the land open for development, the rivers gained importance as shipping routes. In 1837, Chicago, its population now over 4,000, received city status. The expansion of the lake ports, completion of the Illinois and Michigan Canal connecting the Great Lakes with the Mississippi River, and arrival of the railroads spurred rapid growth. Public schools were established in 1840, and by 1847 the new city had two daily newspapers. From 1855 to 1858, Chicago literally pulled itself out of the mud, jacking up downtown buildings and filling in the swamp muck with soil *(see p57)*.

TIMELINE

1673 Explorers Jacques Marquette and Louis Jolliet arrive at "Checaugou"	**1779** First settlement in Chicago established by trader Jean Baptiste Point du Sable *Jean Baptiste Point du Sable*		**1803** Fort Dearborn built	**1848** Illinois & Michigan Canal completed *(see pp118–19)*
1650	**1700**	**1750**	**1800**	**1850**
1682 Frenchman La Salle explores area and establishes forts		**1783** British cede land that is now Chicago to the newly established US government *A Potawatomi chief*	**1825** Erie Canal opens **1837** Chicago incorporates as a city	**1858** Chicago becomes US's chief railroad hub **1847** *Chicago Tribune* newspaper founded

◁ **A contemporary lithograph depicting the Great Chicago Fire of 1871**

Chicago's proximity to both the Mississippi River and the Great Lakes confirmed it as the nation's transportation hub. By 1860, 15 railroad companies had terminals here. Christmas Day 1865 saw the opening of the gigantic Union Stock Yards, the city's largest employer for decades. (It eventually closed in 1971.) Meatpacking laws, along with the Food and Drug Administration, were created after Upton Sinclair's stirring 1906 book, *The Jungle,* revealed the poor conditions of such stockyards.

Detail of cow (1879) on the archway to Union Stock Yards

Although meat processing remained Chicago's major industry, positioning the city as the US's primary supplier, the grain-handling and manufacturing industries were also strong in 19th-century Chicago.

THE GREAT FIRE
The Great Chicago Fire of 1871 burned for 36 hours, October 8 to 10, destroying most of the buildings in downtown Chicago, all of which were made of wood. At least 300 people died, and about 100,000 – one-third of the population – were left homeless. A cow, belonging to a certain Mrs. O'Leary, was blamed for kicking over a lantern and starting the fire. Although an inquiry confirmed that the blaze started in the O'Leary shed, the cause of the fire was not determined.

An 1874 bylaw prohibited the building of wooden structures downtown. Consequently, Chicago architect William Le Baron Jenney *(see pp26–7)* designed the Home Insurance Building (1884), a nine-story structure supported by a steel skeleton, regarded by many to be the first skyscraper. Jenney's design paved the way for the canyons of tall buildings found in city centers today.

SOCIAL UNREST, SOCIAL REFORM
As Chicago's downtown rebuilt and the city continued to expand – to 500,000 inhabitants by 1880 – social divisions grew. In the 1873 Bread Riot, police trapped thousands of protesting hungry workers under a bridge, clubbing many to death. Four years later, during the 1877 national railroad strike, Chicago police fired on demonstrators, killing 30. On May 4, 1886, workers rallied at Haymarket Square to protest the police killing of two laborers demanding the shortening of the workday to eight hours. A bomb exploded in the midst of the police officers, starting a riot that

The aftermath of the Great Fire, as seen from Chicago Harbor

TIMELINE

1860 Abraham Lincoln nominated for US president at Republican Convention

Lincoln Statue, in Lincoln Park

1871 Great Chicago Fire

1874 City council prohibits the building of wooden structures downtown

1880 Chicago's population reaches 500,000

18 Haymark R

| 1860 | 1870 | 1880 |

1861 Civil War begins

1865 Union Stock Yards, world's biggest stockyard, opens

1873 Bread Riot

1879 Art Institute of Chicago *(see pp46–9)* founded as the Chicago Academy of Fine Arts

1884 World's first skyscraper *(see pp26–7)* built

Protesters clash with police in the 1873 Bread Riot

Christopher Columbus' journey to the Americas with the 1893 World's Columbian Exposition, held in Jackson Park *(see p105)*. Over 25 million visitors came to it, the largest fair yet to be held in the Americas. Despite a deep national economic depression, the city built a fabulous fairground, dubbed the "White City" because of its Neo-Classical white marble buildings. It was to have a huge impact on US architecture. Most of the buildings burned down or were vandalized after the fair.

eventually killed seven officers. The ensuing trial, in which eight men were charged with murder and four subsequently executed, is considered one of the worst miscarriages of justice in the US.

Into this social tumult stepped Jane Addams *(see p31)* and Ellen Gates Starr. In 1889, they founded Hull-House to help settle immigrants *(see p116)*. It would soon become a leader in US social welfare and reform.

PROGRESS, AND THE 1893 WORLD'S COLUMBIAN EXPOSITION

Downtown, other initiatives were underway. The Art Institute of Chicago *(see pp46–9)* was founded in 1879, and the Chicago Symphony Orchestra *(see p170)* and the University of Chicago *(see pp100–101)* in 1890. The elevated tramway opened in 1892, its circle around the commercial core giving the downtown the nickname "The Loop."

Chicago celebrated the 400th anniversary of

Guidebook for the 1893 World's Columbian Fair

GROWTH AND GROWING PAINS

By 1890, Chicago's population climbed past one million. Awareness of public health issues led to concern that the city discharged, directly or indirectly, most of its waste into the Chicago River, and from there into Lake Michigan, the source of drinking water. In 1900, the Chicago Sanitary and Ship Canal opened, and the direction of the Chicago River was reversed so that the river flowed away from the lake not into it *(see p57)*.

A 1903 Chicago disaster affected both urban design and bylaws nationwide. Nearly 600 people died when a fire tragically destroyed the Iroquois Theater on December 30 *(see p51)*. Investigators blamed the fatalities on the doors. Many opened inward: impossible to open with a frantic crowd pressed against them. Most US cities now require that doors of public buildings open outward.

By 1914, waves of immigrants from Europe

Speakeasy directions written in chalk

had arrived in Chicago. Industrialization now brought another wave: African Americans from the South, seeking work after being displaced from farm work by the cotton gin and other new machinery. Chicago's Black population skyrocketed, from about 14,000 in 1910 to almost 110,000 by the early 1920s. Previous arrivals did not always welcome the new migrants. A 1919 race riot that started at a segregated South Side beach raged for several days, leaving 38 dead and nearly 300 injured.

Speakeasies, illicit social clubs offering liquor despite the prohibition of alcohol, flourished in the 1920s and made way for the bootlegging gangster. The most famous gangster – and the one most closely linked to Chicago in the public mind – was Al Capone, who arrived in 1919 from New York. Capone is legendary for his bloody gang war. In the notorious 1929 St. Valentine's Day Massacre, seven mobsters from a rival gang were killed execution-style by mobsters loyal to Capone.

Almost as famous were Eliot Ness and his team, who collected the evidence of income-tax evasion that put Capone in prison in 1931, where he died 16 years later.

CHICAGO MILESTONES: 1920S–60S

The Chicago Municipal Airport (now Midway Airport) opened in 1927. From 1945 to 1958, it was the world's busiest airport, before being replaced by O'Hare, which was equipped to handle the new jetliners and is today one of the world's busiest airports.

The old airport brought visitors to the 1933–4 World's Fair. Showcasing innovative uses of electricity, the fair attracted 39 million people. Another kind of energy came to the fore when, in 1942, physicist Enrico Fermi from the University of Chicago conducted the world's first controlled atomic reaction (see p100).

Physicist Enrico Fermi

After World War II, the city's economy boomed, its population peaking at 3.6 million. New arrivals included musicians from the Mississippi Delta and by 1950, they were recording a new form of blues.

The 1950s saw many milestones: Carl Sandburg won the Pulitzer Prize for Poetry in 1951; and Ray Kroc's first McDonald's opened in 1955 in Des Plaines, just outside Chicago.

Chicago's O'Hare Airport, one of the world's busiest

TIMELINE

1920	1930	1940	1950	19
1928 Chicago River straightened to allow for expansion of downtown	**1933** Chicago hosts Century of Progress World's Fair	**1942** First controlled atomic chain reaction, at University of Chicago	**1953** Hugh Hefner publishes first issue of *Playboy* magazine	
1919 Mobster Al Capone arrives	**1929** St. Valentine's Day Massacre	**1931** Eliot Ness succeeds in convicting Al Capone	**1943** Chicago's first subway opens	**1955** Richard J. Daley elected mayor
				1959 White Sox win American League baseball pennant

Eliot Ness

Richard J. Daley, mayor of Chicago for 21 years

TURBULENT POLITICS

In 1955, Chicago elected Democrat Richard J. Daley as mayor, a position he held until his fatal heart attack in 1976. In 1966, Martin Luther King Jr. brought the civil rights movement to Chicago, challenging Daley's Whites-only political machine and the segregation of the Black population. Daley's administration survived the West Side riots, prompted by the assassination of King in Memphis, and the disastrous confrontations between police and demonstrators outside the Democratic National Convention, both in 1968. Daley was equally well known for his commitment to a clean city, in keeping with his motto "Keep Chicago beautiful."

Daley's successors include Jane Byrne, Chicago's first female mayor (1979–83), and Harold Washington, Chicago's first Black mayor (1983–7), called "the people's mayor" because he was considered to be in touch with the grassroots. Washington made significant structural changes in city operations before dying of a heart attack at his desk, shortly after his re-election as mayor in 1987.

In 1989, Chicagoans elected Richard M. Daley, son of former mayor Richard J. Daley, as mayor.

CHICAGO TODAY

In 1990, Chicago's title of "Second City" became an honorific, as the population of Los Angeles surpassed that of Chicago and became the largest in the US after New York. But Chicagoans continue to glory in the city's triumphs. It remains the US's largest transportation center and the financial capital of the Midwest. Chicago Board of Trade, founded in 1848, continues to be the most important grain market in the nation. Willis Tower (see p42) recaptured the title of World's Tallest Building in two of four categories in 1997. The Chicago Bulls won six NBA championships. The 1999 Cows on Parade, a public-art project of 300 fiberglass cows decorated by Chicago artists, delighted locals and visitors alike.

Chicago has had its share of recent disasters. In 1992, the Chicago River poured into a hole pierced in an abandoned tunnel in the Loop. Water filled downtown basements, threatening to sink the city center below the level of the original swampland.

As a mature city, Chicago offers superb public art and architecture, and natural, cultural, and gastronomical delights. The city's dynamism is sure to linger in the memories of its visitors for decades to come.

Willis Tower, one of the iconic sights of Chicago

1966 Martin Luther King Jr. brings civil rights movement to Chicago	1971 Union Stock Yards close	1979 Jane Byrne elected mayor of Chicago	1983 Harold Washington elected mayor of Chicago	1990 Chicago drops in ranking to third-largest US city	2008 Chicago resident Barack Obama becomes US president
					2004 Millennium Park opens (see p53)

1970		1980		1990		2000

1968 Democratic National Convention riots	1973 Willis Tower (see p42) opens as tallest building in world		1986 Refurbished Chicago Theatre reopens (see p54)	1992 Chicago River leaks into abandoned freight tunnel, threatening to collapse downtown	2005 White Sox win the World Series

Willis Tower

CHICAGO AT A GLANCE

More than 100 places of interest are described in the *Area by Area* and *Beyond Chicago* sections of this book. They range from the Gothic–style Rockefeller Memorial Chapel *(see p102)* to the Post-Modern James R. Thompson Center *(see p56),* from the offbeat neighborhood of Wicker Park *(see p114)* to tranquil Washington Park *(see p104).* To help make the most of your stay, the following ten pages are a time-saving guide to the best Chicago has to offer. The guide highlights the city's best museums and architecture, as well as the people and cultures that have given Chicago its unique character over the years. Below are the top ten tourist attractions that no visitor to Chicago should miss.

CHICAGO'S TOP TEN   TOURIST ATTRACTIONS

Museum of Science and Industry
See pp106–109

John G. Shedd Aquarium
See pp96–7

Magnificent Mile
See pp60–61

Willis Tower
See p42

Navy Pier
See p65

Art Institute of Chicago
See pp46–9

Millennium Park
See p53

Lincoln Park Zoo
See pp112–13

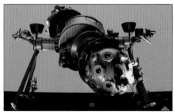

Adler Planetarium and Astronomy Museum
See pp92–3

Field Museum
See pp86–9

◁ View of Chicago's River North district (on the left) and the Loop (on the right)

Chicago's Best: Museums

Chicago has some of the world's finest museums, and
the buildings in which they are housed are often
works of art themselves. The Art Institute of Chicago,
world-renowned for its Impressionist and Post-
Impressionist paintings, and Museum Campus –
consisting of the Field Museum, Adler Planetarium, and
Shedd Aquarium – are prominent on any visitor's itinerary. There are many smaller museums, too, celebrating
Chicago's heritage and giving insight into the people
and events that have left their mark on the city.

North Side

Downtown Core

Chicago History Museum
*This museum traces Chicago's rich
history, beginning with its first explorers
and settlers, through the development of
the city, to major events in modern-
day Chicago (see p74).*

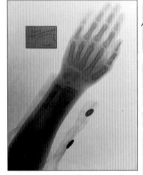

**International Museum of
Surgical Science**
*The history of medicine and
surgery, from blood-letting to
X-rays, is brought to life at this
fascinating museum (see p75).*

Chicago Cultural Center
*The great hall is one of many high-
lights in this much loved center.
Visitors can also enjoy theater, film,
dance, and music. Most productions
are free (see p52).*

Spertus Museum
*This Torah cover is part
of the outstanding
collection of art and
artifacts reflecting 5,000
years of Jewish culture
and ritual exhibited at this
museum (see p84).*

0 kilometers 2

0 miles 1

Museum of Contemporary Art
Cutting-edge modern works by European and American artists such as sculptor Alexander Calder are featured in permanent and rotating exhibits (see p65).

Art Institute of Chicago
One of the largest holdings of Impressionist and Post-Impressionist paintings outside France can be found here (see pp46–9).

Field Museum
An encyclopedic collection of objects relating to the earth's natural and cultural history are explored in vivid displays at this museum (see pp86–9).

Adler Planetarium and Astronomy Museum
One of the world's foremost planetariums, the Adler has a webcam atop its dome – offering a superb view of Chicago – and over 2,000 astronomical artifacts (see pp92–3).

Smart Museum of Art
The specialties within the wide-ranging collection of this compact museum are antiquities and Old Masters (see p103).

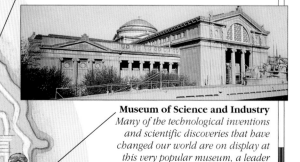

Museum of Science and Industry
Many of the technological inventions and scientific discoveries that have changed our world are on display at this very popular museum, a leader in interactive exhibits (see pp106–9).

Chicago's Best: Architecture

Chicago's downtown skyline is characterized by high-rises, both modern and historic, while a range of residential architecture styles, such as Queen Anne and Prairie, are found in the city's neighborhoods. After the 1871 fire *(see p16)* and subsequent ban on wood as a building material, the use of terra cotta and cast-iron – both fire resistant and durable – became prevalent. Terra cotta was also an excellent material for decorative carving and so sheaths many of the city's steel-frame buildings. A detailed overview of Chicago's architecture is found on pages 26–7.

North S

Downtow
Core

Crilly Court

The Crilly Court row houses (see p71), with their turrets and bays, are one of the finest examples of Queen Anne style in the city.

Newberry Library

Henry Ives Cobb, master of the Richardsonian Romanesque style, designed the library in 1890–93 (see p67). Its heavy stone walls and recessed, arched windows are typical of this style, popular in the second half of the 19th century.

333 Wacker Drive

A Post-Modern structure designed by the architect firm Kohn Pedersen Fox, this building (see pp56–7) was met with critical acclaim and local approval when constructed in 1983.

0 kilometers   2

0 miles   1

Harold Washington Library Cente

This Neo-Classical giant (see p82) allude to Chicago's many historic building through its varied architectural feature

John Hancock Center
The towering glass walls and horizontal beams of the John Hancock Center (see p64) are characteristic of the International Style.

Gage Group
These three buildings reflect different approaches to the Chicago School: two, designed by Holabird and Roche, have minimal exterior decoration; the third, with a façade designed by Louis Sullivan, is more ornate.

Water Tower
The Gothic Revival-style castellated tower is one of the city's best-loved landmarks (see p63).

Field Museum
Designed in white marble by Daniel H. Burnham, this monumental Neo-Classical building (1921) features a long colonnaded façade with Greek-style caryatids (see pp86–9).

South Loop and Near South Side

Christopher Bouton House
This villa-like residence, with its tall windows and dominant cornice, was built in 1873 in the Italianate style popular in 19th-century Chicago.

Robie House
Built 1908–1910, this house is considered by many to be Frank Lloyd Wright's Prairie School masterpiece (see pp102–103).

South Side

Exploring Chicago's Architecture

Carving on the Rookery

Chicago is world famous as a center of architectural innovation, a city where new building techniques have been developed and where architects have pushed the boundaries of creative expression. This reputation had its beginnings in the defining event of Chicago's history – the tragic fire of 1871. With a blank slate on which to build, architects rose to the challenge, transforming devastation into opportunity and reshaping the city. It was in Chicago that the world's first skyscraper was built, and here that Frank Lloyd Wright developed his distinctive Prairie School of architecture.

GOTHIC REVIVAL

Popular in the 1830s and 1840s, Gothic Revival was inspired by the medieval architecture of Europe, particularly of England. Steeply pitched roofs, pointed arches, turrets, and buttresses are typical features. One of Chicago's best examples of this style is the **Water Tower** (1869). Interest in Gothic continued through the 19th century and is reflected in many of the city's most impressive buildings, such as the **Fourth Presbyterian Church** (1914) and those of the **University of Chicago**.

ITALIANATE STYLE

The elegant Drake Hotel, built in the popular Italianate style

Popular from the mid- to late 1800s, the Italianate design style is based on the historic architecture of Italy: the villas of northern Italy and the palaces of the Italian Renaissance. Characteristic features include asymmetrical balancing, low-pitched roofs, projecting eaves, and ornate door and window designs, the windows often grouped into arcades. Two notable examples are the **Samuel M. Nickerson House** (1883) and the **Drake Hotel** (1920).

RICHARDSONIAN ROMANESQUE

Richardsonian Romanesque, or Romanesque Revival, was popularized in the US in the latter half of the 19th century by Bostonian Henry Hobson Richardson (1838–86). His architectural legacy is represented in Chicago by the severe yet subtly ornamented **Glessner House** (1887). Typical features of this style are heavy rough-cut stone, round arches, and deeply recessed windows. Richardson's influence can be seen in the work of Henry Ives Cobb, particularly Cobb's design of **Newberry Library** (1890–93) and the former home of the Chicago History Museum (*see p74*) at Dearborn and Ontario streets.

QUEEN ANNE

Mainly used in residential architecture, Queen Anne style was highly influential in Chicago from the mid- to late 1800s. The name does not reflect a historical period but was coined by English architect Richard Shaw. Queen Anne homes are built on a human scale. A mix of Classical, Tudor, and Colonial elements lead to a hybrid look. Victorian detailing, such as curlicue cutouts on the trim, is often prominent. **Crilly Court** (1885) and the **Olsen-Hansen Row Houses** (1886) are fine examples of Queen Anne style. There are also many Queen Anne houses to be found in the **Pullman Historic District**.

Crilly Court, the name of Crilly's son carved above the door

CHICAGO SCHOOL

Named after the city in which it developed, the commercial style of the Chicago School led to both an engineering and aesthetic revolution in architecture. William Le Baron Jenney created the first skyscraper when he designed the nine-story Home Insurance Building (1884; demolished 1929), using skeletal steel frames rather than the

BALLOON FRAME

Balloon-frame construction was first developed in Chicago by Augustine D. Taylor, in 1833 (though some credit George Washington Snow's 1932 Chicago warehouse as the first such construction). The name refers to the ease of construction: it was as simple as inflating a balloon, although critics said it referred to the ease with which the wind would blow away such structures. Raising a balloon-frame house required simply joining machine-cut lumber with machine-made nails, rather than interlocking time-consuming joints. Various interior and exterior surfaces could then be applied. Chicago's early balloon-frame houses fed the flames of the 1871 fire, but some built after the fire still exist in Old Town (*see pp70–71*).

conventional height-limiting, masonry load-bearing walls.

Jenney trained many of Chicago's celebrated architects, including Louis Sullivan, William Holabird, Daniel Burnham, and John Wellborn Root, whose architect firm designed several Chicago School buildings, such as the **Rookery** (1885–8) and the **Reliance Building** (1891–95). The new window style of these buildings, made possible by Jenney's structural innovation, became known as Chicago windows. Each consists of a large central glass pane, flanked by two slender windows that open.

Reliance Building, Chicago School

NEO-CLASSICAL OR BEAUX-ARTS

Neo-Classical, or Beaux-Arts, style became popular in Chicago once it was chosen as the design style for the 1893 World's Fair. Based on classical Greek and Roman architecture, with its columns, pilasters, and pediments, these buildings are often monumental in scale. Many of Chicago's most notable cultural institutions, such as the **Chicago Cultural Center** (1893–7), are housed in Neo-Classical buildings.

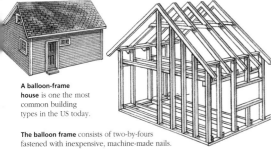

A balloon-frame house is one of the most common building types in the US today.

The balloon frame consists of two-by-fours fastened with inexpensive, machine-made nails.

PRAIRIE SCHOOL

In the first two decades of the 20th century, Frank Lloyd Wright developed a truly indigenous American architectural style. Reflecting the sweeping lines of the Midwestern landscape, Prairie style is characterized by low horizontal lines, projecting eaves, and rectangular windows. It is used mostly in residential architecture.

Oak Park is a treasure-trove of Wright-designed houses. Notable Wright buildings elsewhere in Chicago are **Robie House** (1908–1910) and **Charnley-Persky House** (1892).

Prairie School is considered a part of the Chicago School.

INTERNATIONAL STYLE

The international style developed primarily at Germany's Bauhaus School. Luminary Ludwig Mies van der Rohe immigrated to Chicago in 1938, after the Nazis closed the Bauhaus, and his ideas took root in the US. Simple, severe geometry and large expanses of glass are typical elements. One of the best places to see examples of Mies' "less is more" philosophy is at the **Illinois Institute of Technology** campus. Another landmark Mies building is the austere but beautifully proportioned **IBM Building** (1971).

Chicago firm Skidmore, Owings and Merrill, architects of the **John Hancock Center** (1969), **Willis Tower** (1974), and **Trump International Hotel & Tower** (2009) is famous for its International-style designs.

The Post-Modern Harold Washington Library Center *(see p82)*

POST-MODERN

Post-Modern architecture developed in the 1970s primarily in response to – and as a rejection of – the formal ideals of the International style. It is an eclectic style without strict rules or unified credo, although playful references to architectural styles of the past are typical features of Post-Modern structures.

The building at **333 West Wacker Drive** (1983), designed by the firm Kohn Pedersen Fox, and the **James R. Thompson Center** (1985), designed by architect Helmut Jahn, are notable examples of Post-Modern design.

WHERE TO FIND THE BUILDINGS

Charnley-Persky House pp76–7
Chicago Cultural Center p52
Crilly Court p71
Drake Hotel p64
Fourth Presbyterian Church p63
Glessner House p90
IBM Building p66
Illinois Institute of
  Technology p94
James R. Thompson Center p56
John Hancock Center p64
Newberry Library p67
Oak Park pp114–15
Olsen-Hansen Row
  Houses p71
Pullman Historic District p119
Reliance Building p50
Robie House pp102–103
The Rookery p42
Samuel M. Nickerson House p66
Trump International Hotel &
  Tower p77
333 West Wacker Drive pp56–7
Willis Tower p42
University of Chicago pp100–103
Water Tower p63

Multicultural Chicago

Chinatown street signs

Chicago prides itself on being one of the most ethnically diverse cities in the US. In the 1840s, the Irish, fleeing their country's potato famine, arrived in droves in the young city of Chicago. Since then, successive waves of immigrants from countries around the world have shaped the city's many neighborhoods. These varied ethnic communities continue to celebrate their cultures at various festivals that are held throughout the year *(see pp32–35).*

Spanish sign welcoming visitors to Pilsen, once a Czech community

THE IRISH

Irish police officers joining the St. Patrick's Day celebrations

The first Irish immigrants to Chicago worked as laborers, helping build the Illinois and Michigan Canal *(see p118)* in the mid-1800s. By 1870, the Irish represented over 13 percent of the city's population. Settled mostly in the South Side industrial town of Bridgeport, they soon became a powerful force in city politics. Over the years, there have been eight Irish mayors.

An Irish tradition not to be missed is a foaming glass of Guinness beer at one of the city's many Irish pubs.

THE WESTERN EUROPEANS

Germans were some of the earliest immigrants to Chicago. Settling primarily in the North Side neighborhood of Old Town, by the 1870s they were Chicago's largest ethnic group. Today, the core of Germantown is Old Town's Lincoln Square, teeming with delicatessens and dance halls.

In the mid-1800s a small community of Swedes was established just north of the Chicago River. They later moved to Clark Street and Foster Avenue, an area now known as Andersonville. The community, with its many delicatessens and shops, retains its original character. Midsommarfest is celebrated here each June.

Prosperous Italians arrived in Chicago in the 1860s. By 1900, they were joined by poorer Italian farmers, many of whom settled between Van Buren and 12th Streets. Today, Taylor Street, between Madison and Halsted Streets, on Chicago's West Side, is the nucleus of Little Italy.

Greek immigration was spurred by the 1871 fire, when laborers came to help rebuild the city. By 1927, 10,000 shops, mainly selling fresh produce and flowers, were operated by Greeks. A short stretch of Greek restaurants lies along South Halsted Street near Van Buren Street, on the West Side.

South Side neighborhoods such as Hyde Park and Kenwood *(see pp104–105)* were populated by wealthy

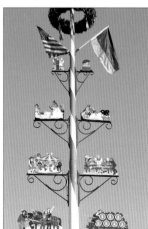

Traditional German maypole at the corner of Linden in Lincoln Square

German Jews. Over 125 Jewish congregations worshipped in the city by the late 1920s, with the Jewish population and synagogues spread throughout the city, much like today.

THE EASTERN EUROPEANS

The political unrest in Czechoslovakia in 1848 led to the first wave of Czech immigrants to the US, many settling in the Midwest. By the 1870s, Chicago had a Little Prague along DeKoven Street on the West Side. Over the next few decades, a thriving Czech community developed nearby, along Blue Island Avenue from 16th Street to Cermak Road (then known as 22nd Street). Named Pilsen, after the west Czechoslovakian city Plzeň, the neighborhood today is predominantly Hispanic. Remnants of the Czech community, however, can be seen in buildings such as Thalia Hall *(see p116).*

The Polish community, which is the largest outside Warsaw, is also the largest White ethnic group in Chicago after the Hispanics. Poles began arriving in large numbers during the 1870s. By the turn of the century, the Polish Downtown had been established at Division Street and along Milwaukee Avenue.

Ukrainians arrived in Chicago during the early 1900s, settling Ukrainian Village, an area bounded by Division Street and Chicago, Damen, and Western Avenues, northwest of the Loop. Two interesting museums in the community celebrate

Ukrainian culture. The Lithuanian community, in the suburban village of Lemont, also has a strong presence in Chicago, as does the smaller Latvian community, west of Lakeview.

Eastern European Jews settled the West Side's Maxwell Street at Halsted Street from the 1880s until the 1910s. Community life focused around the Maxwell Street Market (see p165), which was once the world's largest flea market, with stalls selling their reasonably priced wares.

THE AFRICAN AMERICANS

Jazz legend Nat "King" Cole, son of a Chicago Baptist minister

Despite Chicago's first settler being mulatto (see p15, racist laws significantly affected African-American settlement in the early 1800s. By 1850, Chicago was a destination for fugitive slaves from the South. In the 1890s, a thin strip of the South Side, bounded by Van Buren and 31st Streets, State Street and Lake Michigan, became known as the Black Belt, with about half of the city's Black population living here.

The early 1900s saw another wave of settlement in the Black Belt: the "Great Migration" of Blacks from the South looking for factory work. Over the next decade, a lively jazz and blues scene developed in the area.

In the 1940s and 1950s, the Chicago Housing Authority replaced South Side tenements with public-housing projects, which soon became notorious for crime. But by the 1960s and 1970s, Chicago

also had several middle-class Black communities, such as Park Manor, as well as racially integrated areas, such as Hyde Park. The Black Metropolis Historic District (35th Street and Indiana Avenue) was created in 1984 to commemorate the vibrant Black Belt community of the early 1900s. Today, African Americans represent approximately 40 percent of Chicago's population.

THE HISPANIC AMERICANS

The first flood of Mexican immigrants was early in the 20th century, as laborers came to Chicago to help build the city's railroad. A second wave came after World War II, again as laborers. This time they were accompanied by Puerto Ricans. Cubans, fleeing from the 1959 revolution, joined Chicago's Hispanic community. Today, the Hispanic Americans – nearly 30 percent of the city's population – continue to have an enormous impact on the cultural fabric of Chicago.

In the two southwest neighborhoods of Pilsen (see p116) and Little Village (south of Cermak Road between

Menu and graffiti on the wall of Mi Barrio Taqueria, in Pilsen

Western Avenue and Pulaski Road), the colorful streets are alive with Latin music, and inviting aromas waft from the numerous eateries.

THE ASIANS

In 1870 there were but two Chinese immigrants in Chicago. By the turn of the century, a Chinese community was growing in the South Side vice district of Custom

Colorful Vietnamese and Chinese signs on bustling Argyle Street

House Levee. That Chinatown dissolved in the early 1900s once the vice lords left. Chinese immigrants, faced with anti-Chinese sentiment reflected in excessive rent increases, found themselves forced to the fringes of the district. They settled at 22nd (now Cermak Road) and Wentworth Streets, an area that is now the heart of Chicago's Chinese community (see p94). There is also a new Chinatown on the North Side, marked by a pagoda at the Argyle CTA station entrance.

Chicago's Asian population swelled considerably in the 1980s with the arrival of Vietnamese, Cambodian, and Thai political refugees, as well as Filipino, Indian, Korean, and Japanese immigrants. Many settled in pockets on the North Side, where various Asian communities have developed, such as the Vietnamese neighborhood of Little Hanoi at Argyle Street and Broadway.

THE MELTING POT

Other cultures are represented in Chicago but are not as distinctly defined. Chicago's American Indian population of approximately 17,000, concentrated in Uptown, north of Lakeview, is the highest of any US city after San Francisco and Los Angeles. Chicagoans of Middle Eastern origin are scattered throughout the city.

Remarkable Residents

Chicago has always been a city at the forefront. It has nourished leaders in diverse fields, from music to industry, from architecture to sports. Some have been drawn to Chicago from other parts of the US and abroad; others were born and bred in Chicago. All have left their mark on the city and, indeed, on the world, including, most notably, the current President of the United States, Barack Obama. As the city where the skyscraper was developed in the late 1800s, Chicago has long been a center for architectural innovation, with many of North America's influential architects based here for at least part of their careers. Having nurtured outstanding musicians since the 1910s, the city is also famous for its jazz and blues.

Blues legend Muddy Waters playing his electric guitar

Frank Lloyd Wright, one of the world's most influential architects

ARCHITECTS

Chicago architects have literally shaped the city. Daniel Burnham (1846–1912) was one of Chicago's most successful architects. His partnership with John Wellborn Root (1850–91) led to buildings such as the Rookery *(see p42)*, a stunning early skyscraper. His later partnership with designer Charles Atwood (1849–95) resulted in the groundbreaking Reliance Building *(see p50)*.

Burnham was in charge of designing the 1893 World's Fair. However, it is for the 1909 Plan of Chicago he coauthored that he is best known. This document of civic planning became the vision for Chicago, proposing a series of riverfront public spaces and the widening of major roads to make the downtown easily accessible.

Louis Sullivan (1856–1924) has been called the first truly American architect. Celebrated for his organic style of ornamentation, as seen on the windows of Carson Pirie Scott *(see p50)*, Sullivan declared that form follows function. Indeed, the detailing allowed the architect artistic license while drawing in passers-by.

Sullivan nurtured a young draftsman with whom he worked, Frank Lloyd Wright (1867–1959). Over the next 70 years, Wright played a significant role in modern architecture, fathering the Prairie School *(see p27)* and designing such masterpieces as Robie House *(see pp102–103)*.

Ludwig Mies van der Rohe (1886–1969) moved to Chicago in 1937. The impact of his International style *(see p27)* was profound.

MUSICIANS

An innovator of American music, Louis Armstrong (1901–1971) lived in Chicago from 1922 to 1929. Here he launched a revolution with his trumpet playing, popularizing the new art of jazz.

If Armstrong was the king of jazz, Benny Goodman (1909–1986) was the king of swing. His Russian parents settled in Chicago's West Side, where Goodman joined the Hull-House *(see p116)* youth band. Later, he led the US's first racially integrated band, inviting Black pianist Teddy Wilson to join his orchestra. Jelly Roll Morton (1890–1941), the great pianist from New Orleans, came to Chicago in 1922. Morton claimed to have invented jazz. Muddy Waters (1915–83) didn't claim to have invented blues, but he did take credit for bringing the sound of the Mississippi Delta to Chicago, where his use of electric guitar was seminal.

Nat "King" Cole (1919–65) began his career playing the organ at his father's church. Cole, with his unique and velvety vocals, broke several color barriers in the 1950s. He was the first African American to have a radio show, and later, a weekly TV show.

ACTORS AND COMEDIANS

Paul Sills and Bernie Sahlins opened Chicago's renowned improvisational comedy spot Second City in 1959. Many comics, including Gilda Radner (1946–89), Mike Nichols, Elaine May, Dan Aykroyd, and Joan Rivers, got their start here. Comic genius Jack Benny (1894–1974) and *Saturday Night Live* star John Belushi (1949–82) both lived in Chicago suburbs.

Several Chicago-based actors, including John Cusack and John Malkovich, have

Chicago's Oprah Winfrey, a national TV personality

gone on to international fame. One of the city's best-known TV personalities is talk-show host Oprah Winfrey *(see p169)*, watched by nearly 15 million Americans each weekday. It was in Chicago that the TV talk show was born, in 1949, with NBC's *Garroway at Large*.

ATHLETES

Sports teams in Chicago are not known for their winning streaks, but they do boast a number of superstars. Former Chicago Bulls basketball player Michael Jordan is perhaps most famous, known as much for his product endorsements as for his scoring.

Hockey legend Bobby Hull, as the star of the 1961 Chicago Black-hawks team, helped bring the Stanley Cup to the city – the team's only cup win in more than half a century.

Johnny Weissmuller (1904–1984) may be best known as the star of 18 Tarzan movies; however, the boy who swam at Oak Street Beach *(see p77)* became the man who held every world freestyle swimming record of the 1920s.

Michael Jordan, the Chicago Bulls' No. 1 basketball player

WRITERS

Chicago's most famous literary figure is Ernest Hemingway (1899–1960), who grew up in Oak Park *(see pp114–15)*. He rejected the conservative mindset of this

Chicago suburb at that time, saying it was full of "wide lawns and narrow minds."

Theodore Dreiser (1871–1945), considered the father of American literary naturalism, wrote about Chicago, his home city, in his masterpiece *Sister Carrie*.

African-American novelist Richard Wright (1908–1960) moved to Chicago at age 19, though he wrote his bestselling novel *Native Son*, about a man raised in a Chicago slum, in New York.

Illinois-native poet Carl Sandburg (1878–1967) moved to Chicago in 1912, where he worked as a literary critic. His 1914 poem "Chicago" describes it as the "City of the Big Shoulders." Poet Gwendolyn Brooks (1917–2000) lived in Chicago her whole life, writing exclusively about it. She was, in 1950, the first African American to win a Pulitzer Prize, for *Annie Allen*, her collection exploring the Black experience in Chicago.

Renowned poet Carl Sandburg

GANGSTERS AND CRIMINALS

The city's reputation for lawlessness was secured in the 1920s with the rise of the US's infamous crime lord, Al Capone (1899–1947). Prohibition set the stage for mob warfare as gangsters monopolized the lucrative market of banned alcohol. More than 300 gang-related murders occurred in the 1920s, including the Capone-orchestrated St. Valentine's Day Massacre *(see p18)*.

Bank robber John Dillinger's daring made him a folk hero of sorts. When he was killed by the FBI outside Lincoln Park's Biograph Theatre in 1934, onlookers dipped hand-kerchiefs in his blood for mor-bid mementos.

A bank robber as folk hero, John Dillinger

ENTREPRENEURS AND INDUSTRIALISTS

Young Chicago attracted many enter-prisers. Cyrus Hall McCormick (1809–1884) transformed wheat farming with his inven-tion of the Virginia reap-er. In 1848, he concentrated his farm-imple-ment empire in Chicago. He died the richest man in Illinois.

Charles Wacker, city planner

Real-estate developer Potter Palmer (1826–1902) built luxury hotels and is credited with creating the wealthy Gold Coast area *(see pp72–7)*.

Marshall Field (1834–1906) built his fortune as a depart-ment store owner *(see pp50–51)*, funding some of Chicago's most important institutes.

Brewer Charles H. Wacker (1856–1929), son of Frederick Wacker *(see p71)*, helped shape the city as chair of the Chicago Plan Commission, overseers of the 1909 Plan of Chicago *(see p30)*.

SOCIAL REFORMERS

At the turn of the 20th century, Chicago was home to three of the most influen-tial women in the US.

Black civil-rights activist Ida B. Wells (1862–1931) success-fully sued a railroad company for racial discrimination. Her columns appeared in many of the nation's 200 Black papers during the 1890s *(see p95)*.

Jane Addams (1860–1935) was involved with almost every US social movement of the early 20th century, winning a Nobel Peace Prize for her work. In 1889, she cofounded Hull-House *(see p116)*.

Suffragist Frances Willard (1839–98) helped found the WCTU, the first international women's organi-zation *(see Willard House, p130)*.

CHICAGO THROUGH THE YEAR

Chicago's nickname "Windy City" originally referred to its blustery politicians who lobbied to host the 1893 World's Columbian Exposition. Visitors will be struck by the appropriateness of the label. Chicago is a windy city whatever the season – although it ranks only 14th for wind velocity in the country.

Cyclist on Lincoln Park's lakefront path

Springtime in Chicago begins in late March. The city bursts into bloom after a long winter, living up to its official motto, *Urbs in Horto*, or "City in a garden." In summer, Chicago's beaches offer cooling breezes and the sun-warmed waters of Lake Michigan. These same waters keep the city temperate during autumn. In winter, they lead to "lake effect" storms: plenty of snow and chilling breezes. Intrepid locals bundle up and take advantage of winter attractions such as the Winter Delights festival. City Visitor Centers and the mayor's office *(see p169)* provide event information.

Irish reveler at Chicago's annual St. Patrick's Day Parade

SPRING

Chicagoans welcome the arrival of spring by jogging through Grant Park, enjoying Lincoln Park's magnificent flower displays, and cheering on the city's two baseball teams, the Chicago Cubs and the White Sox, whose seasons begin in April *(see pp170–71)*.

MARCH

Pulaski Day Reception *(1st Mon in Mar),* Polish Museum of America, 984 N Milwaukee Ave. Celebrations in honor of Polish freedom fighter and later US Civil War hero Casimir Pulaski.
St. Patrick's Day Parade *(Sat before Mar 17).* The Loop. The Chicago River is dyed green in celebration.
South Side Irish Parade *(Sun before Mar 17),* Western Ave from 103rd to 114th Sts. One of the largest Irish parades outside Dublin.
Greek Independence Day Parade *(last Sun),* Halsted St from Randolph to Van Buren.

APRIL

Chicago Park District Spring Flower Show *(early Apr–mid-May),* Lincoln Park and Garfield Park conservatories. An exuberant display of colorful flowers.
Chicago Cubs and Chicago White Sox Home Openers *(early Apr).* See both Major League Baseball teams start the season on their home turf.

MAY

Bike Chicago *(May–Sep),* city wide. Five-month-long celebration of cycling.
Mayor Daley's Kids and Kites Fest *(early May),* Lake Shore Dr and Montrose Ave.
Great Chicago Places and Spaces *(mid- or late May),* 224 S Michigan Ave. Architecture in Chicago's downtown is celebrated through walking and lobby tours, special events, and exhibitions.
Wright Plus *(mid- or late May),* Oak Park *(p114).* Tour Frank Lloyd Wright-designed private residences and national historic landmarks in this annual housewalk.

SUMMER

Chicagoans throng to art fairs, neighborhood festivals, and outdoor concerts during the summer. A long-standing Chicago tradition is the free evening concerts – from opera to blues, from country to pop – at Millennium Park's *(see p53)* Pritzker Pavilion.

JUNE

Chicago Gospel Festival *(early Jun),* Millennium Park. A two-day free event featuring gospel composers, singers, and musicians.
Chicago Blues Festival *(early Jun),* Grant Park. A three-day extravaganza of local blues musicians and southern artists.
Printer's Row Book Fair *(early Jun),* Dearborn Ave between Congress Pkwy and Polk St *(p82).* Book dealers,

Navy Pier, Chicago's amusement park for the entire family *(see p65)*

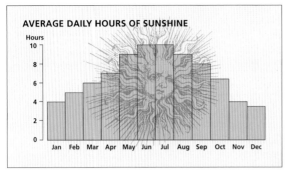

AVERAGE DAILY HOURS OF SUNSHINE

Sunshine
More than 50 days a year on average have clear skies, whereas 240 are overcast. Night descends early during the winter months, but the days can be brilliantly clear. December is the cloudiest month of the year, with an average of just four cloud-free days.

alongside papermaking and bookbinding demonstrations.
Old Town Art Fair *(second weekend)*, 1800 W block of Lincoln Park W. Artists from around the world display and sell their work.
Wells Street Art Festival *(second weekend)*, Wells St between Division and North aves. Crafts and fine art on display and for sale.
Ravinia Music Festival *(mid-Jun–mid-Sep)*, Ravinia Park. Dozens of performances in all musical styles *(p170)*.
Gay and Lesbian Pride Parade *(fourth Sun)*, from Lakeview *(p114)* to Lincoln Park.

JULY

Taste of Chicago *(first week)*, Grant Park *(pp84–5)*. Concerts and cooking lessons accompany the cuisine of some of the city's finest restaurants.
Kwanzaa Summer Festival *(first Sat)*, Abbott Park, 49 E 95th St. Musical entertainment, food, and activities for children of all ages.
Chicago Country Music Festival *(early Jul)*, Grant Park *(pp84–5)*.
Rock Around the Block *(mid-Jul)*, Lakeview *(p114)*. Annual weekend-long neighborhood festivities.
Chicago Folk and Roots Festival *(mid-Jul)*, Welles Park. A mix of musical styles from around the world.
La Fiesta del Sol *(late Jul)*, Pilsen *(p116)*. Carnival rides, arts and crafts, local and visiting musicians, and Mexican cuisine are featured at this festival, one of Chicago's largest.
Jazzfest *(late Jul/early Aug)*, South Shore Cultural Center,

7059 S Shore Dr. Top jazz musicians perform.
Venetian Night *(late Jul)*, Monroe Harbor. Parade of boats and a fireworks display that's synchronized to music.
Chinatown Summer Fair *(mid- or late Jul)*, Wentworth Ave between Cermak Rd and 24th St. Fabulous food to eat, with art and dance displays to admire.
Chicago Oudoor Film Festival *(mid-Jul through Aug)*, Grant Park. Free movie classics are shown on a gigantic outdoor screen.

AUGUST

Lollapalooza *(first weekend)*, Grant Park. Massive alternative rock festival held in Chicago since 2007.
Bud Billiken Day Parade *(second Sat)*, King Dr. from 35th to 55th sts. One of the US's oldest African-American parades culminates with a huge picnic in Washington Park *(p104)*.
Chicago Carifete *(mid-Aug)*, Midway Plaisance *(p104)*. Music, dance, and food from the islands of the Caribbean.

Air maneuvers over the North Side as part of the Air and Water Show

Pilsen Together Chamber of Commerce Art Festival *(mid–late Aug)*, 1617 W 18th St. Tastes, sights, and sounds of Hispanic culture.
Chicago Air and Water Show *(late Aug)*, North Ave Beach. Planes perform maneuvers in the sky and boats do stunts on the water.
Bucktown Arts Fest *(late Aug)*, N Oakley Blvd *(p114)*. Local artists display their work.
Viva! Chicago Latin Music Festival *(last weekend)*, Grant Park *(pp84–5)*.

Visitors sampling delicacies of dozens of restaurants at Taste of Chicago

AVERAGE MONTHLY RAINFALL

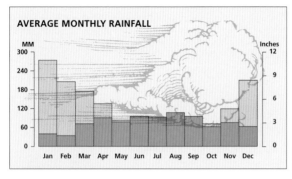

MM		Inches
300		12
240		9
180		6
120		
60		3
0		0

Jan Feb Mar Apr May Jun Jul Aug Sep Oct Nov Dec

Precipitation
Chicago's average monthly precipitation is much the same throughout the year, with a modest peak in early summer. Summer storms are brief but dramatic, and provide relief from humidity. Winter brings blizzards.

▓ Rainfall
▒ Snowfall

Pumpkins at a local farmers' market, a telltale sign of autumn

AUTUMN

Autumn is an invigorating season in Chicago. September's comfortable weather provides an inviting backdrop to the numerous outdoor festivals held throughout the city.

Autumn is also the season when Chicagoans and visitors alike test their mettle and stamina during the internationally celebrated annual marathon.

Football season kicks off the first week of September with the Chicago Bears playing at Soldier Field. The city's many sports enthusiasts also flock to the United Center to see the Chicago Bulls play basketball and the Chicago Blackhawks play hockey *(see p171)*.

In late autumn, the city gets a head start on the Christmas season, with many holiday traditions beginning immediately after Thanksgiving, in November.

SEPTEMBER

Chicago Jazz Festival *(Labor Day weekend)*, Grant Park *(pp84–5)*. Swing to the lively sounds of renowned jazz musicians and singers.
Art on Harrison *(second weekend)*, Oak Park *(pp114–15)*. Showcasing Oak Park's artists, galleries, and studios, with displays, demonstrations, and food.
Celtic Fest Chicago *(mid-Sep)*, Grant Park *(pp84–5)*. A celebration of Celtic music.
Mexican Independence Day Parade *(mid-Sep)*, Little Village. Floats, bands, and dancers join to celebrate Mexico's 1820 independence from Spain.
World Music Festival *(mid- to late Sep)*, various locations. The eclectic sounds of world-beat music.

OCTOBER

Haunted "L" Rides *(weekends)*, Chicago Cultural Center *(p52)*. Free Loop train tour with ghosts and goblins.
Annual House Tour *(second weekend)*, Pullman *(p119)*. A rare opportunity to see inside this historic district's 19th-century houses.
Around the Coyote *(second weekend)*, Wicker Park *(p114)*. Arts festival and gallery tours.
Chicago Marathon *(second Sun)*, downtown. One of the world's largest marathons, with thousands of participants, and spectators in the hundreds of thousands giving support and cheering runners along the 26.2-mile (43-km) course.

Oktoberfest *(early Oct)*, Weed St from Dayton St to Halsted Ave. Celebrates German culture with food and beer gardens.
Chicagoween *(month-long)*, Daley Plaza. An outdoor haunted village that kids will love.

NOVEMBER

Holiday Windows at Macy's *(Nov–Dec)*. Animated Christmas displays in the windows of the State Street store *(pp50–51)* are a Chicago tradition.
Christmas Around the World and Holidays of Light *(mid-Nov–Jan)*, Museum of Science and Industry *(pp106–109)*. Chicago's ethnic groups decorate trees in an "enchanted" forest and share holiday traditions.
Magnificent Mile Lights Festival *(third weekend)*, Michigan Ave from the Chicago River to Oak St. Christmas lights are lit during this annual procession.

The Chicago Marathon, attracting athletes from around the world

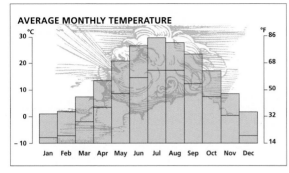

AVERAGE MONTHLY TEMPERATURE

Temperature
Spring in Chicago is generally mild. Most summer days are comfortably warm, but there may be some very hot and humid periods. Autumn is crisp, with unpredictable temperatures. Winter winds are often bitingly cold. This chart shows the average minimum and maximum temperatures for each month.

State Street Thanksgiving Day Parade *(Thanksgiving)*, State St between Congress Pkwy and Randolph St. Santa and his elves delight children.
Holiday Tree Lighting Ceremony *(day after Thanksgiving Day)*, Daley Plaza.
Christkindlmarket *(late Nov–Dec)*, Daley Plaza. Holiday shopping in a German marketplace, complete with an 80-ft (24-m) tree.

WINTER

The city sparkles during winter with elaborate decorations, and buildings and trees festooned with seasonal green and red lights. The Merchandise Mart, on the north bank of the river, looks like a massive wrapped gift.

DECEMBER

Winter Flower and Train Show *(early Dec)*, Lincoln Park Conservatory. Model trains

weave through colorful holiday poinsettia displays.
Zoo Lights *(throughout Dec)*, Lincoln Park Zoo *(pp112–13)*. More than 1.5 million lights illuminate the zoo.
Night of the Luminaria *(third Sat)*, Galena *(pp134–5)*. Thousands of candle-lit Luminaria line the streets of the town's Victorian historic district and surrounding neighborhoods.
New Year's Eve *(Dec 31)*, Navy Pier *(p65)* and Buckingham Fountain *(p85)*. An evening of celebration with laser-lights and fireworks.

JANUARY

New Year's Day *(Jan 1)*, Navy Pier *(p65)*. Family activities and fireworks to start off the New Year.
Winter Delights *(Jan 1–Mar 31)*. City-wide indoor and outdoor events, including themed weekends and the Magnificent Mile Crystal Carnival, with its giant ice sculptures.

Illuminated Christmas tree in front of the Tribune Building

FEBRUARY

Chinese New Year Parade *(date varies)*, Wentworth Ave from Cermak Rd to 24th St. Festivities include colorful floats, traditional music and dancing, and food.

PUBLIC HOLIDAYS

New Year's Day (Jan 1)
Martin Luther King Day (3rd Mon in Jan)
President's Day (3rd Mon in feb)
Pulaski Day (1st Mon in Mar)
Memorial Day (last Mon in May)
Independence Day (Jul 4)
Labor Day (1st Mon in Sep)
Columbus Day (2nd Mon in Oct)
Veterans Day (Nov 11)
Thanksgiving Day (4th Thu in Nov)
Christmas Day (Dec 25)

Ice skaters enjoying a bright winter day outdoors

CHICAGO
AREA BY AREA

DOWNTOWN CORE

Bordered on the north and on the west by the Chicago River, on the east by Lake Michigan, and on the south by the Congress Parkway, the Downtown Core is Chicago's historic and financial center. The downtown's nucleus is the Loop, named for the elevated train tracks encircling it. Even though the area was completely destroyed by the Great Fire of 1871, a mere two decades later it had been rebuilt with pioneering skyscrapers, including the Marquette Building. Along with this architectural legacy, the area is home to such famous museums as The Art Institute of Chicago. State Street is home to landmark department stores.

Picasso sculpture
at the Daley Center

SIGHTS AT A GLANCE

Historic Buildings
Auditorium Building **6**
Chicago Theatre **16**
Fine Arts Building **7**
Marquette Building **3**
Macy's **12**
Monadnock Building **5**
Oriental Theater **13**
Reliance Building **11**
The Rookery **2**
Santa Fe Building **8**
Sullivan Center **10**
35 East Wacker
   Drive **18**

Modern Skyscrapers
Federal Center **4**
James R. Thompson Center **20**
R.R. Donnelley Building **19**
333 West Wacker Drive **21**
Willis Tower **1**

Museums and Galleries
*The Art Institute of Chicago
   pp46–9* **9**
Chicago Cultural Center **14**

Bridges, Parks, and Streets
Michigan Avenue Bridge **17**
Millennium Park **15**
Wacker Drive **22**

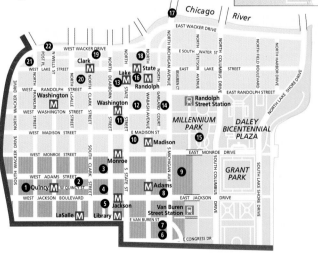

GETTING THERE
The Downtown Core is easily explored on foot. Frequent CTA elevated trains circle the Loop. CTA buses also provide frequent service. Downtown routes include 20, 22, 29, 36, and 56. Twelve Metra lines service Chicago's suburbs. Trains depart from one of five stations surrounding the Loop (*see pp188–91*).

KEY

▦	Street-by-Street map See pp40–41
M	CTA train station
▣	Metra train station

0 meters	500
0 yards	500

◁ **Atrium in Macy's landmark department store**

Street-by-Street: The Loop

Stone lion guarding the doors of the Art Institute

The Loop gets its name from the elevated track system that circles the center of the Downtown Core. Trains screeching as they turn sharp corners and the steady stream of businesspeople during rush hour add to the Loop's bustle. In the canyon vistas through the many tall, historic buildings – and modern edifices such as the Federal Center – you can catch glimpses of the 19 bridges spanning the Chicago River. The conversion of warehouses to condominiums and renovation of historic theaters are helping to enliven the Loop at night.

★ Willis Tower
At a height of 1,454 ft (443 m), this is one of the tallest buildings in the world. Views from the glass-enclosed observation deck on the 103rd floor are stunning ❶

Marquette Building
This early skyscraper (1895) was designed by William Holabird and Martin Roche, central Chicago School figures and architects of more than 80 buildings in the Loop ❸

190 South LaSalle Street (1987), designed by New York architect Philip Johnson, has a white-marble lobby with a gold-leafed, vaulted ceiling.

The Rookery
One of the earliest designs by Burnham and Root, this 1888 building has a lobby was remodeled by Frank Lloyd Wright in 1907 ❷

STREET

CLARK

ADAMS

FRANKLIN

WACKER

STREET

DRIVE

STAR SIGHTS

★ Art Institute of Chicago

★ Willis Tower

Chicago Board of Trade
occupies a 45-story Art Deco building, with a statue of Ceres atop its roof. The frenetic action inside can be observed from a viewers' gallery.

Santa Fe Building
This classic Chicago School building, with an elegant two-story atrium, houses the Chicago Architecture Foundation **8**

★ Art Institute of Chicago
The Impressionist and Post-Impressionist collection at this museum, one of the most important in the country, is world famous **9**

LOCATOR MAP
See Street Finder maps 3 & 4

KEY

– – –   Suggested route

| 0 meters | 100 |
| 0 yards | 100 |

Monadnock Building
The north half of this building (1891) is the tallest building ever constructed entirely of masonry **5**

Federal Center
Ludwig Mies van der Rohe designed this three-building office complex around a central plaza, which holds Alexander Calder's 1973 sculpture Flamingo **4**

Fine Arts Building
Frank Lloyd Wright once had a studio in this 1885 building designed by Solon S. Beman. The building was originally used as a carriage showroom by the Studebaker Company **7**

The "Elevated," or "L," train tracks opened in 1892. Its loop in the city's core is seven blocks long and five blocks wide.

Auditorium Building
The lavish birch paneled theater in this 1889 multipurpose skyscraper, is one of Adler and Sullivan's best interiors **6**

Willis Tower ●

233 S Wacker Dr. **Map** 3 B2.
Tel (312) 875-9696. **M** *Quincy*.
☐ *Apr–Sep: 10am–10pm
daily; Oct–Mar: 10am–8pm
daily; last adm 30 min before
closing.* ⬚ 🔊 🍴 🏛 🅿
www.willistower.com
www.theskydeck.com

In 2009 Sears Tower
was renamed Willis
Tower. It was the tallest
building in the world
from the time of its
contruction in 1973
until 1997 when the
Petronas Twin Towers
were built in Kuala
Lumpur. In 2000 it
regained its status as
the world's tallest
building when one of
its antennas was
extended. The build-
ing held this record
until early 2010
when Burj Khalifa in
Dubai opened as the
world's tallest build-
ing with the highest
occupied floor in the
world. Willis Tower
remains, however,
the tallest building
in the western
hemisphere and a
significant landmark
in Chicago.

The skyscraper
was designed
by Bruce
Graham, a
partner at the Chicago
architectural firm of
Skidmore, Owings and
Merrill, with the assistance of
chief engineer Fazlur Khan.
Construction of the innovative
building took three years,
employing 1,600 people
during the peak period. More
than 110 concrete caissons
anchored in bedrock support
the tower's 222,500 tons.

Today, the tower contains
3.5 million sq ft (0.3 million
sq m) of office space and
more than 100 elevators. It
also contains approximately
43,000 miles (69,000 km)
of telephone cable, almost
enough to encircle the
Earth twice.

The elevator to the Skydeck
travels at a stomach-churning
1,600 ft (490 m) per minute.

**The 110-story
tower** soars to
1,450 ft (442 m) – or
1,730 ft (527 m) if
the higher of the
two antennas is
included.

The tower top
sways 6 inches (15
cm) in strong wind.

The glass-enclosed,
103rd-floor Skydeck,
and The Ledge, the
world's third-highest
observation deck,
provides views of
the far shores of
Lake Michigan and
four states on
clear days.

**The 16,000
bronze-tinted
windows** are
cleaned by six
automatic machines
eight times a year.

Black aluminum
clads the frame-
work, which is
made from 76,000
tons of steel.

**Alexander
Calder's mobile
sculpture** *Universe*
(1974) is on display
in the lobby.

View of the Willis Tower and
Skydeck, looking northeast

The Rookery ●

209 S LaSalle St. **Map** 3 C2. *Tel* (312)
553-6100. **M** *Quincy; Jackson (brown
line).* ☐ *8am–6pm Mon–Fri; 8am–
2pm Sat.* ☒ *major public hols.* ♿

When the Rookery opened
in 1888, it was the tallest
building in the world. The 12-
story building, designed by
the influential firm Burnham
and Root in the Richardsonian
Romanesque style *(see p26)*,
has a dark red brick façade
with terra-cotta trim and a
rough granite base. The
building, now housing offices,
was constructed on a foundation of crisscrossing rails
– necessitated by the clay
soils unable to support the
weight of the massive
structure. While its thick
masonry walls are load
bearing, the iron framing
of the lower stories

During the summer, there are
often lengthy lineups for the
Skydeck and The Ledge, an
observation deck that extends
onto a glass-floored platform
for thrilling views. Diversions include a short movie
on Chicago and an exhibi-
tion on the city's ten
most significant
buildings.

The Loop's glittering skyline as seen at sunset

allows for the use of large windows – a welcome innovation when artificial lighting technology was in its infancy.

Framing the main entrance is a monumental arch with geometric carvings, including eponymous rooks. Inside is a two-tiered court, remodeled in 1907 by Frank Lloyd Wright, who covered the original iron columns and staircases with white marble, inlaid with gold leaf. The central staircase, framed with Wright's signature urns, leads to a mezzanine enclosed by a domed skylight. A magnificent, cantilevered cast-iron staircase leads from the second floor to the top. The building was made a National Historic Landmark in 1988.

The Rookery's spectacular light court

Marquette Building ❸

140 S Dearborn St. **Map** 3 C2. *Tel (312) 422-5500.* Ⓜ *Monroe (blue line).* ◯ *24 hrs daily.* ♿

Considered the premier remaining example of the Chicago School of architecture *(see pp26–7)*, the Marquette Building was designed by Holabird and Roche in 1895.

Entrance to the Marquette Building

Commissioned by the owners of the Rookery, the architects faced the demanding task of equaling the Burnham and Root original sophisticated design of that building.

The grid of this early commercial 17-story high-rise's steel-frame skeleton is easily seen in the terra-cotta and brick exterior.

The building's groundbreaking expansive horizontal windows became known as Chicago windows *(see p27)*. They are one of the few remaining examples of this innovative window design.

Bronze bas-relief panels over the entrance doors, designed by Hermon Atkins MacNeil, illustrate French missionary Father Jacques Marquette's 1673–4 expedition to the area.

In the two-story lobby, mosaic panels of glass and mother-of-pearl designed by J.A. Holzer of Tiffany and Company depict scenes of the French exploration of Illinois. Sculpted heads inset above the elevators on the first and second floors pay tribute to the Native American chiefs and early French explorers of the Chicago area *(see p15)*.

The building underwent restoration in 1980.

Federal Center ❹

Dearborn St, between Adams and Jackson sts. **Map** 3 C2. Ⓜ *Jackson (blue line).* ◯ *7am–6pm Mon–Fri.* ◉ *major public hols.* ♿

The three-building Federal Center complex, designed by Ludwig Mies van der Rohe and completed in 1974, expresses the pared-down functionalism of Mies' International style *(see p27)*. There is little ornamentation to distract from these austere curtain-wall structures made of glass and steel.

The 30-story Dirksen courtroom building stands on the east side of the complex; the 42-story Kluczynski office tower and one-story post office are to the west. The center is interesting for the expert arrangement of its buildings around the plaza and with each other.

The sterile plaza is graced with Alexander Calder's 53-ft (16-m) vermilion sculpture *Flamingo (see p44)*, which seems almost to be dancing – its steel organic form a surprising complement to the rigid geometry of the buildings.

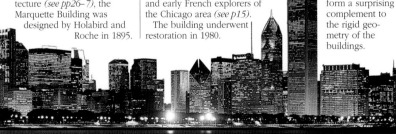

The Monadnock Building's filigree wrought-iron staircase

Monadnock Building ❺

53 W Jackson Blvd. **Map** 3 C2. **Tel** (312) 922-1890. Ⓜ Jackson (blue line). ◯ 7am–6pm Mon–Fri. ◯ public hols. ♿

Constructed in two parts two years apart (and by two different architectural firms), the interestingly bisected Monadnock Building looks both to the past and to the future. The northern half of this office building, designed by Burnham and Root, was built first, in 1891. Sixteen stories tall and with masonry load-bearing walls (the building method at the time), it is the tallest masonry building ever constructed. The southern section, on the other hand, designed by Holabird and Roche, has a steel skeleton sheathed in terra-cotta, an innovation that in the 1890s allowed skyscrapers to soar.

The building is named after one of New Hampshire's White Mountains. "Monadnock" is also a geological term for a mountain surrounded by a glacial plain – an appropriate name for this most solid of buildings, as its walls are 6 ft (2 m) thick at the base. The interior was restored in the 1980s: the mosaic floor is a replica; the

white-marble ceiling and ornate staircase are original. At the north entrance and at the south elevator banks, you can see, under glass, part of the original marble floor. A corridor bordered by shops and restaurants runs the length of the building, much like an interior street.

Auditorium Building ❻

430 S Michigan Ave. **Map** 4 D3. **Tel** (312) 341-3555. Ⓜ Library. 🚌 145, 147, 151. ◯ 7:30am–10:30pm Mon– Thu; 7:30am–6pm Fri; 11am–5pm Sat, Sun. ◯ major public hols. ♿ **Building**: (312) 341-3555; **Theater** : (312) 922-2110. See **Entertainment** p168.

Designed by Dankmar Adler and Louis Sullivan, their first major commission together, the Auditorium Building (1889), with its walls of smooth limestone typical of the Richardsonian Romanesque style (see p26) rising above the rough granite base, broke many records and achieved a number of firsts. Combining a 400-room hotel, a 17-story office tower, and a 4,300-seat theater, it was the tallest building in Chicago and the first building of its size to be electrically lighted and air-conditioned. Not surprisingly, it was also the most expensive, costing over $3 million to build. At 110,000 tons, it was the heaviest building in the world, and the most fireproof.

The building's crowning jewel is the lavish Auditorium

Roosevelt University admissions office in the Auditorium Building

Theatre, the first home of the Chicago Symphony Orchestra. After many years of neglect (World War II servicemen used the stage as a bowling alley), it was restored in the 1960s and is now a venue for performing arts events. Four elliptical arches span the width of the theater, which is ornamented with stenciling, stained glass, and gold-leaf plaster reliefs. Its excellent acoustics enable guests in the last row to hear an unamplified whisper on stage, six stories below.

The grand lobby, with its onyx walls and ornate staircase, contains an exhibition on the building's history. The tenth-floor library, originally the hotel's dining room, has a dramatic barrel-vaulted ceiling and superb lake views.

The building also houses Roosevelt University.

Stained-glass detailing in the Auditorium Building

Façade of the Auditorium Building, with cows from Chicago's public-art project in the foreground

White-marble lobby of the Santa Fe Building

Fine Arts
Building **7**

410 S Michigan Ave. **Map** 4 D2.
Tel (312) 566-9800. M *Library.*
3, 4, 145, 147, 151. ○ *7am–10pm
Mon–Fri; 7am–9pm Sat; 10am–5pm
Sun.* ● *major public hols.* &

Although now closely
associated with fine art
and culture, the Fine Arts
Building was originally
commissioned by Studebaker
Brothers Manufacturing to
house a wagon carriage
showroom. (The name
"Studebaker" inscribed
outside in stone is still visible
above the first floor.)

Designed by Solon S.
Beman and completed in
1885, the building, with its
columns, rough stone, and
arched entranceway and
windows, is typical of the
Romanesque style.

When the Studebaker
Company moved to a new
location, Beman was
commissioned to renovate the
building as a cultural center.
The façade of the eighth floor
was removed and replaced
with a three-story addition.
Inside, studios, shops, and
offices were added, and the
building quickly became a
hub of artistic activity. The
literary magazines *Dial*,
Poetry, and *Little Review* were
published here; the Little
Theater staged dramas; and
painters, sculptors, and
architects (including Frank

Lloyd Wright, *see p30*) had
their studios on the tenth
floor. In 1892, resident artists,
including Frederic Clay
Bartlett and Ralph Clarkson,
formed a group called the
Little Room and produced
eight murals, which still can
be seen on the walls of the
tenth floor.

Today, the building, which
has been given national
historic landmark status, has
a slightly frayed, run-down
charm. Many arts-related
enterprises remain in the
building, including the Fine
Arts Building Gallery in Suite
433, which showcases Chicago
artists, with a new exhibition
each month. There are also
two movie theaters.

The sound of singers
practicing scales can be heard
echoing through the halls,
and a ride in the old elevator
(with an operator) is an
experience not to be missed.

Santa Fe
Building **8**

224 S Michigan Ave. **Map** 4 D2.
Tel (312) 341-9461. M *Adams.* ○
24 hrs daily. ● *major public hols.*

The Santa Fe Building
gleams – inside with white
marble, and outside with
white-glazed terra-cotta.
Designed by D.H. Burnham
and Co. in 1904 and originally
known as the Railway
Exchange Building, it is now
called the Santa Fe because of
the rooftop sign, erected in
the early 1900s by the Santa
Fe Railroad.

Porthole windows line the
top floor; terra-cotta reliefs of
ancient goddesses decorate
the vestibule. The atrium's
balustraded mezzanine, marble
staircase, and elevators with

Decorative elevator door in the
Santa Fe Building

grillwork are all notable. The
building also houses the
Chicago Architecture Center
which is a "mini-museum"
detailing the history of Chicago
architecture and offering
guided tours of the city.

The Artist's Snack Shop on the ground floor of the Fine Arts Building

The Art Institute of Chicago ❾

Frieze on the west façade

The extensive collections at the Art Institute of Chicago represent nearly 5,000 years of human creativity through paintings, sculptures, textiles, photographs, cultural objects, and decorative artifacts from around the world. The museum was founded by civic leaders and art collectors in 1879 as the Chicago Academy of Fine Arts, changing its name to The Art Institute of Chicago in 1882. Outgrowing two homes as wealthy patrons donated collections, it finally settled in a Neo-Classical structure built for the 1893 World's Fair. A new wing for modern and contemporary art, designed by Renzo Piano opened in 2009, increasing gallery space by one third.

Kartikeya sculpture, 12th century
This gray granite sculpture of Kartikeya, Ganesha's brother, is the Hindu God of War.

KEY

- American Art
- Eastern & Islamic Art
- Architecture & Design
- European Modern Art 1900–1950
- African Art
- Ancient Egyptian, Greek & Roman Art
- Photography
- Indian Art of the Americas
- Prints and Drawings
- Contemporary Art after 1945
- European Art before 1900

First floor

McKinlock Court

Indra Statue, 16th century
Originating from Kathmandu Valley, this gilded bronze statue is a fine example of Nepalese handicraft. Indra, the Hindu god of warriors and thunder, was said to ride Airavat, a four-tusked white elephant. Traditionally, followers of Indra would honor him by sacrificing animals.

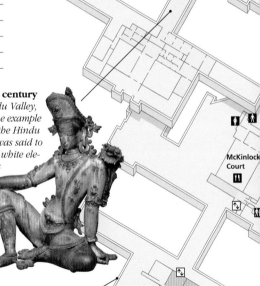

McKinlock Court

Lower level

STAR EXHIBITS

- ★ American Gothic by Grant Wood
- ★ A Sunday on La Grande Jatte–1884 by Georges Seurat
- ★ Old Man in a Gorget and Black Cap by Rembrandt van Rijn

Main Entrance

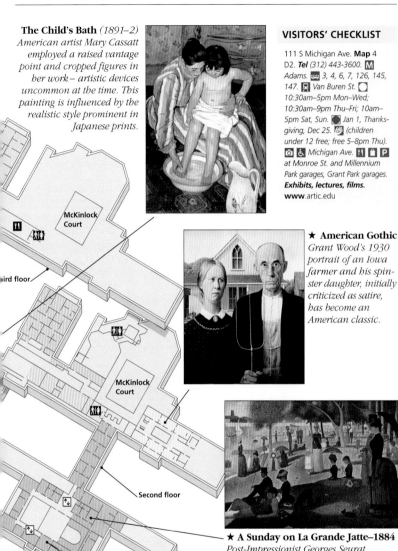

The Child's Bath (1891–2)
*American artist Mary Cassatt
employed a raised vantage
point and cropped figures in
her work – artistic devices
uncommon at the time. This
painting is influenced by the
realistic style prominent in
Japanese prints.*

McKinlock
Court

ird floor

McKinlock
Court

Second floor

The Assumption
of the Virgin

VISITORS' CHECKLIST

111 S Michigan Ave. **Map** 4
D2. *Tel (312) 443-3600.* M
Adams. 3, 4, 6, 7, 126, 145,
147. Van Buren St.
10:30am–5pm Mon–Wed;
10:30am–9pm Thu–Fri; 10am–
5pm Sat, Sun. Jan 1, Thanksgiving, Dec 25. (children
under 12 free; free 5–8pm Thu).
Michigan Ave.
at Monroe St. and Millennium
Park garages, Grant Park garages.
Exhibits, lectures, films.
www.artic.edu

★ **American Gothic**
*Grant Wood's 1930
portrait of an Iowa
farmer and his spin-
ster daughter, initially
criticized as satire,
has become an
American classic.*

★ **A Sunday on La Grande Jatte–1884**
*Post-Impressionist Georges Seurat
composed this image of promenading
Parisians using tiny dots of color.*

★ **Old Man in a Gorget and
Black Cap**
*Rembrandt van Rijn's interest in
the wisdom of age can be seen in
this character study (c.1631).*

MUSEUM GUIDE
*First-floor galleries range from ancient Egyptian
artifacts to Asian collections, American art, and
the modern wing's film, video and new media,
and photography galleries. The second floor is
devoted mostly to European works from the 15th to
20th centuries and to art after 1960. The third floor
houses European modern art from 1900 up to 1950.*

Exploring the Art Institute of Chicago

The museum's holdings span the globe as well as centuries, from 3rd-millennium BC Egyptian and Chinese artifacts to modern American and European art. Almost every major artistic movement of the 19th and 20th centuries is represented. The museum's Early Modernism collection is very strong; its Impressionist and Post-Impressionist collection – one of the most significant in the world – is outstanding. Important Renaissance and Baroque paintings complement these exhibits.

Flower gardens in the grounds behind the Art Institute

Visitor to the European gallery appreciating works of old masters

ASIAN ART

Some of the museum's most exquisite pieces are in its distinguished Asian collection, which comprises 35,000 works of archeological and artistic significance.

The galleries of Chinese, Japanese, and Korean art include celebrated collections of ancient Chinese bronzes and jades, 18th- and 19th-century Japanese woodblock prints, and early Korean ceramic vases.

The art from the Golden Age of the Tang Dynasty (AD 618–907) is the prize of this exhibit, in particular, the magnificent brightly glazed earthenware funerary horses.

Indian, Himalayan, and Southeast Asian art dating from the 2nd to 19th centuries encompasses artifacts of the Hindu and Buddhist faiths. Among the gems here are the nearly life-sized 2nd- and 3rd-century bodhisattva sculptures from Gandhara (present-day Pakistan), and a carved 13th-century stone statute of Saraswati, the Hindu goddess of learning, from Southern India.

The Art Institute also houses Persian 16th-century illuminated manuscripts and miniature paintings, though these are not currently on view.

ARMS AND ARMOR

Remarkable works of late medieval and Renaissance metal-craft are showcased in the George F. Harding Collection. One of the finest such collections in North America, it consists of 3,000 pieces of arms and armor. These include finely etched helmets, chain mail, equestrian equipment, historic weaponry, and decorated breastplates.

One of the earliest pieces in the collection is a breastplate from northern Italy. Dating from 1380, its original fabric covering is still intact. Also striking is a 1575 northern Italian armor, used for foot combat. Made of etched and gilded steel and brass, the suit is decorated with large medallions depicting allegorical figures.

DECORATIVE ARTS

For unparalleled insight into the ever-changing taste of Western society, visit the decorative arts galleries. Their broad array embraces household items, including furniture and tableware, jewelry, and religious artifacts.

The impressive European collection contains 25,000 objects crafted from wood, metal, glass, ceramics, enamel, and ivory dating from 1100 to the present. It also includes sculpture from the medieval period to 1900.

The American collection includes an excellent selection of Arts and Crafts furniture, including a beautiful oak library table (1896) designed by Frank Lloyd Wright *(see p30)*.

The fine European and American textile collection spans 15 centuries and

The grand staircase and foyer of the Art Institute

features vestments, tapestries, and embroideries. Highlights are a 19th-century William Morris-designed carpet and two rare fragments of Coptic cloth dating from between the 5th and 8th centuries.

Two of the quirkiest – and most renowned – collections are the Arthur Rubloff Paperweight Collection and the Thorne Miniature Rooms. The museum's holdings of more than 1,000 French, English, and American glass paperweights, popular in the mid-19th century, are one of the largest in the world.

The Thorne Miniature Rooms consist of 68 model rooms, painstakingly constructed to a scale of 1 inch (2.5 cm) to 1 foot (30 cm). The intricate European and American furnished interiors, ranging from the 16th to 20th centuries, are made with extraordinary technical precision.

The Londonderry Vase (1813), inspired by Roman imperial art

20TH-CENTURY ART

The museum's trove of more than 1,500 20th-century and contemporary paintings and sculptures provides a comprehensive and provocative survey of the development of modern art. Representing every significant artistic movement in Europe and the US, the works are arranged in groupings that highlight stylistic affinities between varied artists.

The collection is divided into pre-1950 and post-1950 works, housed in the Modern Wing.

Particularly strong are the examples of Cubism, the precursor of all abstract art forms; German Expressionism, the embodiment of the search for a strong emotional language in art; and Surrealism, the liberation of the irrational.

Post-World War II art is represented with works by such influential artists as Willem de Kooning and Jackson Pollock.

ARCHITECTURE

When the 1894 Chicago Stock Exchange (Adler and Sullivan) was demolished in 1972, its Trading Room was salvaged and reconstructed at the museum. Its ornate glory can still be seen in the stenciled ceiling and art-glass skylights. There are also pieces from other demolished Chicago buildings.

Special exhibits and a library with a comprehensive collection on Louis Sullivan complement the installations, housed in the Modern Wing.

IMPRESSIONIST AND POST-IMPRESSIONIST ART

Gifts from wealthy patrons such as Bertha Palmer (see p77) and Frederic Clay Bartlett, who astutely began collecting works by Monet, Degas, and Seurat in the late 19th century, led to the Art Institute becoming the first in the US to include a gallery of Post-Impressionist art. Today, it is one of the foremost centers of Impressionist and Post-Impressionist paintings outside France.

United only by their fiercely held belief in artistic experimentation, the French Impressionists were a diverse group who

The Basket of Apples (c.1895) by Paul Cézanne

exhibited together in the 1870s and 1880s. Dedicated to a new form of art – one that eschewed the constraints of the prevailing formal style – these artists attempted to capture the textures and moods of fleeting moments, or impressions. Their final exhibition was in 1886.

The artists who followed in the Impressionists' footsteps – labeled Post-Impressionists by English art critic Roger Fry – created works of art exploring evocative color relationships and rules of composition.

Highlights of the museum's holdings include the highly estimable Helen Birch Bartlett Memorial Collection, featuring Paul Cézanne's The Basket of Apples (c.1895) and Henri de Toulouse-Lautrec's At the Moulin Rouge (1895).

No better illustration of Impressionist and Post-Impressionist principles can be found than Claude Monet's six versions of a wheat field, which combines the basic doctrine of Impressionism – capturing nature's temporality – with the Post-Impressionist concern for reconstructing nature according to art's formal, expressive potential.

On the Seine at Bennecourt (1868) by Claude Monet

Sullivan Center ⑩

1 S State St. **Map** 3 C2.
Tel (312) 675-5500. Ⓜ Monroe;
Washington (red line). ◯ Call for
opening times. ● Easter,
Thanksgiving, Dec 25.

It is appropriate that such
an architectural gem as the
Sullivan Center (formerly
known as the Carson Pirie
Scott Building), which,
until 2007, housed one of
Chicago's oldest department
stores, rests at Chicago's
ground-zero address of State
and Madison, the starting
point for the city's street-
numbering system.

The upper floors of the
building are finished in
white terra-cotta, but it is
the ornamental metalwork
on the first two floors that
give this building, designed
by Louis Sullivan in 1899, its
distinctive character.

A particularly noteworthy
feature of the exterior is the
corner entrance pavilion,
which extends 12 stories to
the top of the building and
has ornamental cast-iron
motifs. Along with intricate
botanical and geometric forms,
Sullivan's initials, L.H.S., can
be seen above the corner
entrance. While this is the
showy heart of the building, it
is worth taking a walk east
along Madison Street to take
time to admire the metalwork
and Chicago windows from a
far less busy vantage point.

The Reliance Building, precursor to
the modern skyscraper

Reliance Building ⑪

32 N State St. **Map** 3 C1. **Tel** (312)
782-1111. Ⓜ Washington (red line).
◯ 24 hrs daily. ♿ Ⓟ See **Where
to Stay, Hotel Burnham** p140.

The Reliance Building's
two-stage construction
(1891–95) was as unusual as
were the structural-support
techniques used. The leases
for the upper floors of the
original building on the site
did not expire until 1894, so

when work on the new
Reliance Building began in
1890, the upper floors of the
old building were supported
on jack screws and the lower
stories demolished. The
ground floors of the Reliance
Building were completed and
in 1894, when the leases
expired, the upper floors
were demolished and the
steel framing for 13 more
stories completed, in 15 days.

The new building, officially
opened in March 1895, was
considered revolutionary
because of its steel frame and
unusual two-story-column
design, allowing for the
masses of windows which
give the building its modern
look. The building's design
was undertaken by John Root
of Burnham and Root. Charles
Atwood completed it upon
Root's death in 1891.

The building was in serious
disrepair in the mid-1990s,
until the City of Chicago
purchased it and began an
exterior renovation, which
involved the replacement of
2,000 pieces of terra-cotta. In
1995, it was designated a
Chicago landmark. In 1998, a
hotel company bought the
building, undertaking a $27.5-
million refurbishment before
opening the Hotel Burnham
in 1999. Root's original bronze
and granite design of the first
floor has been re-created and
the 20-ft- (6-m-) high elevator
lobby reconstructed using
Italian marble, ornamental
metal elevator grills, and
elaborate mosaic floor tiles.

Macy's ⑫

111 N State St. **Map** 4 D1.
Tel (312) 781-1000. Ⓜ Washington
(red line). ◯ 10am–8pm Mon;
9am–9pm Tue, Wed; 10am–8pm
Thu–Sat; 11am–6pm Sun. ● Easter,
Thanksgiving, Dec 25. ♿ ☑ 🍴
Ⓟ See **Shops and Markets** p163.

No other retail establishment
is, perhaps, as important to
Chicago's cultural history as
Marshall Field's department
store, which became part of
the Macy's chain in 2006.
The original Marshall Field
plaques remain on the building but, despite protests by

Ornamental metalwork above the entrance to Sullivan Center

Christmas window display at Macy's

loyal customers, the name Macy's remains ubiquitous elsewhere. Originally a dry-goods shop begun by wealthy businessman Marshall Field *(see p77)*, the store now occupies an entire city block. Built in five stages as the company grew, the original building, a Renaissance Revival-style design by Charles B. Atwood of D.H. Burnham, still stands at Washington and Wabash.

Field is credited with transforming State Street into the retail heart of Chicago in the early 1900s and for coining the commercial credo "Give the lady what she

Superb Tiffany glass dome in Macy's southern atrium

wants." When the store opened in 1907, it was considered the largest in the world, with 1,339,000 sq ft (124,400 sq m) of retail space, including the basement (such use was until then unheard of in US merchandising), 35,000 electric lights, 50 elevators, and 12 street-front entrances.

The store's most spectacular feature is its Tiffany mosaic dome, believed to be the largest piece of glass mosaic in the world. With more than 1.6 million pieces of iridescent glass covering 6,000 sq ft (557 sq m), it took 18 months and 50 artisans, supervised by designer Louis Comfort Tiffany, to complete.

Oriental Theater ⓭

24 W Randolph St. **Map** 3 C1.
Tel *(312) 782-2004.* Ⓜ *Washington (red line).* ♿ 📷 *11am Sat. See* **Entertainment** *pp170–71.*

The Oriental Theater occupies the site of one of the worst theater fires in US history: just weeks after opening in 1903, fire broke out in the Iroquois Theater, claiming almost 600 lives *(see p17)*. The theater was rebuilt and operated until 1925,

when it was demolished. The Oriental, built on the site, opened in 1926. The 22-story building, with its 3,238-seat auditorium, was designed by renowned theater architects Cornelius W. and George L. Rapp.

The theater was used both as a movie palace and for live performances. Judy Garland, Jackie Gleason, and Bob Hope all performed here.

Inspired by the East Indian carnival-festival Durbar, the theater's interior is full of fantastic decorative elements, such as the elephant-head light fixtures in the foyer.

The Oriental is in what, for more than a century, was Chicago's bustling theater district: Randolph Street between Michigan Avenue and Wacker Drive. The Rice Theatre was the first to open in the area, in 1847 (since

Signs such as this mark the Loop's theatrical district

burned down). By the 1880s, more than 25 entertainment palaces were offering vaudeville, musicals, opera, and drama. Although few of the original theaters remain, the district is being revitalized, spurred by the restoration of the Oriental, which reopened as the Ford Center for the Performing Arts Oriental Theater. Restoration of the theater was completed in 1998 after a 17-year closure; 62,500 sq ft (5,800 sq m) of gold leaf were used in the theater's renovation.

Façade of Chicago Cultural Center's Randolph Street entrance

Chicago Cultural Center ⓮

78 E Washington St. **Map** 4 D1.
Tel (312) 744-6630. Ⓜ Randolph.
◷ 8am–7pm Mon–Thu; 8am– 6pm
Fri; 9am–6pm Sat; 10am–6pm Sun.
● public hols. ♿ via Randolph St
entrance. 🎟 1:15pm Wed, Fri, Sat.
▢ ▢ ℹ **Weekly arts events;**
call (312) 346-3278.
www.chicagoculturalcenter.org

Built between 1893 and
1897 as the city's main library,
the building was dedicated in
1991 as the Chicago Cultural
Center to showcase and
celebrate the performing,
visual, and literary arts.

Designed by the Boston
firm Shepley, Rutan and
Coolidge, this massive Neo-
Classical (see p27) edifice
features soaring arches of
white marble and classical
Greek columns. The 3-ft-
(1-m-) thick masonry walls,
clad with Bedford limestone,

rise 104 ft (32 m) above a
granite base. The elegant
building cost almost $2
million to construct.

There are two entrances to
the building. The north
entrance, at 77 East Randolph
Street, with Doric columns
and a massive portico, serves
the four-story north wing; the
deeply arched Romanesque
portal with bronze-framed
doors at the south entrance,
at 78 East Washington Street,
serves the five-story south
wing. The Garland Court
corridor connects the wings.

The interior of the building,
which includes a grand
Carrara marble staircase just
inside the Washington Street
entrance, is a monument to
elegant ornamentation. Inset
in the staircase are small
medallions made from a
rare Irish emerald marble.
On the underside of the
staircase, seen by looking up
from each landing, are
intricate mosaics.

Two spectacular glass
domes complete the opulent
detailing. At the south end of
the building, on the third
floor in Preston Bradley Hall,
is a huge Tiffany dome. This
38-ft (11.5-m) jewel of
sparkling colored glass, stone,
and mother-of-pearl is valued
at an incredible $35 million.
It is the largest stained-glass
Tiffany dome in the world.
At the north end of the
building, in the second-floor
G.A.R. Rotunda, is a stained-
glass dome in an intricate
Renaissance pattern. It was
created by the local firm
Healy and Millet. Both domes
were originally skylights but

have since been sheathed
with copper and backlit
to protect and preserve
the glass.

On the fourth floor is the
Sidney R. Yates Gallery, a
replica of an assembly hall
in Venice's 14th-century
Doge's Palace. Arched,
bronzed doorways are inlaid
with antique marble, and
the ceiling is coffered. The
stairway leading to the fifth
floor is modeled on the
Bridge of Sighs in Venice.

Although the building
itself deserves many hours
of architectural exploration,
allow enough time to view
the center's many exhibits
that reflect the city's rich
cultural heritage and
showcase local and
international artists. Along
the western corridor on the
same floor is the Landmark
Chicago Gallery, displaying
photographs of the city's
architectural heritage.

The center also contains
two concert halls, two
theaters, a cabaret space,
and a dance studio.
Hundreds of programs and
exhibitions are presented
annually. Each week, there
are many concerts, literary
readings, and cultural events
held here.

One of two Visitor Infor-
mation Centers operated
by the Chicago Office of
Tourism is on the first floor
of the Chicago Cultural
Center, near the Randolph
Street entrance.

Grand staircase leading to the
third-floor Preston Bradley Hall

Stained glass dome by Healy and
Millet in the G.A.R. Rotunda

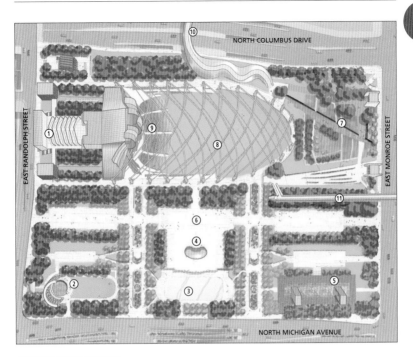

KEY TO MAIN SIGHTS

① Harris Theater for Music & Dance
② Wrigley Square
③ McCormick-Tribune Ice Rink
④ AT & T Plaza

⑤ South Terrace and Crown Fountain
⑥ Chase Promenade
⑦ Lurie Garden
⑧ Great Lawn

⑨ Jay Pritzker Pavilion
⑩ BP Bridge
⑪ Nichols Bridgeway

Millennium Park ⓯

Bounded by Randolph & Monroe Sts, Michigan Ave, & Columbus Dr. **Map** 4 D1. **Tel** *(312) 742-1168.* **M** *Madison; Randolph.* 🖪 *11am & 1pm Jun–Oct.* 🖳 **P** *Concerts.* www.millenniumpark.org

A project to celebrate the 21st century, Millennium Park has provided year-round recreational opportunities since it opened in summer 2004. A northern expansion of Grant Park *(see pp84–5)*, it covers more than 1 million sq ft (93,000 sq m). This park-within-a-park has transformed an unsightly rail yard into a world-class cultural destination for families, tourists and convention-goers.

The showpiece is the outdoor **Jay Pritzker Pavilion**, which was designed by internationally acclaimed architect Frank Gehry in association with the park's own designers. The bandshell includes a special sound system that reaches the whole audience. The Pavilion is the home of the Grant Park Orchestra and Chorus summer concerts *(see p169)*. It can accommodate up to 14,000 people, while its stage allows for up to 120 musicians and a chorus of 150 singers to perform at the same time. Nearby, connecting the **Great Lawn** with the third floor of the Art Institute's Modern Wing, is the **Nichols Bridgeway**.

The 1,500-seat **Harris Theater for Music and Dance** was built mostly below ground so as not to obscure views through the park. Designed by Hammond Beeby Rupert Ainge, the theater offers ballet and other dance performances, in addition to classical, chamber, opera, and folk music.

Designed to pay homage to the city's motto *Urbs in Horto* (City in a Garden), the **Lurie Garden**, with its graceful wooden footbridge and groves of trees, is a pleasant landscape of plants and flowers. This 2.5-acre garden was the result of an international design competition and has become a popular meeting place.

The **Crown Fountain** consists of two 50-ft (15-m) towers that project video images of Chicago citizens, whose mouths open to spout water on those visitors splashing below.

The **McCormick-Tribune Ice-rink** converts to an outdoor restaurant and activity plaza in the summer, becoming a venue for Chicago's summer dance program *(see p168)*.

Beside the Ice Rink is the **AT & T Plaza**, featuring the huge *Cloud Gate* sculpture by renowned British artist Anish Kapoor. This giant elliptical structure (nicknamed *The Bean*) has a highly polished surface, which is designed to reflect the park and surroundings. It is Kapoor's first public work installed in the US.

Chicago Theatre

175 N State St. **Map** 4 D1. *Tel (312)
462-6363.* M *Lake (red line), State
and Lake (brown, green, & orange
lines).* 🚌 *29, 36, 62, 145, 146.*
⭘ *10am–6pm Mon–Fri.* 🎭
*Apr–Sep: noon Tue & Thu; Oct–Mar:
noon Tue. 3rd Sat of month:11am &
noon. See* **Entertainment** *pp170–1.*

Slated for demolition in the
1980s but reprieved, this
grand 3,800-seat theater has
been restored to its former
glory. The oldest surviving
theater in Chicago, it was
designed by Rapp and
Rapp in 1921 and
originally was a
vaudeville movie
palace. It now hosts
musicals and other
live performances.
   Along with its
Beaux-Arts white
terra-cotta façade,
the theater has the
last cast-iron
building front in
Chicago. In 1902,
architects Hill and
Woltersdorf
remodeled the west
façade and added
another floor. The decoration
of the entranceway, triumphal

**Chicago Theatre's
marquee and sign**

arch (inspired by Paris' Arc de
Triomphe), and palatial lobby
reflect the opulence of early
theater design. The six-story-
high sign above the marquee
has become a city symbol.

Michigan Avenue Bridge ⑰

Map 2 D5. 🚌 *151.*

Linking the loop with the
Magnificent Mile, Michigan
Avenue Bridge, the first
double-deck trunnion bascule
bridge ever built, was
completed in 1920.
Spanning the Chicago
River, the bridge's two
leaves, each weighing
3,340 tons (3,030
tonnes), open by
turning on enormous
trunnion bearings on
the banks. In 1991, it
was designated a
Chicago landmark.
   The bas-relief
sculptures, one on
each of the four
bridgehouses, com-
memorate important
events in Chicago's
history. A plaque on the
southwest corner marks the

**Henry Hering's Defence depicting
the 1812 massacre, on bridgehouse**

site of Fort Dearborn
(1803–12); brass markers
embedded in the concrete
outline the shape of the
original fort.
   At the bridge's north end,
in the 401 North Michigan
Avenue plaza, a plaque marks
the homestead of Jean
Baptiste Point du Sable,
Chicago's first permanent
non-American Indian resident.
   Michigan Avenue Bridge is
one of 20 downtown bridges
spanning the Chicago River,
in a city that has the greatest
number of movable bridges
of any city in the world.

The opulent interior of the restored Chicago Theatre

Visitors can also stroll along nearby Riverwalk, parallel to Wacker Drive from Wabash Avenue to Wells Street.

35 East Wacker Drive ⑱

Map 4 D1. *Tel* (312) 726-4260. Ⓜ Lake; State. ◯ 24 hrs daily. ♿

This sandy-colored terra-cotta office building, which became a Chicago landmark in 1994, has been described as a "confection" –

Frieze on 35 East Wacker Drive

the dome at the top really does resemble a birthday cake! The building, designed by Thielbar and Fugard, opened in 1926. During Prohibition, the dome housed mobster Al Capone's notorious speakeasy, the Stratosphere Club.

The building once had private parking garages on each of the first 22 floors; jeweler tenants, concerned about security, drove into the elevator and were lifted up to their floors. A 1988 renovation restored the marble interior. Outside, a 6-ton (5.4-tonne) clock with the gilded bronze figure of Father Time overhangs the Wacker Drive sidewalk.

35 East Wacker Drive, seen from across the Chicago River

Corberó's *Three Lawyers and a Judge* in the R.R. Donnelley Building

R.R. Donnelley Building ⑲

77 W Wacker Dr. **Map** 3 C1. *Tel* (312) 917-1177. Ⓜ Clark. ◯ 24 hrs daily. ♿

The R.R. Donnelley Building (1992), a modern 50-story office tower overlooking the Chicago River, is one of the more recent skyscrapers to be built in the Downtown Core.

Designed by Chicago architect James DeStefano, with famed Catalan architect Ricardo Bofill as the design consultant, the building combines classical aesthetic with Chicago School *(see pp26–7)* functionality. The many classical references to ancient Greece and Rome include the four-pedimented roof, a contemporary take on a classically proportioned Greek temple. The building materials likewise conjure the classics: a grid of Portuguese white granite frames the exterior curtain wall of silver reflective glass.

The ground-floor marble lobby, with its 42-ft- (13-m-) high ceiling and huge, classical windows, is a monumental space housing

two sculptural groupings: Ricardo Bofill's *Twisted Columns* (1992), a set of three Modernistic columns hand-carved from white Italian marble, and Catalan sculptor Xavier Corberó's *Three Lawyers and a Judge* (1992), rough-hewn basalt figures suggesting human forms.

At night, 540 high-intensity lamps dramatically illuminate the building in a lighting scheme designed by Pierre Arnaud, who also illuminated the Pyramids, the Parthenon, and the Louvre Museum.

View of buildings along waterfront Wacker Drive, at twilight

The towering atrium in the James R. Thompson Center

James R. Thompson Center 🔀

100 W Randolph St. **Map** 3 C1.
Tel (312) 814-6684. **M** Clark/Lake.
🕐 6:30am–6pm (atrium 8am–6pm)
Mon–Fri. 👍 🅰 **Art exhibits**.

The James R. Thompson Center (1985) is a refreshing change from the rectangular skyscrapers that make up Chicago's Downtown Core. Architect Helmut Jahn designed the center as a symbol of open democratic government, one with no barriers between it and the people. The all-glass walls and roof in this multishaped structure provide a monumental, dazzling – and some say, chaotic – transparency.

Originally called the State of Illinois Building, and often still referred to as such, the building was later renamed after the former Illinois governor who commissioned it. The tricolor (patriotic but often criticized salmon, silver, and blue) center is home to

almost 70 government offices and numerous restaurants and shops. Performances and fairs are often held in the atrium.

The interior rotunda, at 17 stories and 160 ft (49 m) in diameter, is one of the largest enclosed spaces in the world. A cylindrical skylight soaring 75 ft (23 m) above the roofline caps the rotunda. Its steel frame weighs almost 10,500 tons (9,525 tonnes).

Exposed escalator and elevator machinery echo the building's no-barriers theme.

Elevators run up glass shafts to a viewing platform on the 16th floor. Here, visitors brave enough to look down will have a stunning view of the marble rosette in the granite concourse floor marking the building's center.

Throughout the building are 14 specially commissioned artworks showcasing Illinois artists, and selections from the building's permanent art collection are also on view. Ask for a directory at the information desk.

On the second floor is the Illinois Art Gallery, with visiting exhibitions, and the Illinois Artisans Shop, selling artworks and crafts.

Not on view to the public are eight ice banks – each 40 ft (12 m) long, 12 ft (3.5 m) wide, and 14 ft (4 m) tall – in the sub-basement. In summer, up to 400 tons (363 tonnes) of ice are frozen each night in these giant ice cubes, then used to cool the building.

Outside the building, at the Randolph Street entrance, sits Jean Dubuffet's 29-ft (9-m) lighthearted fiberglass sculpture *Monument with Standing Beast* (1984) (see p125).

333 West Wacker Drive 🔀

Map 3 B1. **M** Washington (brown, orange, purple lines). 🕐 7am–6:30pm Mon–Fri. 👍 🅿

Located at a bend in the Chicago River, this prominent Post-Modern, 36-story edifice echoes the curving form of its natural neighbor. Designed in 1983 by the architectural firm of

The massive James R. Thompson Center, *Standing Beast* in foreground

Kohn Pedersen Fox, the office tower is sheathed with reflective, green-tinted glass that changes shade depending on the levels of sun and water. Broad horizontal bands of brushed stainless steel run every 6 ft (2 m). Green marble and gray granite form the base of this elegant, wedge-shaped building, materials used again in the two-story lobby.

A cityscape reflected on 333 West Wacker Drive's convex surface

Wacker Drive ❷

From N Wacker Dr to N Michigan Ave. **Map** 3 C1. **M** *Clark*.

Wacker Drive's east-west segment offers one of the loveliest downtown walks of any US city. Running alongside the south bank of the main branch of the Chicago River and connecting to 17 of the city's bridges, this two-tiered street was the first of its kind in the world.

Named in honor of Charles Wacker, one of Chicago's civic planners *(see p71)*, the drive was built in 1926 to replace the run-down South Water Street Market.

The lower level is reserved for through traffic, but the upper level consists of a roadway, sidewalks, and a pleasant riverwalk, lined with public art.

Wacker Drive affords a splendid view across the river of impressive architecture, including the massive Merchandise Mart. Built for Marshall Field in 1930, it is, at

The fortresslike Merchandise Mart, best viewed from Wacker Drive

4.2 million sq ft (390,000 sq m), the world's largest commercial building.

State Street Bridge Gallery, in the bridge's mechanical room (open daily, no admission charge), offers visitors a rare opportunity to see the machinery at work behind this famous movable bridge. The gallery also displays local artwork.

At 75 East Wacker Drive is the city's thinnest skyscraper. This Gothic-style, 1928 build-ing is clad in white terra-cotta.

The Chicago Architecture Foundation's river cruise tours, departing from Michigan Avenue Bridge at Wacker Drive, offer fantastic views of Chicago's towers.

CHICAGO'S RIVER

No other natural feature played as important a role in the early development of Chicago as did the Chicago River. For Native Americans and settlers alike, the river served as a trade route connecting the Great Lakes and the heart of the continent. By the mid-1800s, as shipping became a major economic activity in the area, the Chicago River was the main thoroughfare of a growing metropolis.

One unsanitary result of such growth was that the Chicago River also served as the city's sewer, a dumping ground for waste. The swampy conditions, with the surface of the land near to the level of standing water, made it impossible to construct an underground sewer system.

In the mid-1800s, a Boston engineer, Ellis Chesbrough, was hired to fix the problem. Chesbrough developed the country's first

comprehensive sewer system – above ground. The streets, along with the buildings on them, were raised above the new system, sometimes by as much as 12 ft (3.5 m). The city's largest hotel at the time, the Tremont, was raised while still open for business, with-out breaking a pane of glass or cracking a plaster wall.

This new sewer system did not entirely eradicate the city's unsanitary conditions, however. In 1885, a devas-tating cholera and typhoid epidemic killed thousands of Chicagoans (12 percent of the population by some estimates) when sewage flowed into Lake Michigan, the city's source of drinking water.

In response to this tragedy, the city initiated the largest municipal project in the US at the time – the construction of the 28-mile- (45-km-) long Sanitary and Ship Canal. Built between Damen Avenue and the town of Lockport, the canal connected the Chicago

River to the Des Plaines and Illinois Rivers and involved the digging out of more rocks, soil, and clay than was excavated for the Panama Canal. This massive project reversed the flow of the main and south branches of the river, which now drain away from Lake Michigan and into the Sanitary and Ship Canal.

Drawbridge spanning the Chicago River opening for water traffic

NORTH SIDE

Just north of the Chicago River, Chicago's North Side encompasses several neighborhoods, most settled in the mid-1880s by Irish, German, and Swedish immigrants. Tragically, the 1871 fire razed the entire area. The communities

Ornate detailing on Present Bridge

rose from the ashes, and today the Magnificent Mile, Gold Coast, Streeterville, and River North are all upscale residential and shopping districts. Modest Old Town is an eclectic mix of residences, shops, and entertainment venues.

SIGHTS AT A GLANCE

Historic Buildings and Streets
Charnley-Persky House ❷❾
Crilly Court and Olsen-Hansen Row Houses ❷❷
Drake Hotel ❾
Edward P. Russell House ❷❽
1500 North Astor Street ❷❼
1550 North State Parkway ❷❹
Hotel InterContinental Chicago ❸
Menomonee Street ❷⓿
Newberry Library ❶❽
Residence of the Roman Catholic Archbishop of Chicago ❷❺
Samuel M. Nickerson and Ransom R. Cable Houses ❶❺
Tribune Tower ❷
Wacker Houses ❷❶
Water Tower and Pumping Station ❺
Wrigley Building ❶

Modern Skyscrapers
John Hancock Center ❼
Marina City and IBM Building ❶❸
Trump International Hotel & Tower ❸❶

Churches and Cathedrals
Archdiocese of Chicago and Chapel of St. James ❶❼
Fourth Presbyterian Church ❻
St. James Episcopal Cathedral ❶❻
St. Michael's Church ❶❾

Museums and Galleries
Chicago Children's Museum ❶❷
Chicago History Museum ❷❸
Hershey's Chicago ❹
International Museum of Surgical Science ❷❻
Museum of Contemporary Art ❶⓿
River North Gallery District ❶❹

Shopping Streets
Oak Street ❽

Piers and Beaches
Navy Pier ❶❶
Oak Street Beach ❸⓿

GETTING THERE

The Magnificent Mile is a short walk from the Loop. CTA stations Grand and Chicago are nearby, and buses 3, 145, 146, 147, and 151 run along Michigan Avenue to farther destinations. A free trolley circles Streeterville. CTA red line serves River North and the Gold Coast; Sedgwick station serves Old Town.

KEY

▮ Street-by-Street map
See pp60–61

Ⓜ CTA train station

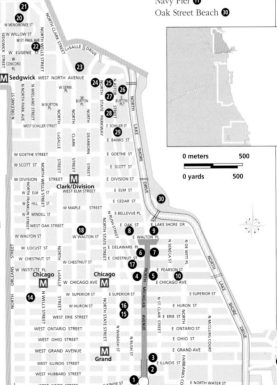

◁ Aerial view of the Gold Coast, looking north to Lincoln Park

Street-by-Street: The Magnificent Mile

The magnificent mile, a stretch of Michigan Avenue north of the
Chicago River, is Chicago's most fashionable street. Although
almost completely destroyed in the 1871 fire, by the early 1900s,
Michigan Avenue had become a major traffic artery. The 1920
opening of Michigan Avenue Bridge led to a retail boom. In 1947,
developer Arthur Rubloff, predicting that the street would be
Chicago's premier shopping district, dubbed it the Magnificent
Mile. His prediction came true and the name stuck. Exclusive
shops line the wide boulevard, while modern retail
complexes and mixed-use skyscrapers rub shoulders
with historic buildings.

★ John Hancock Center
*This tower offers spectacular
views from its open-air
skywalk on the 94th floor.
The ground-level plaza has
a fountain, cafés, and,
occasionally, live music* **7**

**Fourth Presbyterian
Church**
*Fourteen carved stone
angels, each holding a
musical instrument, adorn
the nave of this Gothic
Revival-style church, the
oldest structure on the
Magnificent Mile after the
Water Tower. A large fountain sparkles at the center of
its inner courtyard* **6**

KEY

– – – Suggested route

STAR SIGHTS

★ Hotel Inter-
　Continental
　Chicago

★ John Hancock
　Center

★ Water Tower and
　Pumping Station

**★ Water Tower and
Pumping Station**
*These two historic
castellated structures,
the station housing a
café, theater and visitors'
center, sit on an island in
the street – a relaxing,
shady retreat from busy
Michigan Avenue* **5**

Chicago Place
*Contains specialty shops and
an airy food court with an
excellent view of Michigan
Avenue. Historical murals
decorate the building's lobby.*

Water Tower Place

The shopping area of this 1970s tower block is centered around an eight-story terraced atrium and includes upscale boutiques, numerous restaurants, and two major department stores.

LOCATOR MAP
See Street Finder map 2

★ Hotel InterContinental Chicago

An eclectic mix of detailing – from Mesopotamian-inspired carvings to knights in armor – vie for attention in this 1929 hotel **❸**

Tribune Tower

Rock fragments from famous sites around the world, including St. Peter's Basilica in Rome, are embedded in the exterior of this Gothic-style tower **❷**

NORTH MICHIGAN AVENUE

The Westfield North Bridge

development houses shops, restaurants, a movie theater, and several hotels.

0 meters 200

0 yards 200

Wrigley Building

This structure, one of Chicago's most beloved, boasts a giant four-sided clock and a quiet courtyard, which is open to the public. The building is particularly dazzling at night, when it is illuminated **❶**

View of the two-part Wrigley Building, to the left of Tribune Tower

Wrigley Building ❶

400–410 N Michigan Ave. **Map** 2 D5. **Tel** (312) 923-8080. M Grand (red line). 🚌 3, 11, 145, 146, 147, 151. **North lobby** ⏰ 24 hrs daily; **South lobby** ⏰ 7am–6pm Mon–Fri. **South building** ⏰ public hols. ♿

The Wrigley Building rests on a historical site: it was to here that Jesuit missionary Jacques Marquette and explorer Louis Joliet made their first portage west of the Great Lakes in the 1670s, and here that La Salle planted the flag of France *(see p15)*.

Chewing-gum manufacturer William Wrigley, Jr. commissioned the architectural firm Graham, Anderson, Probst and White to design the building. The 30-story south tower was built in 1920, the 21-story north tower in 1924. They are connected by three arcades. The circular temple and cupola rising above a massive four-faced clock were inspired by Seville's Giralda Tower.

Six shades of white enamel, from gray to cream, were baked onto the terra-cotta cladding; at night, it shimmers.

Tribune Tower ❷

435 N Michigan Ave. **Map** 2 D5. **Tel** (312) 222-3232. M Grand (red line). ⏰ 24 hrs daily. ♿ 🚻

The 36-story limestone Tribune Tower is the winning design of a 1922 international competition sponsored by the Tribune Company to celebrate the 75th anniversary of the *Chicago Tribune*. Architects were challenged to create the most beautiful office building in the world. From 263 submissions, that of New York firm Howells and Hood was chosen. Their Gothic design, reflected in the flying buttresses of the crowning tower, echoes France's Rouen Cathedral.

The building's ornate three-story arched entrance is carved with figures from Aesop's fables. Gargoyles, such as the monkey symbolizing human folly (below the south-side fourth-floor windows), embellish the façade. More than 100 rock fragments from famous sites, including Beijing's Forbidden City and London's Westminster Abbey, are embedded in the exterior walls, as is a 3.3-billion-year-old piece of moon rock, collected by the Apollo 15 mission. A guide to the rocks is available in the lobby.

Hotel InterContinental Chicago ❸

505 N Michigan Ave. **Map** 2 D5. **Tel** (312) 944-4100. M Grand (red line). ⏰ 24 hrs daily. ♿ 🐾 🚻 🖥 ▼ 🅿 See **Where to Stay** p143.

Originally the Shriners' Medinah Athletic Club, this magnificent building was renovated at a cost of $130 million, reopening in 1990 as the Hotel InterContinental Chicago. Designed in 1929 by Walter W. Ahlschlager, it is topped with a large onion-shaped gilt dome.

Many of the building's exterior and interior details reflect the Shriners' interest in all things Egyptian, medieval, and Renaissance. Ask the concierge for the free self-guided tour audiotape, which explains historic features.

Carved on the 2nd-floor staircase to the Hall of Lions, two lions guard the intricate terra-cotta fountain. Inside the King Arthur Foyer and Court on the 3rd floor, colorful paintings on the ceiling beams depict King Arthur's life. On the 5th floor, classical Renaissance paintings adorn the walls of the Renaissance Room Foyer.

The Johnny Weissmuller Pool at Hotel InterContinental Chicago

The Spanish Tea Court features a fountain lined with Spanish Majolica tiles.

A gem is the 11th-floor swimming pool, named after the swimmer and actor Johnny Weissmuller. A recent renovation created a common entrance for the north and south towers.

Sign for the giant chocolate store on Magnificent Mile

Hershey's Chicago ❹

822 North Michigan Avenue. **Map** 2 D4. **Tel** (312) 337-7711. Ⓜ Chicago (red line). ⏰ 10am–8pm Sun–Thu (to 10pm in summer); 10am–10pm Fri & Sat.

When candy-maker Milton Hershey visited the city of Chicago in 1893, he purchased the equipment that he would use to revolutionize the chocolate industry. With mass production he was able to lower the cost of manufacturing milk chocolate, once a luxury item, making it affordable to all. Today, the Hershey Foods Corporation is the largest North American producer of confectionary.

Hershey's Chicago is a huge themed store located in a Loyola University building on Magnificent Mile. It stocks all the well-known brands such as Hershey's, Reese's, and Kit Kat, as well as the latest products and goods unique to the Chicago store. Sugar-free versions of the most popular products are also available. The store's interactive "bake shoppe", where visitors can customize cookies, cupcakes, and brownies, is popular with children.

The Chicago store is the latest addition to the world-famous chain which includes Hershey's Time Square in New York and the Hershey's Chocolate World in Hershey Pennsylvania.

Water Tower and Pumping Station ❺

806 N Michigan Ave. **Map** 2 D4. Ⓜ Chicago (red line). **Tower Tel** (312) 742-0808. ⏰ 10am–6:30pm Mon–Sat; 10am–5pm Sun. ⚫ public hols. **Station Tel** (312) 744-2400. ⏰ 7:30am–7pm daily. ⚫ Thanksgiving, Dec 25. ♿ station only. 🖥 🛍 ℹ️

Built just before the fire of 1871, the Water Tower (1869) and the Pumping Station (1866), housing Chicago's original waterworks, were two of the few buildings in the city to survive the conflagration.

Designed by William W. Boyington, these structures look like Gothic castles. The 154-ft (47-m) tower consists of limestone blocks rising in five sections from a square base. The tower originally housed a standpipe that stabilized the mains water pressure. It is now home to a City Gallery which specializes in photography. Lookingglass Theatre is also based here.

In addition to housing a Visitor Information Center (163 E. Pearson St.), the Pumping Station fulfills its original purpose, pumping up to 250 million gallons (946 million liters) of water per day.

The Water Tower survived Chicago's Great Fire of 1871

Fourth Presbyterian Church ❻

866 N Michigan Ave. **Map** 2 D4. **Tel** (312) 640-2573. Ⓜ Chicago (red line). 🚌 10, 143, 144, 145, 146, 147, 151. ⏰ 9am–6pm Mon–Fri; 8am–7:30pm Sun. 🎵 8am, 9:30am, 11am, 6:30pm Sun. ♿ via 126 E Chestnut St. **Concerts** 12:10pm Fri.

The 1871 fire destroyed the original Fourth Presbyterian Church, at Wabash and Grand, the night it was dedicated. The current building (1914) is the oldest surviving structure (after the Water Tower) on Michigan Avenue, north of the river.

Designed by Ralph Adams Cram, architect of New York's Cathedral of St. John the Divine, the church is Gothic Revival in style (see p26). Its exposed buttresses, stone spire, and recessed main window all reflect the influences of medieval European churches.

Angels, 7 ft (2 m) tall, stand just below the illuminated timber ceiling; the stained-glass windows are magnificent.

A covered walkway leads to a tranquil courtyard designed by Howard Van Doren Shaw.

Weekly Friday concerts, some including the church's magnificent organ, are free.

The peaceful courtyard of the Fourth Presbyterian Church

John Hancock Center **7**

875 N Michigan Ave. **Map** 2 D4.
Observatory Tel (312) 654-2891.
M Chicago (red line). ⬤ 9am–11pm
daily. 🎟 to observatory (children
under 5 free). ♿ ❚❚ ⛾ 🅿

Affectionately called
"Big John" by Chicagoans,
John Hancock Center
stands out as a bold feature
of the Chicago skyline. The
100-story building has 18-
story-long steel braces
crisscrossing the tapering obe-
lisk tower like stacked Xs.

The center's major attraction is the Hancock
Observatory, located on
the 94th floor. Here, 1,127 ft
(343 m) above the Magnificent
Mile, you can actually
go outside, onto Chicago's only

open-air
(screened)
skywalk.
Designed by
architect
Bruce
Graham of
Skidmore,
Owings and
Merrill and
engineer
Fazlur R.
Khan,
the John
Hancock
Center
opened in
1969, and
houses
offices,
condo-
miniums,
and shops in
2.8 million

**Open-air deck topping
the Hancock Center**

sq ft (0.26 million sq m) of
space. The elevator ride to
the top is touted as the fastest
in North America. At 20 miles
(32 km) per hour, you reach
the observatory in just 40
seconds. On a clear day,
you can see for up to 80
miles (130 km). The view
is especially dazzling during
the late-afternoon when the
sun falls upon the downtown
buildings. A wall-to-wall
exhibition in the observatory
traces Chicago's history.

The center's lower court-
yard has several cafés, with
patios in summer.

Entrance to the 1920s Drake Hotel

Oak Street **8**

Between Rush St & N Michigan Ave.
Map 2 D3. M Chicago (red line).
See **Shops and Markets** pp162–3.

Tree-lined Oak Street at the
north end of the Magnificent
Mile is home to many upscale
boutiques: Prada, Hermès,
Sonia Rykiel, Luca Luca, and
Jil Sander. The Daisy Shop
specializes in vintage couture
resale clothing. Wolford
Boutique sells European
hosiery and swimwear.

Along with its chic fashion
boutiques, Oak Street has
numerous art galleries, such
as the Colletti Antique Poster
Gallery, specializing in original works from 1880 to 1940.
Perhaps the grandest one-stop
shop in Oak Street is Barneys
New York, which opened its
spacious store here in 2009.
Luxury brands and Barneys'
in-house label attract distinguished shoppers.

The 20-story apartment
building (1929) at No. 40 was
designed by Ben Marshall,
architect of the Drake Hotel.

Drake Hotel **9**

140 E Walton Pl. **Map** 2 D3. **Tel** (312)
787-2200. M Chicago (red line). ♿
❚❚ ⬚ ⛾ See **Where to Stay** p145.

The essence of luxury in the
heart of the Magnificent Mile,
the 537-room Drake Hotel
opened in 1920. Designed by
Marshall and Fox in the
Italian Renaissance style *(see
p26)*, this 13-story hotel is
clad in limestone.

The lobby, paneled in
marble and oak, is graced
with grand chandeliers,
elegant red carpets, and a
magnificent fountain.

The elegant Palm Court, in
the lobby, offers traditional
afternoon tea and is also a
fashionable place for cocktails, with live jazz Fridays
and Saturdays. The Cape Cod
Room has an extensive
seafood menu.

The hotel's splendid piano
bar, the Coq d'Or, has live
music every night. When
Prohibition ended in 1933,
this bar served the second
drink in Chicago.

Upscale boutiques lining Oak Street

The Museum of Contemporary Art's grand entrance

Museum of Contemporary Art ❿

220 E Chicago Ave. **Map** 2 D4. *Tel (312) 280-2660.* Ⓜ *Chicago (red line).* 🚌 *10, 66.* 🕙 *10am–8pm Tue; 10am–5pm Wed–Sun.* ● *Jan 1, Thanksgiving, Dec 25.* 🎟 *(free Tue).* ♿ 🛍 📷 🏪 🅿
www.mcachicago.org

Founded in 1967, the Museum of Contemporary Art offers innovative exhibits that interpret and present contemporary art. Designed by Berlin architect Josef Paul Kleihues, the sleek building has four floors of naturally lit exhibition space. On display are selections from the museum's extensive collection of works by internationally acclaimed artists, including Andy Warhol, René Magritte, Cindy Sherman, and Alexander Calder. Don't miss Richard Long's *Chicago Mud Circle* (1996), an exuberant application of mud on the gallery wall. The museum also hosts evenings of dance, theater, and live music.

Navy Pier ⓫

600 E Grand Ave. **Map** 2 F5. *Tel 800-595-7437.* 🚌 *29, 65, 66, 124.* 🕙 *10am; closing times vary by day and season.* ● *Thanksgiving, Dec 25.* ♿ 🍴 🛍 🍷 🅿 🚻 *Lake cruises.* **www.navypier.com**

Navy Pier is a bustling recreational and cultural center. Designed by Charles S. Frost, the 3,000-ft- (915-m-)

Tranquil fountains and palms at Navy Pier's Crystal Gardens

long and 400-ft- (120-m-) wide pier was the largest in the world when built in 1916. Over 20,000 timber piles were used in its construction.

Originally a municipal wharf, the pier was used for naval training during World War II. After a four-year renovation, Navy Pier opened in its present incarnation in 1995.

Navy Pier Park has a 150-ft- (45-m-) Ferris wheel; old-fashioned carousel; outdoor amphitheater; ice skating; miniature golf; and IMAX 3D theater. The Smith Museum displays stained glass.

Free trolleys run between Navy Pier and State Street.

Chicago Children's Museum ⓬

700 E Grand Ave. at Navy Pier. **Map** 2 F5. *Tel (312) 527-1000.* 🚌 *29, 56, 65, 66, 124.* 🕙 *10am–5pm daily; 10am–8pm Thu & Sat.* ● *Thanksgiving, Dec 25.* 🎟 *(free 5–8pm Thu & 1st Mon of month).* ♿ 🅿
Special activities daily.
www.chichildrensmuseum.org

Chicago Children's Museum, focusing on activating the intellectual and creative potential of children age 1 to 12, is an activity center for the whole family. All exhibits are hands-on. Kids can build a fort in the Under Construction exhibit, climb three stories of rope-rigging on the Kovler Schooner, or make a flying machine in the Inventing Lab. In the WaterWays, they can channel water with dams and locks. The Dinosaur Expedition is where kids can dig for bones in an excavation pit. Along with educational exhibits, kids can simply have fun.

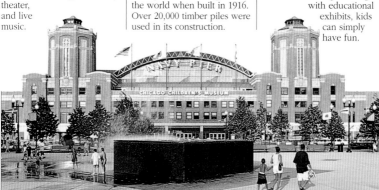

Chicago Children's Museum, at the main entrance to Navy Pier

Marina City and IBM Building ⓭

Marina City: 300 N State St.
Map 1 C5. Ⓜ *State and Lake.*
⬤ *24 hrs daily.* ♿ 🍴 🅿
IBM Building: 330 N Wabash Ave.
Map 2 D5. Ⓜ *State and Lake.*
⬤ *24 hrs daily.* ♿

The two towers of Marina City pay symbolic tribute to the Midwest's farming economy – they look like giant corncobs. Designed by Bertrand Goldberg Associates and opened in 1967, these twin circular towers function like a city within a city, with apartments, offices, shops, parking, a marina, and even a bowling alley.

To the east of Marina City, and in stark contrast to its organic form, rises the IBM Building, a sleek modern monument. Designed by Mies van der Rohe *(see p30)* with C.F. Murphy Associates and opened in 1971, the 52-story office tower has an exposed steel frame and dark bronze-tinted glass walls.

A small bust of Mies van der Rohe, who died before construction of the building was complete, is located in the lobby. In winter, the exterior plaza can be quite bleak and frigid. There are strung ropes to prevent people from being blown into the Chicago River.

Marina City's twin towers, flanked on the right by the IBM Building

Shops and galleries lining the streets of the River North Gallery District

River North Gallery District ⓮

Between N Wells & N Orleans Sts, from W Erie St to W Chicago Ave.
Map 1 B4. Ⓜ *Chicago (brown, purple lines).* ☎ 649-0065.
See **Shops and Markets** pp162–7.

River North is home to more than 65 art galleries – the largest concentration outside New York City. Some of Chicago's finest antique and home-furnishing shops are also located here.

West Superior Street is the center of the district. Galleries here and on adjoining streets offer a wide range of artwork by both international and local artisans. Unusual pieces by American folk artists, African-American art, glass sculpture, photography, and contemporary paintings are just some of the treasures to be found. Most galleries are closed Sundays and Mondays.

Samuel M. Nickerson and Ransom R. Cable Houses ⓯

40 & 25 E Erie St. **Map** 2 D4.
Ⓜ *Chicago (red line); Grand (red line).*
Nickerson House ⬤ *Tue, Wed, Sat for tours.* **Cable House** ⬤ *to public.*

Samuel M. Nickerson House offers a glimpse into the wealthy world of late-1800s Chicago high society. Commissioned by Nickerson, a distillery owner and banker, this Italian Renaissance palazzo was designed in 1883 by Chicago church-architects Burling and Whitehouse. Recently restored, it is now home to the Richard H. Driehaus Museum.

The mansion has 23 rooms on its three floors, each room seemingly more opulent than the next. More than 20 varieties of marble, along with onyx and alabaster, were used to build the main hall and great staircase. Even the ceiling is marble. The largest room is the first-floor Picture Gallery, illuminated by a domed, Tiffany leaded-glass skylight.

Across the street, the Ransom R. Cable House now quarters a securities and capital management corporation. Designed by Cobb and Frost, the 1886 Richardsonian Romanesque *(see p26)* mansion was built for the president of the Chicago, Rock Island and Pacific Railway Company. It features rough-hewn rusticated masonry. Both houses are designated as Chicago landmarks.

Charming coach house belonging to the Ransom R. Cable House

St. James Episcopal Cathedral  🔟

65 E Huron St. **Map** 2 D4. **Tel** *(312) 787-7360*. Ⓜ *Chicago (red line)*. ◯ *for mass only.* **Cathedral** 🔲 *10:30am Sun;* **Chapel** 🔲 *12:10pm Thu–Fri; 5:30pm Wed.* 🔳 🔲 **Concerts**. **www**.stjamescathedral.org

The parishioners of St. James have worshiped at this site since 1857. After their original building was destroyed in the Great Fire of 1871 (only the 1867 bell tower survived), architects Burling and Adler were hired to design a new building. The St. James Episcopal Cathedral, a Gothic Revival *(see p26)* structure of Joliet limestone, was completed in 1875.

Inside is a fine example of Victorian stencil work (1888), designed by Edward J. Neville Stent, a student of British designer William Morris. The stencils were restored in 1985 by the Chicago architects Holabird and Root.

The Chapel of St. Andrew is at the north end of the cathedral. Designed by Bertram G. Goodhue in 1913, it is said to be based on a private oratory in an ancient Scottish abbey. The painted-glass windows portray the figures of St. Paul, Mary Magdalene, and St. Francis.

The majestic altar and windows in the Chapel of St. James

Statue of Archbishop Quigley outside Quigley Seminary

Archdiocese of Chicago and Chapel of St. James 🔟

835 N Rush St. **Map** 2 D4. **Tel** *(312) 534-8200*. Ⓜ *Chicago (red line)*. **Archdiocese office** ◯ *to public.* **Chapel** 🔲 *mandatory: noon, 2pm Tue, Thu–Sat.* **Concerts**.

The Archdiocese of Chicago is in the process of moving into the former Quigley Seminary, which closed in 2007. Designed by Zachary T. Davis (architect of Wrigley Field) and Gustave E. Steinback and completed in 1919, this Gothic building has carved buttresses and spires.

Ten statues in the niches along the north wall represent saints, such as St. Cecilia, patron of music, and St. Elizabeth, patron of pregnant women. On the spire of the library tower is a statue of St. George, his iron spear serving as the building's lightning rod. A statue of Archbishop James E. Quigley (1854–1915), known for his commitment to building Catholic schools in Chicago, is at the northwest corner of the grounds.

Also on the site is the Chapel of St. James, inspired by the Gothic Sainte-Chapelle in Paris. The spectacular Rose Window, 28 ft (9 m) in diameter, depicts the life of the Virgin Mary. Smaller windows relate stories from the Bible and the pictorial scheme represents 245 events of scriptural and church

history. More than 700,000 pieces of glass are set in limestone frames. The magnificent 50-ft- (15-m-) tall limestone altar, adorned with sculptures, was hand-carved in France.

Newberry Library 🔟

60 W Walton St. **Map** 1 C3. **Tel** *(312) 943-9090*. Ⓜ *Chicago (red line)*. ◯ *Hrs for lobby, book rooms, and exhibits vary; call ahead.* ⬤ *public hols.* 🔳 🔳 *3pm Thu; 10:30am Sat.* 🔲 **Exhibits, lectures, concerts**. **www**.newberry.org

At the north end of Washington Square Park is the impressive Newberry Library. Founded in 1887 by Walter Newberry, a merchant and banker, this independent research library for the humanities – one of the best in the US – opened to the public in 1893. Henry Ives Cobb, master architect of the Richardsonian Romanesque style, was the designer.

Strengths of the collection include cartography, Native American history, Renaissance studies, and geneology. Rarities include a 1481 edition of Dante's *Divine Comedy*, first editions of Milton's *Paradise Regained*, and the King James Version of the Bible.

Through the triple-arched entrance, the lobby has a grand staircase, terrazzo flooring, galleries, and a bookstore.

Jeweled cover of the first edition of Milton's *Paradise Regained*

St. Michael's Church ⓰

1633 N Cleveland Ave. **Map** 1 B1.
Tel *(312) 642-2498.* **M** *Sedgwick.*
🕇 *9am, 11am, 7pm Sun; 5:30pm
Mon, Wed–Sat.* **&** *weekends or by
arrangement.* **P**

The original St. Michael's
Church was a small brick
building built in 1852. As
St. Michael's small
congregation
expanded, it outgrew
the building. The
cornerstone for a
new church was laid
in 1866. In just three
years the building's
construction,
overseen by builder
August Wallbaum, was
complete. Later, the
Great Fire of 1871
destroyed the roof and
interior of the church.
However, the thick, brick
walls survived and remain
to this day.

**Angel in
St. Michael's**

The steeple, added to
the bell tower in 1888, rises
290 ft (88.5 m) above the

ground. The bell tower is
adorned with a large four-
faced clock. Each of the
five bells in the tower
weighs between 2,500
and 6,000 lbs (1,135 and
2,720 kg). By tradition, if
you can hear the bells
of St. Michael's, you are
in Old Town.

Restoration of the church
began in the 1990s. The
first phase involved
removing a ton of
pigeon excrement from
inside the bell tower.

The colorful, vaulted
interior features Mayer
stained glass, frescoes,
and sculptures depicting
the life of Christ and
the Virgin Mary. The
carved high altar
and its four subsidiary
altars illustrate St.
Michael, flanked
by the archangels Gabriel
and Raphael, triumphant
over Lucifer.

Located on the church
grounds is a small monu-
ment dedicated to Catholic
war veterans.

335 Menomonee Street, a wooden
cottage typical of Old Town

Menomonee Street ⓴

From N Sedgwick St to Lincoln Park
W. **Map** 1 B1. **M** *Sedgwick.*

Menomonee Street lies in
the heart of Old Town
Triangle Historic District
(bounded by Cleveland Street
and North and Lincoln
Avenues), a delightful area of
vintage cottages and Queen
Anne-style *(see p26)* row
houses settled in the mid-
1800s by working-class
German immigrants.

In the 1940s, community
concern over the area's falling
fortunes led to one of the
city's earliest neighborhood
revitalization efforts. Today,
the Old Town Triangle's
narrow tree-lined streets are
home to picturesque houses
and numerous interesting
shops and restaurants.

Walk along Menomonee
Street to view the residences
that typify mid- to late-19th-
century Old Town. Most of
the original houses in the area
were small cottages built
using the method of balloon
framing, so-called because
such structures were reportedly as easy to construct as
blowing up a balloon *(see
p27)*. The lightweight wood-
en frames provided ample
kindling when the 1871 fire
swept through the area.

The whitish gray clapboard
house at No. 350 is a rare
surviving example of the fire-
relief shanties the Chicago
Relief and Aid Society built
for people made homeless by
the fire. These one-room

The high-domed interior and main altar of St. Michael's Church

◁ **Giant ferris wheel and merry-go-round at Navy Pier, illuminated at night**

structures, costing the City about $100 each, were transported on wagons to charred lots, providing fire victims with instant lodging.

The shanties were later replaced with permanent wooden cottages, constructed before an 1874 city ordinance prohibited the building of wooden structures. The high basements and raised front staircases typical of these cottages were designed to accommodate the above-ground sewage system (see p57). The cottages at Nos. 325–45, although built after 1871, are typical of those in the neighborhood before the ravages of the Great Fire.

Wacker Houses ㉑

1836 & 1838 N Lincoln Park W. **Map 1 B1.** Ⓜ Sedgwick. ⬤ to public.

Both the Charles H. Wacker House and the Frederick Wacker House, designed in the early 1870s by an unknown architect, are highly ornate examples of the Chicago cottage style.

Commissioned by Frederick Wacker, a Swiss-born brewer, No. 1836 was built as a coach house but served as the Wacker's temporary home until No. 1838, a wood-frame structure built just before the ban on wood as a building material, was completed.

Charles Wacker, Frederick's son and the city planner after whom Wacker Drive is named (see p57), remodeled the

The elaborate Queen Anne-style Olsen-Hansen Row Houses

coach house after moving it to its present location beside the main family home.

No. 1838's elaborately carved trim is an excellent example of the handcrafted details on many houses in the Old Town neighborhood.

Crilly Court and Olsen-Hansen Row Houses ㉒

Crilly Court: north of W Eugenie St between N Wells St & N Park Ave; **Olsen-Hansen Row Houses**: 164–172 W Eugenie St. **Map 1 C1.** Ⓜ Sedgwick. ⬤ to public.

Representing two different approaches to Queen Anne-style row-house design are Crilly Court and the Olsen-Hansen Row Houses.

Crilly Court was created in 1885 by real-estate developer Daniel F. Crilly, when he bought a city block and cut a north-south street through it, which he named after himself. Over the next ten years, Crilly built a residential and retail development, creating what is now one of the quaintest streets in Chicago.

Two columns frame the entrance to the court. On the court's west side are two-story stone row houses. On the east side is a four-story apartment building, the names of Crilly's four children carved above the doors.

The renovation of the development in the 1940s, led by Crilly's son Edgar, included

Frederick Wacker House, with its alpine-style overhanging porch

closing off alleys behind the residences to create private courtyards and replacing wooden balconies with wrought-iron ones, giving the complex a New Orleans-like atmosphere. This redevelopment of Crilly Court initiated the renewal of the Lincoln Park neighborhood.

The Olsen-Hansen Row Houses, on West Eugenie Street, are more elaborate expressions of the Queen Anne style (see p26). The row houses were designed by Norwegian-born architect Harald M. Hansen in 1886 for Adolph Olsen. Only 5 of the original 12 remain.

Turrets, various window styles, Victorian porches, irregular rooflines, and a mixture of building materials – ranging from red brick to rough stone – give each of the row houses a distinctive identity. Hansen himself lived here, at No. 164.

Daniel F. Crilly, developer of Chicago's handsome Crilly Court

Astor Street

For more than 100 years, Astor Street, named for fur tycoon and real-estate magnate John Jacob Astor, has been the heart of fashionable Gold Coast. Wealthy Chicagoans flocked to the area in the 1880s and built over the next 60 years the striking houses in myriad architectural styles that line the street, though interspersed today with more modern buildings. Just six blocks long, the charming Astor Street district, designated a Chicago landmark in 1975, is ideal for leisurely strolling.

STAR SIGHTS

★ Charnley-Persky House

★ Edward P. Russell House

★ Residence of the Roman Catholic Archbishop of Chicago

JOHN JACOB ASTOR

German-born John Jacob Astor (1763–1848) made his fortune in the fur trade. In 1808 he chartered the Chicago-based American Fur Company, creating a monopoly in the Great Lakes area. Astor's successful fur business helped fund later, highly profitable, real-estate ventures. When he died, he was the richest man in the US.

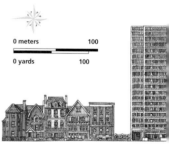

0 meters	100
0 yards	100

Astor Street East Side < < < < < < < < < < < < < < < <

VISITORS' CHECKLIST

From North Ave to W Division St.
Map 2 D1–D2. Ⓜ *Clark/ Division.*

0 meters	100
0 yards	100

May House (No. 1443) is a granite Romanesque Revival-style mansion designed in 1891 by celebrated residential architect J.L. Silsbee, one of Frank Lloyd Wright's *(see p30)* first employers. The mansion's grand arched entranceway with ornate carving is one of its most striking features.

John L. Fortune House (No. 1451)

William D. Kerfoot
This real-estate business-man lived at No. 1425. The first Chicagoan to reopen for business in the Loop after the fire of 1871, he posted outside his hastily erected shanty a sign the day after the fire: "All gone but wife, children, and energy."

1400 Block North Astor Street
The buildings lining this handsome block of the Gold Coast reflect an eclectic mix of architectural styles, ranging from a Tudor Revival country-style house at No. 1451 to a Gothic-style chateau at No. 1449.

Astor Street West Side   < < < < < < < < < < < < < < < < < < < < < < < < < < < < < <

KEY

<<<<< East side walking south

>>>>> West side walking north

★ **Edward P. Russell House**
Carvings in a floral motif decorate the Art Deco façade and window metalwork of this 1929 Holabird and Root-designed townhouse (No. 1444) **28**

★ **Residence of the Roman Catholic Archbishop of Chicago**
Built in 1880 of red brick, this massive Queen Anne-style mansion is the oldest home in the area. Decorative exterior features include floral carvings and limestone trim **25**

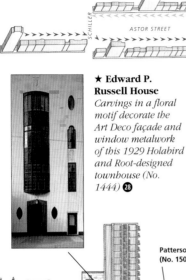

Patterson-McCormick Mansion (No. 1500; *see p76)*

★ **Charnley-Persky House**
This superb house (No. 1365) is, appropriately, now the national headquarters of the Society of Architectural Historians. The building reflects the architectural styles of its two collaborators, Louis Sullivan and Frank Lloyd Wright, and is a masterpiece of Prairie School design (see p27) **29**

Astor Court
This Georgian-style mansion (No. 1355) was designed in 1914 by Howard Van Doren Shaw for William C. Goodman, who also commissioned Shaw to design the Goodman Theatre. A decorative iron gate opens to a courtyard. The building now contains luxury apartments.

Edwin J. Gardiner House (No. 1345)

Chicago History Museum ㉓

1601 N Clark St. **Map** 1 C1. *Tel* (312) 642-4600. 🚌 11, 22, 36, 72, 151, 156. ⏰ 9:30am– 4:30pm Mon–Sat (to 8pm Thu); noon–5pm Sun. ⏰ Jan 1, Thanksgiving, Dec 25. 🎫 *(free Mon, children under 12 free)* 📷 ♿ 🎁 *(call for times).* 📋 📺 🅿 *Concerts, lectures.* www.chicagohistory.org

Founded in 1856, the Chicago History Museum, formerly known as the Chicago Historical Society, is the city's oldest cultural institution. A major museum and research center, it boasts more than 22 million objects, images, and documents relating to the history of Chicago and Illinois.

Permanent exhibits, supplemented with temporary displays, trace the early recorded history of the Chicago area, beginning with the expeditions of 17th-century French explorers such as Father Jacques Marquette.

Among the highlights of the collection are the Chicago history dioramas on the first floor. Behind glass in a darkened room, eight minia-ture scenes show Chicago's rapid growth in the 18th and 19th centuries. The dioramas illustrate great events, such as the Great Fire of 1871 and the 1893 World's Columbian Exposition, as well as historic scenes, such as bustling LaSalle Street in the mid-1860s.

American-history buffs shouldn't miss the American Wing, on the second floor, which features 1 of only 23 surviving copies of the

The original, Neo-Georgian entrance to the History Museum

Declaration of Independence (the version printed in Phila-delphia on July 4, 1776). As well, there is a rare copy of the American Constitution first printed in a Philadelphia newspaper, alongside the Bill of Rights drafted in 1789. Abraham Lincoln's deathbed is also on display. The Chicago History Museum also has a Research Center library, which is open for public research.

Along with the fascinating exhibits, the building itself is noteworthy, as it presents two dramatic faces to the world. The original Neo-Georgian structure, designed by architects Graham, Anderson, Probst and White in 1932, is best appreciated from Lincoln Park. The 1988 addition faces North Clark Street with a three-story, glass-and-steel atrium entrance. The most dramatic feature is the curving glass section at the south end.

In 2006, the museum completed extensive renova-tions and celebrated its 150th anniversary with a new permanent exhibit entitled "Chicago: Crossroads of

America." Offering a fresh perspective on the city, it interprets Chicago as a dynamic hub of commerce, industry, and culture that shaped modern America. A centerpiece is Chicago's first "L" car, which transported riders to the 1893 World's Columbian Exposition. As the title suggests, its galleries focus on Chicago first as a crossroads of commerce and industry, from fur to meat-packing. It also portrays Chicago as a city in crisis, from the fire of 1871 to the Democratic National Convention of 1968, and as a home for many generations of every race, ethnicity, and class; as a breeding ground for such innovations as skyscrapers, the Prairie School, Marshall Field's, Wrigley gum, and Weber grills; and finally, as a cultural hub, offering baseball to jazz, blues, and classical music.

1550 North State Parkway, once the epitome of Gold Coast luxury

1550 North State Parkway ㉔

Map 1 C1. Ⓜ *Clark/Division.* ⬤ *to public.*

When it opened in 1912, this apartment building overlooking Lincoln Park epitomized the luxury of the Gold Coast. Designed by Marshall and Fox (architects of the Drake Hotel, *see p64*), the 12-story Beaux-Arts *(see p27)* structure is faced with white terra-cotta.

Depiction of the 1871 Great Fire from the museum's excellent collection

Originally, each of the floors comprised a separate apartment with 15 rooms (5 for servants) and 9,000 sq ft (835 sq m) of living space – more than four times the size of the average modest home. The luxurious apartments have since been subdivided.

The black grillwork of the iron balconies, bowed windows, and the large urns on top of the balustrade are all interesting features.

The imposing home of Chicago's Roman Catholic archbishop

Residence of the Roman Catholic Archbishop of Chicago ㉕

1555 N State Pkwy. **Map** 2 D1. Ⓜ *Clark/Division*. 🚫 *to public.*

Built in 1880 on the site of an early Catholic cemetery, the building is home to the archbishop of Chicago's Roman Catholic diocese. Archbishop Patrick A. Feehan was the first resident of this, the area's oldest home.

The two-and-a-half-story Queen Anne-style *(see p26)* mansion was designed by Alfred F. Pashley. Although not highly ornamented, its decorative features include Italianate windows and 19 chimneys rising from a peaked and gabled roofline, a landmark of the area.

The property surrounding the archbishop's residence was subdivided in the late 1800s by the Chicago Archdiocese and sold to Chicago's wealthy, who built their houses on the lots.

Today, the archbishop's residence has attractive landscaped grounds, complete with papal flag.

International Museum of Surgical Science ㉖

1524 N Lake Shore Dr. **Map** 2 D1. *Tel* (312) 642-6502. Ⓜ *Clark/Division (red line), Sedgwick (brown and purple lines).* 🚌 *151.* ⭕ *May–Sep: 10am–4pm Tue–Sun; Oct–Apr: 10am–4pm Tue–Sat.* ⚫ *Mon, public hols.* 🎫 *(free Tue)* 📷 🚻 ℗ **www**.imss.org

The International Museum of Surgical Science, with its cranial saws and bone crushers, is an unusual museum and well worth a visit. Where else can one marvel at the variety, size, and intriguing shapes of gallstones and bladder stones?

Opened to the public in 1954, the museum is handsomely lodged in a historic (1917) four-story mansion designed by Howard Van Doren Shaw.

Fascinating exhibits from around the world trace the history of surgery and related sciences. Some of the earliest artifacts are 4,000-year-old Peruvian trepanning tools used to release evil spirits from the

Hope and Help, **by Edouard Chaissing, at museum entrance**

skull. Amazingly, some of the trepanned skulls on display show bony tissue growth, proof that patients survived the procedure. Less grisly exhibits include a re-creation of a turn-of-the-20th-century apothecary, complete with medicine bottles, labels claiming to cure every ill.

The Hall of Immortals showcases 12 larger-than-life sculptures of important figures in medical history, such as the earliest-known physician, Imhotep (c.2700 BC), and Marie Curie.

An unusual exhibit is the 1935 Perfusion Pump created by Charles A. Lindbergh and Alexis Carrel, a device that enabled biologists to keep a human organ functioning outside of the body.

"Beyond Broken Bones," presents a historical overview of orthopedic treatments and prosthetics with a range of documents and artifacts, from ancient bone-cutting tools to artificial limbs and their histories. A new exhibit, "The Universal Condition," chronicles attempts to alleviate pain and includes pre-historic skulls and patent drugs. The library contains more than 5,000 books, including rare and antique volumes.

Turn-of-the-20th-century apothecary shop, Museum of Surgical Science

Façade of 1500 North Astor Street, with its Classical detailing

1500 North Astor Street ㉗

Map 2 D1. **M** *Clark/Division then bus 22, 36.* ● *to public.*

This opulent four-story Italian Renaissance palazzo was built in 1893 for *Chicago Tribune* publisher Joseph Medill as a wedding gift for his daughter. Designed by McKim, Mead and White, it is built of orange Roman brick, with terra-cotta trim. The most impressive feature of this house, the largest on Astor Street, is the two-story front porch with Doric and Ionic columns.

Cyrus Hall McCormick II, son of the inventor of the Virginia reaper *(see p31),* bought the mansion in the 1920s. He then commissioned an addition to be built at the north end, doubling the building's size. It now contains luxury condominiums.

Edward P. Russell House ㉘

1444 N Astor St. **Map** 2 D2. **M** *Clark/Division.* ● *to public.*

A unique, four-story townhouse, the Edward P. Russell House was designed in 1929 by the architect firm of Holabird and Root.

Designed in the Art Deco style popular in the 1920s and 1930s, the house is, perhaps, the finest example of this architectural style in Chicago.

Graceful carvings in a floral motif decorate the building's smooth, white stone façade. These carvings are repeated in the metalwork on the windows. Although the shapes of the windows vary, they all unite to create a harmonious balance.

The stone on the townhouse's façade, which was quarried in Lens, France, is trimmed with polished granite. A subtle three-story bay of black metal embodies the grace and elegance of this truly refined, much-admired, building.

Art Deco window on the exterior of Edward P. Russell House

Charnley-Persky House ㉙

1365 N Astor St. **Map** 2 D2. **Tel** *(312) 573-1365.* **f** *(312) 915-0105.* **M** *Clark/Division.* 🗹 *mandatory.* ● *public hols.* 📷 📷

Frank Lloyd Wright called Charnley-Persky House (1892) "the first modern house in America." Two of America's most influential architects collaborated on the design: Wright *(see p30),* then a draftsman in the early stages of his career, and Louis Sullivan *(see p30),* known for his architectural detailing. They were commissioned by lumberman James Charnley and his wife Helen.

Charnley-Persky House is a pivotal work in the history of modern architecture. Its design embraces abstract forms, every interior view providing a perfectly balanced composition. The house's relatively simple façade of brick and limestone contrasts with the elaborate fronts of the exclusive Astor Street neighborhood.

An atrium reaching from the oak-paneled entry hall to a skylight two floors above is the interior's focal point. Dramatic arches frame the rooms on the first floor.

Along with bold geometrical forms and organic abstractions there are surprising details, such as windows in the closets. One striking feature of the house is the elegantly tapering wooden screen on the second floor.

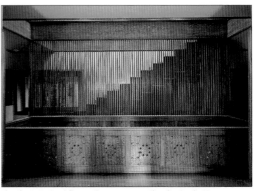

The elegant second-floor stairway screen at Charnley-Persky House

View of the Gold Coast skyline from Oak Street Beach

Restored in 1988 by the architect firm of Skidmore, Owings and Merrill, the house now headquarters the Society of Architectural Historians. It was renamed in honor of Seymour Persky, who bought it for the society.

Oak Street Beach ③⓪

Between E Division & E Oak Sts, at N and E Lake Shore Dr. **Map** 2 D3. **Tel** (312) 742-7529 (Chicago Park District). Ⓜ Chicago (red line) then bus 36; Clark/Division. 🚌 145, 146, 147, 155.

Just steps from Chicago's Magnificent Mile is the fashionable Oak Street Beach, one of the city's several beaches that together form a sandy chain along the lakefront.

As well as providing a great view of Lake Michigan, the Gold Coast, and towering North Side buildings, Oak Street Beach presents a good opportunity to don swimsuit and sandals. Throngs of joggers, cyclists, dog walkers, and in-line skaters make the broad expanse of Oak Street Beach a lively place to enjoy the sun and watch the waves. At the southern end of the beach is a pleasant promenade.

To reach the beach, use the pedestrian tunnels at Oak or Division Streets. There are washrooms at the beach, but the nearest changing rooms are at North Avenue Beach.

Trump International Hotel & Tower ③①

401 N Wabash Ave. **Map** 1 D5. **Tel** (312) 588-8000. Ⓜ Grand (red line). ♿ 🛎 🍸 🍴 🅿 See **Where to Stay** p145.

Completed in 2009 as the second-tallest building in Chicago after Willis Tower, Trump Tower stands sleek and shiny on the edge of the Chicago River, reflecting the skyline in its stainless steel and glass façade. At 92 stories and 1,392 ft (425 m) tall, it is a significant addition to the Chicago skyline. It houses shops, a hotel, and condominiums, breaking the John Hancock Center's record as Chicago's tallest residence.

Non-residents can enjoy dinner at the hotel restaurant on the 16th floor, which has floor-to-ceiling windows and an outdoor terrace, and offers spectacular panoramic vistas of Lake Michigan, the Chicago River, and the city.

Trump International Hotel & Tower by the Chicago River

OLD MONEY

Chicago has a beautiful sound because Chicago means money – so the late actress Ruth Gordon reputedly said. By the turn of the century, 200 millionaires flourished in the city. One of the most prominent was dry-goods merchant and real-estate mogul Potter Palmer, who with his socialite wife Bertha Honore, had an enormous impact on the city's social, cultural, and economic life. Chicago's wealthy began to flock from the Prairie Avenue District, to the Gold Coast after Palmer built, in 1882, his opulent home (since demolished) at present-day 1350 North Lake Shore Drive.

Department-store owner Marshall Field (see pp50-51), was less ostentatious in his display of wealth. Although he rode in a carriage to work, he always walked the last few blocks so people wouldn't see his transport. Likewise, he asked the architect of his $2-million, 25-room mansion not to include any frills. The influential Field also provided major funding to the Field Museum (see pp86-9) and the 1893 World's Fair.

SIGHTS AT A GLANCE

Historic Buildings and Churches
Dearborn Station ❸
Glessner House ⓮
Henry B. Clarke House ⓰
Hilton Chicago ❺
Ida B. Wells-Barnett House ㉑
Pilgrim Baptist Church ⓳

Historic Streets and Districts
Calumet-Giles-Prairie District ⓴
Chinatown ⓱
Prairie Avenue Historic District ⓭
Printing House Row Historic District ❷
South Michigan Avenue ❹

Modern Architecture
Chicago Public Library, Harold Washington LibraryCenter ❶
Illinois Institute of Technology ⓲

Museums, Galleries, and Aquariums
Adler Planetarium and Astronomy Museum pp92–3 ⓬
Field Museum pp86–9 ❿
John G. Shedd Aquarium pp96–7 ⓫
Museum of Contemporary Photography ❼
National Vietnam Veterans Art Museum ⓯
Spertus Museum ❻

Parks and Fountains
Buckingham Fountain ❾
Grant Park ❽

GETTING THERE

The South Loop is a short walk from the Downtown Core and is easily accessible from the Harrison and Roosevelt CTA stations, and via the State Street and Clark Street buses. The Near South Side, 3 miles (5 km) south of the city center, is best reached by car, taxi, or Michigan Avenue bus 3.

◁ T. Thomas Memorial, Grant Park

SOUTH LOOP
AND NEAR SOUTH SIDE

Two of Chicago's neighborhoods have always been areas of diversity, with dereliction and gentrification coexisting side by side. South Loop developed as an industrial area in the late 1800s. But after World War II, manufacturers left and the area declined. Not until the 1970s did it again show signs of prosperity. The Near South Side also had cycles of boom and bust. After the 1871 fire, the city's elite created a wealthy enclave here that lasted until the early 1900s. Decay followed, as brothels and gambling houses formed the Levee vice district. In the 1940s, the Illinois Institute of Technology (IIT) transformed the area yet again.

The contrasts remain striking. The oldest residence in the city, the Henry B. Clarke House, is minutes from the sleek IIT campus; the city's teeming Chinatown borders the historic Black Metropolis.

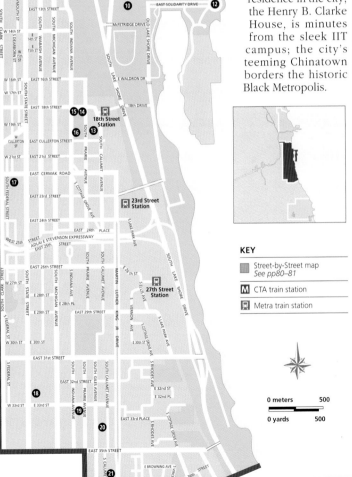

KEY

▨	Street-by-Street map *See pp80–81*
Ⓜ	CTA train station
🚉	Metra train station

0 meters 500
0 yards 500

Street-by-Street: South Loop

Just south of downtown, the South Loop has changed dramatically in recent decades, from a run-down industrial area to a residential and retail neighborhood. With the 1970s conversion of the district's derelict warehouses to fashionable lofts, businesses sprang up as Chicagoans took advantage of the area's proximity to downtown. Today, the South Loop's diversity is evident in its industrial heritage, the green expanse of Grant Park, and the lively retail scene next door to several outstanding museums.

Sculpted owl on the roof of Harold Washington Library

★ Harold Washington Library Center
Dominating the South Loop is the world's largest public library building, artwork displayed throughout ❶

★ Printing House Row Historic District
Many of this area's historic warehouses, built for the printing trade, have been converted into fashionable apartments, with numerous shops and cafés at street level ❷

The Transportation Building was one of the earliest buildings in Printers' Row to be converted to residential use and helped start the area's revival.

DEARBORN ST

CONGRESS PKWY

HARRISON STREET

Details on the *Lakeside Press Building, at 731 S Plymouth Street, are typical of the rich decoration of buildings in this area.*

CLARK STREET

LASALLE

POLK STREET

STREET

STAR SIGHTS

★ Harold Washington Library Center

★ Printing House Row Historic District

★ Spertus Museum

The Second Franklin Building
Handsome tilework illustrates the history of printing over its entranceway.

Museum of Contemporary Photography
Focusing on American photography produced since 1959, the museum presents selections from its extensive collection and excellent temporary exhibitions ❼

★ Spertus Museum
This world-renowned collection of Judaic art highlights decorative objects and religious artifacts that span centuries of Jewish history ❻

LOCATOR MAP
See Street Finder maps 3 & 4

KEY

- - - - Suggested route

South Michigan Avenue
Featuring a spectacular row of historic buildings, this is one of Chicago's grandest streets, an excellent place to window shop and from which to admire the varied architectural styles for which the city is famous ❹

Hilton Chicago
Decorated in the French Renaissance style, this 25-story building is one of Chicago's most opulent hotels and was the largest in the world when it opened in 1927 ❺

Buddy Guy's Legends
This club presents both big-name and local blues acts. Proprietor and blues legend Buddy Guy can often be found among its patrons.

Dearborn Station
Chicago's oldest surviving passenger train station building, an 1885 Richardsonian Romanesque design, has been converted into a shopping mall. Its square clock tower is a local landmark ❸

0 meters	100
0 yards	100

Harold Washington Library Center's ninth-floor Winter Garden

Chicago Public Library, Harold Washington Library Center **❶**

400 S State St. **Map** 3 C2.
Tel (312) 747-4300. Ⓜ Library.
🚌 2, 6, 29, 36, 62, 145, 146, 147,
151. 🕐 9am–9pm Mon–Thu; 9am–
5pm Fri–Sat; 1pm–5pm Sun. 🌑
major hols. 🚻 call (312) 747-4136.
🖥 🎬 **Exhibits, lectures, films**.
www.chipublib.org

This, the largest public library
building in the world, was
designed by Thomas Beeby –
winner of a competition
voted on by Chicagoans –
and opened in 1991. It is
named in honor of Chicago's
first Black mayor.
  Inspired by Greek and
Roman structures – with five-
story arched windows, vaulted
ceilings, and decorative
columns – the design also
pays tribute to many of
Chicago's historic buildings:
the rusticated granite base
recalls the Rookery *(see p40)*,
for example. Perched on each
roof corner is a gigantic
sculpted barn owl representing wisdom; over the main

entrance, a great horned owl
with a 20-ft (6-m) wingspan
grips a book in its talons. The
library holds close to two million books and periodicals on
its 90 miles (145 km) of
shelving. Artwork is displayed
throughout the building,
including work by Cheyenne
artist Heap of Birds. On the
ninth floor is the beautiful
light-suffused Winter Garden.

Rowe Building on Dearborn Street,
in the Printing House Row District

Printing House Row Historic District **❷**

S Federal, S Dearborn, & S
Plymouth sts; between W
Congress Pkwy & W Polk St.
Map 3 C3. Ⓜ *Harrison*.

By the mid-1890s, Chicago
was the printing capital of the
US. The majority of this
industry centered in a two-
block area now known as
Printing House Row Historic
District. Nearby Dearborn
Street railroad station *(see p83)*
facilitated rapid industrial
development in the
neighborhood. However, by
the 1970s, when the station
closed, most of the printing
companies had already
moved out of the area.
  Many of the massive, solid
buildings erected to hold
heavy printing machinery
remain today. Their
conversion into stylish
condominiums and office lofts
has led to the revitalization of

Carved detail on façade of the
historic Lakeside Press Building

the neighborhood and an
influx of commercial activity.
  The landmark Pontiac
Building (542 South Dearborn
Street; 1891) is the oldest
surviving Holabird and Roche
(see p27) building in Chicago.
Several other noteworthy
buildings line South Dearborn
Street. The 1883 Donohue
Building (Nos. 701–721) has
an impressive arched
entranceway, Romanesque
Revival styling *(see p26)*, and a
birdcage elevator in the
lobby. The Rowe Building
(No. 714, c.1882) houses the
excellent Sandmeyer's
Bookstore, specializing in
local authors and travel
literature. The Second
Franklin Building (No. 720) is
significant for the ornamental
tilework gracing its façade.
Above the entrance is a
delightful terra-cotta mural of
a medieval print shop.

Dearborn Station ❸

47 W Polk St. **Map** 3 C3.
Tel 554-4408. M *Harrison.*
◯ *7am–9pm Mon–Fri; 8am–5pm*
Sat. ◉ *major hols.* 🍴 🛍 🍸

Dearborn Station, built
in 1885, is the oldest
surviving passenger railroad
station building in Chicago,
and is a monument to the
historic importance of the
nation's coast-to-coast rail
system. By the turn of the
century, more than 100 trains
(from 25 different railroad
companies) and 17,000
passengers passed through
the station each day.

Designed by Cyrus L.W.
Eidlitz, the station features
masonry walls and terra-cotta
arches in the Richardsonian
Romanesque style *(see p26)*.
A 1922 fire destroyed the
roof, attic, and upper story.
The clock tower was rebuilt
and stands today as the
striking terminus of Dearborn
Street, visible from the
northern Loop.

The station closed its
passenger service in 1971.
After a period of neglect, in
1986, amid much controversy,
the building's train shed was
demolished. The building
was subsequently converted
into a dynamic shopping
mall and office complex,
which helped to revitalize
the area. Today, many of its
original features have since
been restored.

**The former Dearborn Station's
high-ceilinged atrium**

View along South Michigan Avenue looking north

South Michigan Avenue ❹

S Michigan Ave from E Madison St
to E Balbo Ave. **Map** 4 C2–C3.
M *Madison.*

South Michigan Avenue is the
place to revel in the
monumental solidity of late
19th- and early 20th-century
architecture. This historic street
has been described variously
as a "cliff" and a "wall." Be
warned: you may strain your
neck gazing up to the tops of
these massive structures. The
longest span of pre-1920
buildings in Chicago, South
Michigan Avenue contains
numerous architectural styles,
from the Gothic-inspired *(see
p26)* Chicago Athletic
Association Building (No. 12)
to the Chicago School *(see
pp26–7)* Gage Building (No.
18), one of three buildings
making up the Gage Group.
The Gage Building was
designed by Holabird and
Roche; Louis Sullivan designed
the terra-cotta façade.

At Nos. 24 and 30 are
striking examples of Chicago
windows *(see p27)*, which
allowed in plenty of light
for the milliners once
working here.

The School of the Art
Institute of Chicago
residence (No. 112)
contains a frieze of the
Greek god Zeus
overseeing athletic games,
a decorative detail that
reflects the original 1908
purpose of the building as
the home of the Illinois
Athletic Club.

Hilton Chicago ❺

720 S Michigan Ave. **Map** 4 D3.
Tel (312) 922-4400. M *Harrison.*
◯ *24 hrs daily.* 🛗 🍴 🍸 🅿 *See*
Where to Stay p146.

When it opened in 1927,
this 25-story hotel had 3,000
rooms, a rooftop
18-hole miniature golf course,
its own hospital, and a 1,200-
seat theater. After the owner
went bankrupt in the mid-
1930s, the World War II Army
Air Corps purchased the
Holabird and Roche-
designed redbrick building,
converting the grand
ballroom to a mess hall.

In 1945, Conrad Hilton
acquired the building,
reopening the hotel in 1951.
Further renovations from 2000
to 2004 secured the hotel's
reputation for opulence. Its
lofty centerpiece is the
ballroom, a space decorated
in the French Renaissance
style, featuring mirrored
doors and walls, arched
windows, and huge crystal
chandeliers. The hallway is
equally ornate, with fluted
columns, a marble stairway,
and a cloud mural painted on
the ceiling.

**Marble fountain, lobby of
the Hilton Chicago**

Spertus Museum **6**

610 S Michigan Ave. **Map** 4 D3.
Tel *(312) 322-1700.* **M** *Harrison.*
◯ *10am–6pm Sun–Wed;*
10am–7pm Thu; 10am–3pm Fri.
● *Sat, major public and Jewish hols.*
▨ *(free 10am–noon Tue, 3–7pm*
Thu). **&** **♿** **◻** *Concerts, lectures,*
films. www.spertus.edu

Spertus Museum, Chicago's
Jewish museum, is in the
superb Spertus Institute of
Jewish Studies building.

An eternal light (*ner tamid***), in
silver-plated brass and ruby glass**

Designed by Chicago architects Krueck and Sexton, it
opened in November 2007.
This innovative facility
features a 10-story faceted
window wall that stands out
among the masonry-faced
buildings surrounding it. The
building contains interlocking
interior spaces and offers
spectacular views of Chicago's
skyline, Grant Park, and Lake
Michigan. Highlights of the
museum include a unique
visible storage depot that
showcases its world-class
collection of art and artifacts,
including ritual objects,
textiles, and jewelry; changing
special exhibitions that explore
identity and contemporary
culture; site-specific installations of work commissioned
from international artists; an
innovative Children's Center
designed with Redmoon
Theater's artistic director Jim
Lasko; and a resource center
for parents and teachers.
   The institute also contains
the research facilities of the
Asher Library and Chicago
Jewish archives. A green roof
and a tenth-floor sky garden
offer sweeping views. The

Interior of the Museum of Contemporary Photography

second-floor Wolfgang Puck
café is the only kosher café in
downtown Chicago. On the
first floor a gift- and bookshop
offers items created by some
of Israel's hottest designers.
The Feinberg Theater provides
programs of performance,
film, comedy, as well as
lectures by today's leading
thinkers, writers, and scholars.

Museum of Contemporary Photography **7**

600 S Michigan Ave. **Map** 4 D3.
Tel *(312) 663-5554.* **M** *Harrison.*
▭ *1, 2, 3, 3L, 4, 6, 10, 14, 29, 127,*
130, 146. **◯** *10am–5pm*
Mon–Wed, Fri & Sat; 10am–8pm
Thu; noon–5pm Sun. **●** *major hols,*
Dec 25 –Jan 1. **◻** **&** *1st, 2nd*
floors only. *Lectures, films.*

Founded by Columbia
College Chicago in 1984 to
collect, exhibit, and promote
contemporary photography,
the Museum of Contemporary
Photography is the only
museum in the Midwest
devoted exclusively to the

medium of photography.
Wide-ranging provocative and
innovative exhibitions,
housed in the college's
historic 1907 building, change
regularly as do selections
from the collection of more
than 5,000 American photographs produced since 1945.
   Temporary exhibitions
explore photography's many
roles: as artistic expression, as
documentary chronicler, as
commercial industry, and as a
powerful scientific and technological tool. The Midwest
Photographers Project, work
by regional photographers,
rotates annually.

Grant Park **8**

From Randolph St to Roosevelt Rd,
between Michigan Ave & Lake
Michigan. **Map** 4 E2–E4. ***Tel*** *(312)
742-7648.* **M** *Randolph; Madison;
Adams.* **◪** *See* *Through the Year
pp32–5.*

Grant Park is the splendid
centerpiece of the 23-mile-
(37-km-) long band of green
stretching along the Lake
Michigan shoreline from the

The main entrance to Grant Park, Ivan Mestrovic's *Bowman* to the right

View of Grant Park, looking north

city's south end to its northern suburbs. Although bisected by busy streets, the park offers a tranquil retreat from noisy downtown, serving as Chicago's playground, garden, promenade, and sculpture park all in one, and hosting summer concerts and festivals.

The park is built on landfill and debris dumped after the 1871 Fire. Originally called Lake Park, it was renamed in 1901 for the 18th US president, Ulysses S. Grant, who

Reading Cones by Richard Serra in Grant Park

lived in Galena *(see p134)*. In 1893, the World's Columbian Exposition was held in the south end of the park.

Although the park was intended as public ground, free of buildings, various structures were erected. Not until 1890, when businessman Aaron Montgomery Ward initiated a series of lawsuits which dragged on for more than 20 years, was the preservation of Grant Park for public recreation secured.

Daniel H. Burnham and Edward H. Bennett's 1909 Plan of Chicago *(see p30)* envisioned the park as the

"intellectual center of Chicago." The renowned landscape-architecture firm Olmsted Brothers designed the park in a French Renaissance style reminiscent of the gardens at Versailles. The symmetrical layout includes large rectangular "rooms," grand promenades, formal tree plantings, sculptures, and the central Buckingham Fountain.

A noteworthy footnote is that the park was the site of the 1968 Democratic Convention riots, when anti-Vietnam War protesters clashed with police.

Buckingham Fountain ❾

In Grant Park, east of Columbus Dr, at the foot of Congress Pkwy. **Map** 4 E3. *Tel* 742-7529. Ⓜ *Harrison.*

Throughout the summer one of the showiest and most impressive sights in Chicago is the water shooting from the 133 jets of Grant Park's

Buckingham Fountain, culminating dramatically in a spray 150 ft (45 m) high. The fountain's one-and-a-half million gallons (5.7 million liters) of water recirculate through a computer-operated pumping system at a rate of 14,000 gallons (53,000 liters) per minute.

Hundreds of spotlights hidden within the fountain are used to create a dazzling show of colored lights. The 20-minute shows, set to music, are held from dusk to 10pm every hour on the hour, from April to October.

Financed by Kate Sturges Buckingham (1858–1937) in honor of her brother, Clarence (1854–1913), a trustee and benefactor of the Art Institute of Chicago, the fountain was designed by Marcel Francois Loyau (sculptor), Jacques Lambert (engineer), and Edward H. Bennett (architect).

The design, based on the Latona Basin in the gardens of Versailles but twice the size of that fountain, incorporates a ground-level pool 280 ft (85 m) wide, with three concentric basins rising above. In 1927, it was dedicated as the world's largest decorative fountain.

Constructed of pink marble, the Beaux-Arts fountain symbolizes Lake Michigan. The four pairs of 20-ft- (6-m-) tall seahorses diagonally across the fountain from each other represent the four US states bordering the lake: Illinois, Wisconsin, Indiana, and Michigan.

Buckingham Fountain, sculpted seahorses in the foreground

Field Museum ⓾

Xochipilli, Aztec
god of flowers

The Field Museum is one of the world's great
natural history museums, with a collection
of over 20 million objects (just under one
percent are displayed). Following the
success of the 1893 World's Columbian
Exposition, a group of prominent Chicagoans decided to create a museum with
objects from the fair. With funding from
Marshall Field (see p77), they opened, in
1894, the Columbian Museum of Chicago
in Jackson Park's Palace of the Fine Arts,
one of the fair's finest buildings. This
lodging soon proved too small for the
museum. In 1921, its current home – a
white-marble Neo-Classical structure designed by
Daniel H. Burnham – was built, and the Field Museum,
with its celebrated collection of anthropological,
botanical, zoological, and geological objects, opened to
the public.

**★ Underground
Adventure**
*Walk through worm
tunnels, meet giant bugs,
and feel reduced to insect
size in this "subterranean"
exhibit.*

**Egyptian Mummy
Mask**
*This decorative linen-
and-plaster burial
mask encased a
mummified
child.*

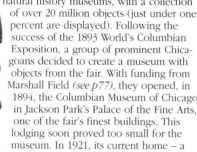

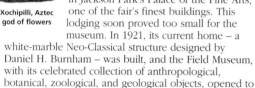

KEY TO FLOORPLAN

☐	Animals, plants, and ecosystems
☐	Rocks and fossils
☐	Ancient Egypt
☐	Americas
☐	Pacific cultures
☐	Special exhibits
☐	Nonexhibition space

Ground Level

MUSEUM GUIDE

*The museum has three levels: ground, main,
and upper. Most of the exhibition galleries are
on the main and upper levels. Each level has
east and west wings; those of the main and
upper are bisected by a large central hall. The
upper level features exhibitions on nature
(plants and earth sciences), dinosaurs, and
Pacific cultures. Exhibits on the main level
focus on animals, birds, and American
Indians. The highlight of the ground level is
the Underground Adventure exhibition.*

Lions of Tsavo
*The two lions that, in 1898, terrorized a
Kenyan outpost, killing 140 workers before
being shot, are on display in the Mammals
of Africa gallery.*

Hall of Jades
This impressive collection of over 500 jade artifacts includes items from Neolithic burial sites, the Chinese Dynasties, and the early 20th century.

Upper Level

VISITORS' CHECKLIST

1400 S Lake Shore Dr. **Map** 4 E4.
(312) 922-9410.
Roosevelt then free trolley.
12, 146. Roosevelt then free trolley.
9am–5pm daily (last adm. 4pm). Dec 25. Check website for free days. via east entrance. 11am, 2pm Mon–Fri. **Lectures, films, special events.**
www.fieldmuseum.org

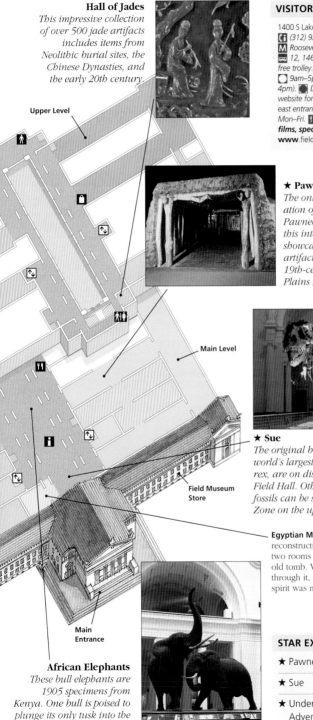

★ Pawnee Earth Lodge
The only precise recreation of a fully furnished Pawnee earth lodge, this interactive exhibit showcases traditional artifacts used by 19th-century Great Plains Indians.

Main Level

★ Sue
The original bones of Sue, the world's largest tyrannosaurus rex, are on display in the Stanley Field Hall. Other spectacular fossils can be seen in the Dino Zone on the upper level.

Field Museum Store

Egyptian Mastaba is a reconstruction incorporating two rooms from a 4,400-year-old tomb. Visitors can roam through it, as the deceased's spirit was meant to.

Main Entrance

African Elephants
These bull elephants are 1905 specimens from Kenya. One bull is poised to plunge its only tusk into the other as it rears.

STAR EXHIBITS

★ Pawnee Earth Lodge

★ Sue

★ Underground Adventure

Exploring the Field Museum

With its encyclopedic collection of cultural objects and biological specimens from around the globe, the Field Museum warrants many trips. More than 40 permanent exhibitions are supplemented with fascinating temporary shows. Particular strengths of the museum are dinosaur fossils – highlighted by the exhibit on Sue, the most complete *Tyrannosaurus rex* skeleton ever found – American Indian artifacts, botanical specimens, and displays relating to mammals and birds. Major crowd pleasers, especially for children, are Underground Adventure, which explores the rich diversity of life in the soil, and Inside Ancient Egypt, focusing on that civilization's funerary practices.

Tlatilco female figurine

The monumental Neo-Classical entrance to the Field Museum

ANIMALS, PLANTS, AND ECOSYSTEMS

One of the museum's missions is to encourage prudent stewardship of our environment. This theme is highlighted in the animal, plant, and ecosystem exhibits, which emphasize the interconnectedness of all life on Earth. The Messages from the Wilderness gallery is a good place to start your exploration. Eighteen wilderness park settings, from the Arctic to Argentina, incorporate representative mammals and their habitats.

Also here is the Local Woodlands Four Seasons Diorama, completed in 1902 by taxidermist Carl Akeley, who transformed the way museums displayed animals.

For Akeley, habitat accuracy and the authenticity of background details were equally important. Thus, each of the 17,000 wax leaves in the diorama is cast separately from a real one.

The main-level galleries in the west wing provide an overview of animal biology, behavior, and habitats, with samples from the museum's 17 million zoological specimens. Outstanding exhibits are Mammals of Asia and Mammals of Africa. Suspended from the ceiling in the World of Mammals gallery is the massive skeleton of a Right whale. The museum's collection of birds is also particularly strong, with its informative Bird Habitats, World of Birds, and North American Birds galleries.

A popular attraction is Bushman, a lowland gorilla brought from West Africa to Lincoln Park Zoo in the 1920s. So beloved by Chicagoans that the mayor gave him a voter's registration card, Bushman died in 1951. He was then moved to the museum where, preserved, he continues to delight visitors.

The museum's 2.6 million botanical specimens encompass all major plant groups and every continent. Particularly rich in flowering plants and ferns of the Americas, this is the world's largest museum exhibit dedicated exclusively to plants. Be sure to stop at the

tropical aerial garden. Its reproductions made from wax, glass, and wire look remarkably lifelike.

ROCKS AND FOSSILS

Two of the 12 Martian meteorites on display in museums around the world are here at the Field Museum. You can touch non-Martian meteorite pieces on the upper floor, in the Earth Sciences galleries. Other fascinating

A collection of marine skeletons, exoskeletons, and fossils

and beautiful rocks in the 500-specimen display are a topaz the size of a pear, in the sparkling Grainger Hall of Gems, and a 312-lb (142-kg) block of lapis lazuli, one of the largest ever found and its origin still a puzzle.

Dino Zone houses the museum's renowned collection of dinosaur fossils. The center-piece, displayed in the Stanley Field Hall, is 67-million-year-old Sue, the largest, most complete *Tyrannosaurus rex* skeleton ever found. It was discovered near the Black Hills of South Dakota in 1990 by fossil-hunter

A golden eagle clutching its prey, by taxidermist Carl Akeley

A gargantuan *Apatosaurus* dinosaur skeleton

Sue Hendrickson. The restored skeleton, the skull alone weighing 600 lb (270 kg), was unveiled in 2000. Interactive exhibits tell the story of its discovery. Scientists now know that Sue was 28 years old at the time of her death. By counting the rings in one of her rib bones, they determined Sue went through a teenage growth spurt between the ages of 14 and 18, during which she gained 4.6 lb (2.1 kg) each day.

The newly-renovated Hall of Jades displays jade artifacts along a chronological storyline from Neolithic burial sites through the Bronze Age, the Chinese Dynasties, and into the early 20th century. A 300 lb (136 kg) jar that once stood in the Imperial Palace of Emperor Qianlong is a highlight of the exhibit.

ANCIENT EGYPT

The museum's Ancient Egyptian holdings consist of more than 1,400 rare artifacts, including statues, hieroglyphics, and mummies. The predynastic burial exhibit

Isty's Book of the Dead, an ancient papyrus scroll

reveals Egypt's intriguing burial practices before the development of intricate pharaonic tombs. Here, the remains of a 5,500-year-old woman are displayed, along with items such as pottery jars thought to be needed in the afterlife. A partial reconstruction of a *mastaba*, a multiroom "mansion of eternity," features a false door at which the earthbound and the wandering spirits meet.

Other extraordinary artifacts include the fully preserved inner coffin of Chenet-a-a, a woman who lived between 945 BC and 712 BC. It is not known what is inside the coffin since it has never been opened or X-rayed.

A Pacific Coast Indian carved figure, once a house entranceway

AMERICAS

The museum's holdings of artifacts from North American Indian tribes reflect one of the Field's main missions: to encourage improved understanding among cultures. Ceremonial objects and splendid totem poles – two Haida examples rise to the ceiling of Stanley Field Hall – are just some of the treasures in this exhibit.

The Pawnee Earth Lodge, a life-size reproduction, was built in conjunction with the Pawnee, a group of American Indians based in Oklahoma.

The 19th-century cedar Kwakiutl transformation masks are colorful and vivid. Such masks are often used

Ceremonial dance mask worn by Alaskan Eskimo shamans

during the ceremonies of this Pacific Northwest tribe. Panels on the mask are opened and closed by the dancer wearing it to show various faces.

PACIFIC CULTURES

The highlight of the Pacific cultures exhibits, with a section on headhunting and a re-creation of a Tahitian market, is the sacred Maori meetinghouse, Ruatepupuke II. Built in 1881 in New Zealand, it was acquired by the museum in 1905. The 55-ft- (17-m-) long, beautifully carved house symbolizes the body of the Maori ancestor Ruatepupuke, credited with sharing the art of woodcarving with the world. The house's ridgepole represents his spine, the rafters his ribs, and the expansive roof-boards his arms, open in greeting. It is the only Maori meetinghouse in the western hemisphere and remains governed by Maori customs.

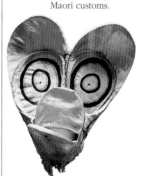

Spirit mask from Papua New Guinea

John G. Shedd Aquarium ⓫

See pp96–7.

Adler Planetarium and Astronomy Museum ⓬

See pp92–3.

Prairie Avenue Historic District ⓭

Prairie Ave, from 18th to Cullerton sts. **Map** 6 D1. Ⓜ *Cermak-Chinatown then bus 21.* Ⓟ *Jul–Sep: 2pm 2nd & 4th Sun; call (312) 326-1480.* ⓗ

When the city of Chicago was incorporated in 1837, the area now known as the Prairie Avenue Historic District was not much more than a strip of sandy prairie bordering Lake Michigan. Its fortunes changed dramatically when the 1871 fire destroyed the city center. Chicago's wealthy, including George Pullman *(see p119)* and Marshall Field *(see p77)*, moved to the Near South Side, building their grand mansions along Prairie Avenue. It remained a mecca for the city's socialites until the late 1800s and early 1900s, when the rapidly

Elbridge G. Keith House on Prairie Avenue

The imposing Richardsonian Romanesque façade of Glessner House

growing Gold Coast area superseded Prairie Avenue as the address of choice. Many mansions fell to the wrecker's ball (plaques along Prairie Avenue mark the sites of demolished houses), but those that remain offer a glimpse into 19th-century splendor.

Along with Glessner House, highlights of the district include the Kimball House (No. 1801). This mansion, designed by Solon Spencer Beman in 1890, is one of the best remaining examples in the US of the Chateauesque style. Clarke House, the oldest house in Chicago, was moved to its current location on Indiana Avenue in 1977 to provide an additional attraction for the district.

Elbridge G. Keith House (No. 1900) is the oldest extant mansion on Prairie Avenue. Built in 1870, it was designed by John W. Roberts in the Italianate style *(see p26)*.

At 1936 South Michigan Avenue is the magnificent neo-Gothic Second Presbyterian Church, designed by James Renwick in 1874. Inside are 22 stained-glass windows by Louis C. Tiffany and 2 windows painted by British Pre-Raphaelite artist Edward Burne-Jones.

The district is reputedly close to the site of a grim event: the 1812 massacre of settlers fleeing Fort Dearborn *(see p15)*.

Glessner House ⓮

1800 S Prairie Ave. **Map** 6 D1. **Tel** (312) 326-1480. Ⓜ *Cermak-Chinatown.* Ⓟ *mandatory: 1pm, 3pm Wed–Sun (except public hols).* ⓗ *(free Wed).* 🎧 **Lectures**.

The only extant residential design in Chicago by Boston architect Henry Hobson Richardson, whose signature style became known as Richardsonian Romanesque *(see p24)*, Glessner House helped change the face of residential architecture.

Commissioned by farm-machinery manufacturer John J. Glessner and his wife, Frances, in 1885 and completed in 1887, the two-story house represented a radical departure from traditional design and created a furor in the exclusive Prairie Avenue neighborhood. George Pullman is said to have proclaimed: "I do not know what I have ever done to have that thing staring me in the face every time I go out of my door."

A fortress-like building of rough-hewn pinkish gray granite with three modified turrets, the house dominates its corner site. The main rooms and many of the large windows face a southern courtyard. The striking simplicity of the design is perhaps best reflected in the main entrance arch, which frames a heavy oak door ornamented with grillwork. The beautifully restored interior boasts a world-class collection of decorative art objects. Most were purchased or commissioned by the Glessners, who were keenly interested in the British Arts and Crafts movement of the late 19th and early 20th centuries. Adherents of the philosophy that everyday objects should be artistically crafted, they filled the house with tiles, draperies, and wallpaper designed by William Morris. Handcrafted pieces, from furniture to ceramics, by American designer Isaac E. Scott grace the rooms.

Untitled (1995) by Stephen Ham, at the Vietnam Veterans Art Museum

National Vietnam Veterans Art Museum ⓯

1801 S Indiana Ave. **Map** 6 D1. *Tel* (312) 326-0270. M Cermak-Chinatown then bus 21. 🚌 1, 3, 4. 🕙 11am–6pm Tue–Fri; 10am–5pm Sat. ⬤ major hols. 🏷 📷 ♿ 📷 (for groups). 🖥 🛍

The National Vietnam Veterans Art Museum is the only museum in the world with a permanent collection that focuses on the subject of war from a personal point of view. Bringing together more than 700 works of art in diverse media created by 140 artists who participated in one of America's most divisive wars, this collection presents a humanist statement on behalf of veterans of all wars.

This adamantly apolitical museum began when two Chicago veterans, Ned

Broderick and Joe Fornelli, began collecting artworks created by fellow veterans. The City of Chicago donated an abandoned warehouse and the museum opened in its new home in 1996.

The artworks explore powerful themes with unflinching honesty. The belongings of prisoner-of-war Major General John L. Borling, who lived in captivity in North Vietnam for seven years, is documented in the display *My Cup Runneth Over*. In 2001, the museum dedicated a permanent memorial honoring all Americans killed in the Vietnam War. The memorial is called "Above and Beyond."

Henry B. Clarke House ⓰

1827 S Indiana Ave. **Map** 6 D1. *Tel* (312) 326-1480. M Cermak-Chinatown then bus 21. 📷 mandatory: noon, 2pm Wed–Sun (departs from Glessner House). ⬤ public hols. 🏷 (free Wed). ♿

Built in 1836, Clarke House is Chicago's oldest surviving building, a Greek Revival-style house constructed for merchant Henry B. Clarke and his wife Caroline. The house originally stood on what is now South Michigan Avenue but was then an old Indian path. When the house sold in 1872, the new owners moved it 28 blocks south, to 4526 South Wabash Avenue. In 1977, the City purchased the house and then, in a feat of engineering, hoisted the

The dining room in the Henry B. Clarke House

120-ton structure over the 44th Street "L" tracks, moving it to its present location one block southeast of the original Clarke property.

Four Roman Doric columns mark the east entrance to the house. Solidly constructed of timber frame, with a white clapboard exterior, the two-story house was damaged in a 1977 fire. It now has been painstakingly restored, even adhering to the original color scheme, which researchers determined by delving under 27 layers of paint.

Now a museum showcasing an interior reflecting the period 1836–60, Clarke House offers a fascinating glimpse into early Chicago domestic life. It is so historically accurate that the first-floor lighting simulates gas lighting, and the upper floor has no artificial lights. A gallery in the basement documents the history of the house.

Behind the house is the Chicago Women's Park and Garden *(see p194)*.

The classical façade of the Henry B. Clarke House

Adler Planetarium and Astronomy Museum ⑫

Diptych sundial,
c.1665–1700

The Adler Planetarium and Astronomy Museum has one of the finest astronomical collections in the world, with artifacts dating as far back as 12th-century Persia. It also has the world's first virtual-reality theater. Spectacular sky shows complement displays on navigation, the solar system, and space exploration. State-of-the-art technology enables visitors to explore exhibits hands-on.

When the Adler opened in 1930, it was the first modern planetarium in the western hemisphere. Businessman Max Adler funded the 12-sided, granite-and-marble Art Deco structure, designed by Ernest Grunsfeld. This original building, with its copper dome and a bronze depiction of a sign of the zodiac on each of the 12 corners, is now a historical landmark.

★ StarRider Theater
The world's first digital theater offers an unrivaled virtual-reality environment in which visitors can participate in a journey beyond the solar system.

★ Atwood Sphere
Step into North America's only walk-in planetarium, built in 1913. Light enters through the 692 holes in the surface of this huge metal ball, representing the stars in Chicago's night sky. The "stars" move across the "sky" as the sphere, powered by a motor, slowly rotates.

Lower
Level

Universe in Your Hands
Learn about a time when people believed that Earth was the center of the universe. Astrolabes, armillary spheres, and sundials illustrate medieval conceptions of the world.

KEY TO FLOOR PLAN

- ☐ Landmark exhibition space
- ☐ Sky Pavilion exhibition space
- ☐ Sky Pavilion special exhibits
- ☐ Zeiss Sky Theater
- ☐ StarRider Theater
- ☐ Nonexhibition space

Our Solar System
Investigate through interactive exhibits the worlds that orbit the Sun, and program a computer-activated Rover to move across simulated Martian terrain.

VISITORS' CHECKLIST

1300 S Lake Shore Dr.
Map 4 F4. *Tel* (312) 922-7827.
M Roosevelt then free trolley.
12, 146. ◯ 10am–4pm
Mon–Fri; 10am–4:30pm Sat–
Sun (to 6pm daily in summer).
● Thanksgiving, Dec 25. 🎫
see website for various free days
(though there will still be separate
adm to theaters).
📷 ♿ 🎫 🛍 🍴 📽 P
Lectures, films, light shows.
www.adlerplanetarium.org

The Milky Way Galaxy

★ **Milky Way Galaxy**
Immerse yourself in a 3-D, computer-animated trip through the Milky Way.

Middle Level

Upper Level

★ **Shoot for the Moon**
Stories of space exploration and future plans to return to the moon are covered in this exhibition. Includes the fully restored Gemini 12 spacecraft.

Zeiss Sky Theater is the Adler's original planetarium theater. The night heavens are cast by a modern version of the historic Zeiss projector onto a screen suspended from its dome.

Main Entrance

Sky Pavilion
A stunning view of the city's skyline can be seen from Galileo's café, in the Sky Pavilion. This two-story 1999 addition to the east side of the landmark building also houses exhibition space and the StarRider Theater.

STAR SIGHTS

★ Atwood Sphere

★ Milky Way Galaxy

★ Shoot for the Moon

★ StarRider Theater

A Chinatown grocery shop

Chinatown 🔟

S Wentworth Ave, north & south of Cermak Rd. **Map** 5 B1–C1. *Tel (312) 326-5320.* Ⓜ *Cermak-Chinatown.* 🍴 See **Restaurants and Cafés** *p150.* **www**.chicagochinatown.org

A red and green gateway decorated with Chinese characters inscribed by Dr. Sun Yet-Sen, founder of the Republic of China, arches over Wentworth Avenue just south of Cermak Road. It marks the entrance to the largest Chinatown in the Midwest. A lively area full of Asian grocery and herbal shops, bakeries, and restaurants, this densely packed neighborhood of approximately 10,000 residents has been home to Chicago's highest concentration of Chinese people since just before World War I.

Traditional Chinese architecture is evident throughout the colorful streetscape. The temple-like **Pui Tak Center** (2216 South Wentworth

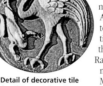

Detail of decorative tile on the Chinese Cultural Center

Avenue) was originally the On Leong Chinese Merchants' Association Building; it is now a cultural center. Sculpted lions at the doorway guard its street-level shops; terra-cotta ornaments bedeck the walls. Modern **Chinatown Square Mall** (Archer, Cermak, 18th, and Wentworth) quarters shops and a plaza surrounded by zodiac sculptures and a mosaic mural. Annual Chinatown celebrations include the Dragon Boat Races in the summer and the Moon Festival in September.

Illinois Institute of Technology 🔟

31st to 35th Sts, between Dan Ryan Expy & S Michigan Ave. **Map** 5 C4–D4. *Tel (312) 567-3000.* Ⓜ *Sox-35th; 35-Bronzeville-IIT.* 🚌 *29, 35.* **www**.iit.edu

The Illinois Institute of Technology (IIT) is a world leader in engineering, technology, and architecture. The main campus is an outstanding example of the work of influential architect Ludwig Mies van der Rohe *(see p30)*, who was hired by architect John A. Holabird to direct the Armour Institute's architecture school and design the new campus.

In the campus plan, along with the 22 IIT buildings he designed, Mies expressed his modernist view that form follow function. Geometric and unadorned glass-sheathed curtain-wall structures epitomize Mies' International style. One of Mies' masterpieces is the **S.R. Crown Hall** (1956). This glass-walled pavilion is an early example of a large clear-span structure, the four exterior columns supporting the girders from which the roof is hung. The building appears to float in space. Of it, Mies said: "This is the clearest structure we have done, the best to express our philosophy."

Alumni Memorial Hall, Mies' first classroom building on the campus, is another notable example of structure also functioning as ornament. The steel grid of the curtain wall suggests the steel structure within. In **Wishnick Hall**, the curtain wall stops short of the corner to reveal the load-bearing column.

St. Saviour's Chapel, known waggishly as the "God box," is believed to be Mies' only church design.

The campus is also home to the magnificent redbrick Richardsonian Romanesque **Main Building**. Designed by Patten and Fisher (1891–3), it is IIT's most visible landmark.

There are two new complexes of note. The McCormick Tribune Campus

S.R. Crown Hall on the Illinois Institute of Technology campus

Center, designed by Rem Koolhaas, features a sound-buffering, concrete and steel tube that encloses the "L" tracks passing directly over the building. A residence hall complex designed by Helmut Jahn consists of terrace- topped buildings joined by glass walls that muffle train noise. A map of the campus is available from Hermann Union Hall.

Pilgrim Baptist Church ⑲

3301 S Indiana Ave. **Map** 6 D4.
Office Ⓜ 35-Bronzeville-IIT.
⬤ until further notice.

This landmark building was built in 1890–91 and designed by Adler and Sullivan for Chicago's oldest Jewish con-gregation, Kehilath Anshe Ma'ariv. It then became the Pilgrim Baptist Church from 1926 until January 2006 when it was destroyed by fire.

The magnificent arched doorway was the only surviving example of an ecclesiastical arch by Adler and Sullivan and reflected the strong masonry forms of the exterior. Terra-cotta panels of foliage designs provided ornament. Plans are being drawn up for its renovation but no date has been set for its reopening to the public.

Calumet-Giles-Prairie District ⑳

Calumet to Prairie Aves, from 31st to 35th Sts. **Map** 6 D4. Ⓜ 35-Bronzeville-IIT.

This small enclave of restored Victorian houses was granted national landmark status in 1980. Of particular interest is Joseph Deimel House (3141 South Calumet Avenue), designed in 1887 by Adler and Sullivan and the only remaining residential commission by the firm in this area.

The Joliet limestone row houses (3144–8 South Calumet Avenue), built in 1881, are a fine example of Victorian row-house architecture. However, only three of the original eight houses are still standing.

A block to the south are the only row houses Frank Lloyd Wright designed (1894) – the Robert W. Roloson Houses (3213–19 South Calumet Avenue). Like Robie House (see pp102–103), Wright used Roman bricks for the walls, here decorated with terra-cotta panels between the upper-story windows. A trio of Richardsonian Romanesque (see p26) town-houses in sandstone, green-stone, and limestone are found at 3356–60 South Calumet Avenue.

Victory monument in the Calumet-Giles-Prairie District

Ida B. Wells-Barnett House

Ida B. Wells-Barnett House ㉑

3624 S King Dr. **Map** 6 E5. Ⓜ 35-Bronzeville-IIT. ⬤ to public.

Civil rights and women's suffrage advocate Ida B. Wells (1862–1931) lived in this house with her husband from 1919 to 1930. Born a slave in Mississippi, Wells became a teacher at age 14 but was dismissed for protesting segregation.

Wells' work as a columnist for *Memphis Free Speech* brought her to Chicago in 1893 to report on the lack of African-American repre-sentation at the World's Columbian Exposition. She moved to Chicago in 1895 and married Ferdinand Lee Barnett, the founder of Chicago's first Black newspaper, the *Conservator*.

Playing a key role in the 1909 founding of the National Association for the Advance-ment of Colored People, Wells is perhaps best known for her anti-lynching campaign, which brought national attention to the issue.

The house, designed in 1889 by Joseph A. Thain in the Romanesque style, was designated a national historic landmark in 1973 in Wells' honor. One of its most inter-esting features is the corner turret made of pressed metal.

Façade of the Pilgrim Baptist Church, with its distinctive doorway

John G. Shedd Aquarium ⓫

Nearly 19,000 saltwater and freshwater animals, representing 1500 species of fish, reptiles, amphibians, invertebrates, birds, and mammals, live at the John G. Shedd Aquarium.

Named after its benefactor, an influential Chicago businessman, the aquarium opened in 1930 in a Neo-Classical building designed by the firm Graham, Anderson, Probst and White. The Oceanarium and its magnificent curved wall of glass face Lake Michigan, whose water flows into its tank. This pavilion showcases beluga whales and dolphins while Wild Reef houses sharks and other large predators.

Aerial view of the Shedd Aquarium, looking north toward Grant Park

Neptune's trident atop the dome of the aquarium

Beluga Whales
Several whales live in the Oceanarium's Secluded Bay, some of which were born at the aquarium.

The Nature Trail leads visitors along winding paths through a re-creation of a Pacific Northwest coastal forest, complete with streams and replicas of 70 species of plants.

KEY

- ☐ Aquarium
- ☐ Oceanarium
- ☐ Animal underwaterviewing
- ☐ Special exhibits
- ☐ Nonexhibition space

STAR SIGHTS

★ Amazon Rising

★ Caribbean Reef

★ Oceanarium

Sea Otter Cove features Habitat Chats about these, the smallest of marine mammals.

★ Oceanarium
Beluga whales, Pacific white-sided dolphins, Alaskan sea otters, tidal-pool creatures, and other marine animals live in this gigantic saltwater habitat, which seems to extend into Lake Michigan, a dramatic effect created by the stunning 475-ft- (145-m-) long glass wall. Watch dolphins and whales during daily educational presentations, or come face to face with them in the Underwater Viewing gallery.

Animals of the Great Lakes Region showcases cold water fish, including the Lake Whitefish, that dwell in the Great Lakes.

Oceans

As part of the Waters of the World galleries, here you can see an array of animals from tide pools, shadowy kelp forests, and all the way from the ocean floor. Particularly fascinating is the Pacific octopus, one of the largest in the world.

VISITORS' CHECKLIST

1200 S Lake Shore Dr. **Map** 4 E4.
Tel 939-2438. M Roosevelt
then free trolley. ☷ 6, 12, 127,
130, 146. 🚆 Roosevelt then
free trolley. ○ Memorial
Day–Labor Day: 9am–6pm daily
(mid-Jun–Aug: 9am–10pm Thu).
Labor Day–Memorial Day: 9am–
5pm Mon–Fri; 9am–6pm Sat,
Sun, public hols. ● Dec 25. 🌐
(see website for various free
days). 🗺 ♿ 🕐 🍴 📷 P
Lectures.
www.sheddaquarium.org

Wild Reef

The blue spot stingray is among the 500 species of reef fish on view in this underground wing. Also housed here is one of the most diverse displays of sharks in North America.

★ Amazon Rising

Experience all four seasons affecting the floodplain forest of the mighty Amazon River, and encounter stingrays, dart frogs, lizards, and many more creatures of the Amazon.

Main Entrance

Asia, Africa, and Australia highlights fish such as the aggressive Nile knifefish that inhabit the warm freshwaters of the eastern hemisphere.

★ Caribbean Reef

More than 250 tropical animals, including nurse sharks and barracudas, live in this reef habitat, one of the aquarium's most popular exhibits. Visitors can watch as a diver feeds the creatures.

SOUTH SIDE

Settled in the mid-1800s as suburban estates, the South Side was soon transformed when the 1893 World's Fair, held in Jackson Park, brought tourists, money, and real-estate and transit development. Hyde Park in particular experienced dramatic change, as the City's preparation for the fair led to an influx of Chicago's elite. By the 1920s, however, pollution from nearby industry and the encroachment of poorer neighborhoods caused the wealthy to depart. By the 1950s, Kenwood and Hyde Park were in decline. That same decade, the University of Chicago led a massive urban-renewal program. Today, the area contains many classic Prairie School homes, superb museums, and two of Chicago's largest greenspaces.

St. George and the dragon, detail from the University of Chicago

SIGHTS AT A GLANCE

Historic Buildings
Robie House ❷
Rockefeller Memorial Chapel ❶
University of Chicago Quadrangles ❺

Historic Districts
Hyde Park ❾
Kenwood ❿

Museums
DuSable Museum of African American History ❽
Museum of Science and Industry pp106–109 ⓬
Oriental Institute Museum ❸
Smart Museum of Art ❹

Parks
Jackson Park ⓫
Midway Plaisance ❻
Washington Park ❼

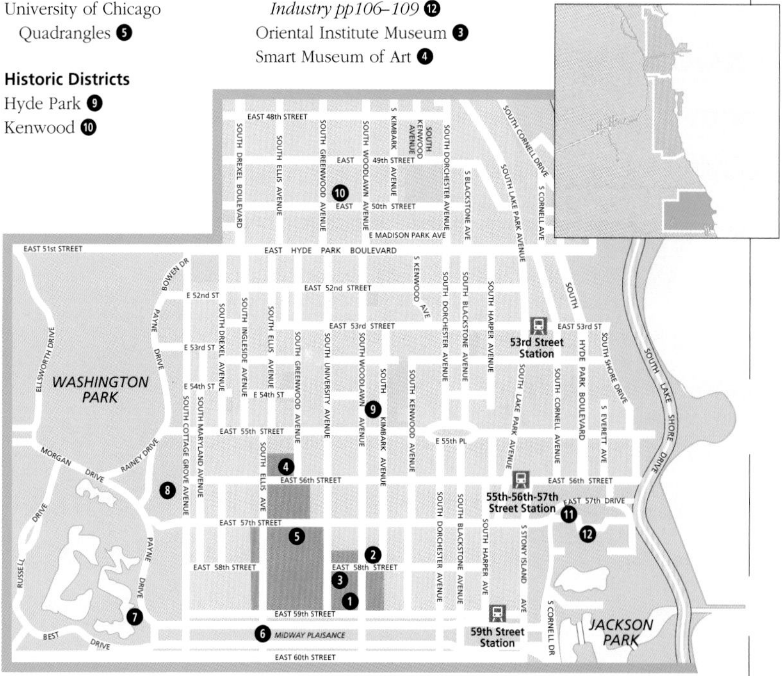

GETTING THERE
Eight miles (13 km) south of the Loop, the South Side is accessible by car via I-94/I-55 or South Lake Shore Drive. Metra trains depart from the Randolph Street, Van Buren Street, and Roosevelt Road stations to 55th-56th-57th and 59th Street stations. CTA buses 6 and 10 offer express service to the South Side. CTA green line trains also service the area.

KEY
Street-by-Street map
See pp100–101

Metra train station

0 meters 500
0 yards 500

◁ **Lower cloister hall in the Chicago Theological Seminary, University of Chicago**

Street-by-Street: University of Chicago

Angel with harp, Bond Chapel

The University of Chicago, founded in 1890 on land donated by Marshall Field, opened its doors to students – male and female, White and Black – in 1892. Today, it has the greatest number of Nobel laureates among faculty, alumni, and researchers of any US university and is particularly lauded in the fields of economics and physics. Over the years, John D. Rockefeller gave $35 million to the university. Henry Ives Cobb designed 18 of the university's limestone buildings before the Boston firm Shepley, Rutan and Coolidge took over as the main architects in 1901. Today, the campus boasts the designs of more than 70 architects. While large, it is easily explored on foot (for walking tours, *see pp176–7*).

Nuclear Energy, by sculptor Henry Moore, marks the spot where, in 1942, a team of scientists led by Enrico Fermi ushered in the atomic age with the first controlled nuclear reaction.

Bond Chapel
(1926) contains beautiful stained-glass windows by Charles Connick and elaborate wood carvings.

Main Quadrangle
The university's tranquil central quadrangle is the largest of seven designed by Henry Ives Cobb ❺

Midway Plaisance
This is the site of the 1893 World's Columbian Exposition amusement park ❻

STAR SIGHTS

★ Oriental Institute Museum

★ Robie House

★ Smart Museum of Art

Cobb Gate
was donated to the university by Henry Ives Cobb, the campus' master planner. It is ornately decorated with gargoyles.

LOCATOR MAP
See Street Finder maps 7 & 8

KEY

- - - - Suggested route

★ **Smart Museum of Art**
This light-filled, intimate museum offers a rich, balanced survey of Western art ④

Regenstein Library
the university's main library, holds treasured rare book and manuscript collections, along with millions of other volumes.

★ **Oriental Institute Museum**
Three millennia of ancient Near East civilization are showcased at this fascinating museum ③

Rockefeller Memorial Chapel
Elaborate carvings and intricate stained-glass windows grace the interior of this limestone-and-brick chapel ①

58TH STREET

WOODLAWN AVENUE

0 meters   100

0 yards   100

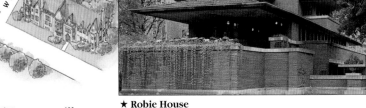

★ **Robie House**
This Frank Lloyd Wright-designed home (1908–1910) is a masterpiece of the Prairie School of architecture ②

Rockefeller Memorial Chapel ❶

5850 S Woodlawn Ave. **Map** 7 C4.
Tel (773) 702-2100. **M** Garfield
(red line) then bus 55. **R** 59th. **O**
8am–4pm daily. **↑** 11am Sun,
10am daily in summer. **& ✔**
Concerts.
www.rockefeller.uchicago.edu

Rockefeller Memorial Chapel
is Bertram G. Goodhue's 1928
interpretation of Gothic *(see
p26)*. The chapel is topped
with a 207-ft (63-m) tower.
It is the tallest building on
campus: John D. Rockefeller,
as a condition of his bequest,
required that this structure be
the university's dominant
feature. Contributing to its
tradition of musical excellence
is one of Chicago's oldest
choral ensembles, and the
stunning E.M. Skinner organ.
The 72-bell tower, the bells
weighing from 10.5 lb (5 kg)
to 18.5 tons, is the second-
largest in the world. The bells
ring at noon and 6pm weekdays, after service, and during
the annual carillon festival.

Bust of a Man (c.1840 BC), at the Oriental Institute Museum

Oriental Institute Museum ❸

1155 E 58th St. **Map** 7 C4. **Tel** (773)
702-9520. **M** Garfield (red line)
then bus 55. **R** 59th. **O** 10am–
6pm Tue, Thu–Sat; 10am–8:30pm
Wed; noon–6pm Sun. **●** public hols.
& ✔ ▯ www-oi.uchicago.edu

The Oriental Institute
Museum is the exhibition arm
of the Oriental Institute, its
scholars having excavated in
virtually every region of

the Near East since 1919. The
museum presents the institute's famed collection of
over 100,000 artifacts from the
earliest civilizations of the
world. It is also one of only
three places in the world
where you can see a
reconstruction of an Assyrian
palace (c.721–705 BC).

Other highlights of the
museum include a monu-
mental sculpture (c.1334–25
BC) of King Tutankhamen
from a Luxor temple. At 17 ft
(5 m), it is the tallest ancient

Robie House ❷

5757 S Woodlawn Ave. **Map** 8 D4.
Tel (773) 834-1847. **M** Garfield
(green & red line) then bus 55.
R 59th. **O** daily. **●** Jan 1, Thanksgiving, Dec 25. **▨ ✔** mandatory:
11am, 1pm, 3pm Mon–Fri;
11am–3:30pm every 30 minutes at
weekends; additional tours in
Jun–Aug: 4pm, 5pm, 6pm Thu. **▯**
www.wrightplus.org

Frank Lloyd Wright's world-
famous Robie House is the
quintessential expression of
the Prairie School movement
(see p27). Designed in 1908
for Frederick Robie, a bicycle
and motorbike manufacturer,
and completed in 1910, the
home is one of Wright's last
Prairie School houses: Wright
left both his family and his
Oak Park practice during its
three-year construction.

Robie House has three
distinct parts combining to
create a balanced whole.
Two, two-story rectangular
concrete blocks sit parallel to

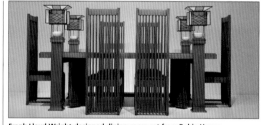
Frank Lloyd Wright-designed dining-room set from Robie House

each other; a smaller square
third story is positioned at
their junction. There is no
basement and no attic. The
exterior design of the house
perfectly captures the prairie
landscape of flat, open fields.
The roof's sweeping planes
embody the house's
aesthetic of bold
rectilinear simplicity.
Steel beams, some 60 ft
(18 m) long, support
the overhanging roof.
Their use was
unorthodox in
residential architecture
at the time.

**Leaded stained-glass windows and
doors**, which run the length of the
living room, allow for both privacy
and natural light.

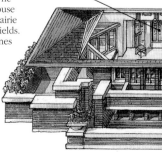

Egyptian statue in the western hemisphere.

The museum's Egyptian collection, which includes objects of ancient Egyptian daily life and religious and funerary practices, is one of the largest in the US.

Smart Museum of Art ➍

5550 S Greenwood Ave. **Map** 7 C4. **Tel** (773) 702-0200. Ⓜ *Garfield (red line) then bus 55.* ◻ *10am–4pm Tue, Wed, Fri; 10am–8pm Thu; 11am–5pm Sat, Sun.* ● *public hols.* ♿ 🎫 ▢ 🏠 Ⓟ ***Special events.*** **www**.smartmuseum.uchicago.edu

If you are feeling over-whelmed by the crowds at Chicago's major museums, this is the place to come for an intimate encounter with art. Named after David and Alfred Smart, founders of *Esquire Magazine* and the museum's benefactors, the Smart Museum was estab-lished in 1974 as the art museum of the University of

Henry Moore's *Nuclear Energy*, **outside the Smart Museum**

Chicago. It holds more than 8,000 artworks and artifacts, including antiquities and Old Master prints, Asian paintings, calligraphies, and ceramics. By showing its works in rotating, thematic displays, the museum ensures its collection is made available to the public. The museum also owns important post-war Chicago artwork, furniture and glass from Robie House, and early modern and contemporary painting and sculpture. A 1999 renovation has allowed for more compre-hensive displays of the

museum's collection of important 20th century and Asian artworks.

The museum's café, with tall windows overlooking the tranquil sculpture garden, is a great spot for a quiet lunch.

University of Chicago Quadrangles ➎

Bounded by 57th & 59th Sts, Ellis & University Aves. **Map** 7 C4. Ⓜ *Garfield (green line) then bus 55.* 🚆 *59th.*

The cloistered quadrangle plan for the University of Chicago – in the 1890s, one of the first in the US – was developed by architect Henry Ives Cobb. He patterned the unified campus after British universities Cambridge and Oxford. Despite years of development and modifica-tion, the six broken quadran-gles surrounding a seventh still reflect Cobb's vision.

Cobb Gate, at the north entrance, is a gargoyled ceremonial gateway donated by Cobb in 1900.

A huge chimney crowns the intersection of the house's three sections, uniting the parts.

A large hearth is the focal point of the living room.

Also bold but simple, the interior is furnished with Wright-designed furniture. The innovative dining-room set is on view at the Smart Museum *(see above)*. The house is a *Gesamtkunstwerk*, a total work of art. Every item in the house contributes to its

beauty. The house is an organic whole, underscored by the harmonious interplay between the exterior and interior and is admired by architects worldwide.

A massive restoration plan was undertaken in 2000 and is expected to take ten years.

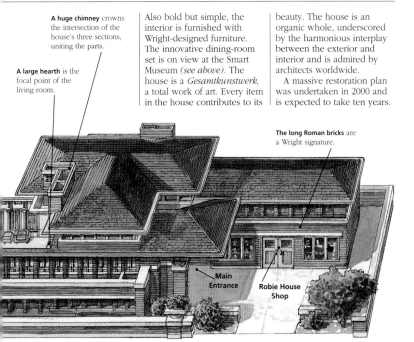

The long Roman bricks are a Wright signature.

Main Entrance

Robie House Shop

University students playing soccer on the Midway Plaisance

Midway Plaisance ❻

Bounded by 59th & 60th Sts, Cottage Grove & Stony Island Aves. **Map** 7 B5–8 E5. 🚇 *59th.*

Midway Plaisance, a mile- (1.6-km-) long greenway at the south end of the University of Chicago campus and the city's broadest boulevard, serves as the university's recreation grounds. The Midway is also an excellent vantage point from which to view the university's Gothic buildings.

Designed by Frederick Law Olmsted and Calvert Vaux as the link between Washington and Jackson parks, the Midway was the site of the 1893 exposition's Bazaar of Nations. It was here that the Ferris wheel – 250 ft (76 m) high – made its debut.

Washington Park ❼

Bounded by 51st & 60th Sts, Martin Luther King Jr. Dr & Cottage Grove Ave. **Map** 7 A2–A5. 🚇 *51st; Garfield (green line).*

Named after the first US president, Washington Park was originally intended to be part of a grand South Park, comprising both Washington Park and Jackson Park, connected by a canal

running through Midway Plaisance. Landscape architects Frederick Law Olmsted and Calvert Vaux, designers of New York's Central Park, developed the South Park plan in 1871. The park commission balked at creating a canal and so the original plan was never realized in its entirety. In 1872, Horace W.S. Cleveland was hired to oversee the completion of Washington Park.

Combining expanses of meadows with borders of trees and shrubs, Washington Park's pastoral landscape also has a pond and lagoon. At the northeast end of the park is Drexel Fountain, one of the oldest fountains in Chicago. It was designed in 1881–2 by Henry Manger.

The park's most magnificent feature is the sculpture *Fountain of Time* at the south end, where Washington Park meets Midway Plaisance. Designed in 1922 by the Chicago artist Lorado Taft (1860–1936), this haunting monument depicts the cloaked figure of Time watching the endless march of humanity. It was erected to celebrate 100 years of US-British peace.

Detail of Taft's *Fountain of Time*, Washington Park

DuSable Museum of African American History ❽

740 E 56th Pl. **Map** 7 B4. **Tel** (773) 947-0600. 🚇 *Garfield (green line) then bus 55.* 🚌 *4.* ⏰ *10am–5pm Tue–Sat; noon–5pm Sun.* ⚫ *major public hols.* 💰 *(children under 6 free; free Sun).* ♿ 📷 *book in advance.* 🏛 🅿 *Lectures, films.*

As part of its mission to celebrate the rich and diverse history and culture of African Americans and their contributions to the nation, the DuSable Museum highlights accomplishments of the ordinary and

extraordinary alike. Founded in 1961, the museum is the oldest such institution in the US.

The museum's permanent exhibit "Songs of My People" brings together diverse images by Black photojournalists of African-American lives.

Memorabilia from the life and political career of Chicago's first Black mayor, Harold Washington, make up the "Harold Washington in Office" exhibit.

Disturbing pop-culture materials are collected in "Distorted Images: Made in USA?," an exhibit focusing on contrived and demeaning images of African Americans.

"Africa Speaks" presents art from Africa, much of which has a functional purpose. Handcrafted door panels, for example, are given to a Nigerian bride on her wedding day so she may close her boudoir while decorating it. The ritual masks from closed West African societies are particularly striking.

Hyde Park ❾

Bounded by Hyde Park Blvd, 61st St, Washington Park, & Lake Michigan. **Map** 8 D3. 🚇 *53rd; 55th-56th-57th; 59th.* 📞 *call (312) 922-3432.* 🍴 🏛

Hyde Park is one of Chicago's most pleasant neighborhoods. The University of Chicago's presence contributes a collegiate atmosphere, while the many shops, restaurants, theaters, and galleries provide a broad array of attractions.

The area was open countryside in 1853 when Chicago lawyer Paul Cornell established the community on a swath of lakeside property.

Unruly gardens characteristic of the Rosalie Villas, in Hyde Park

Isidore Heller House, in Hyde Park, by Frank Lloyd Wright

The quiet suburb was transformed by three events: its 1889 annexation by the City of Chicago, the 1890 founding of the University of Chicago, and the 1893 World's Columbian Exposition. Many of the houses from this 1890s spurt of development survive. Isidore Heller House (5132 South Woodlawn Avenue) is a Frank Lloyd Wright design (1897) that precedes his celebrated Robie House *(see pp102–103)* by a decade yet reveals his characteristic Prairie style.

Rosalie Villas (Harper Avenue, from 57th to 59th), designed by Solon S. Beman between 1884 and 1890, was Hyde Park's first planned community. It consists of about 50 Queen Anne-style residences, each unique in architectural detail.

The retail heart of Hyde Park is 53rd Street, while ethnic restaurants cluster on 55th Street. Bookstores thrive in Hyde Park; it has been called the largest center for books in the Midwest.

Kenwood ⓿

Bounded by 47th St, Hyde Park Blvd, Cottage Grove Ave & Lake Park Ave. **Map** 7 C1. Ⓜ *47th (green line) then bus 28.* Ⓡ *47th.* 🗓 *call (312) 922-3432.* 🚻 🚻

Historic Kenwood was established in 1856 when dentist Jonathan A. Kennicott bought and subdivided a large plot of land near 43rd Street. Over the next three decades it became one of the most fashionable South Side communities. In the 1920s,

many middle-class African Americans moved to the area, but the late 1940s saw a period of decline. A massive urban renewal project was begun in the early 1950s, and by the 1980s, the neighborhood had undergone a revival. Kenwood's rise has further been spurred by the election of its most famous resident, Barack Obama, as President of the United States.

The neighborhood has some of the finest mansions constructed in Chicago, along with many Prairie School *(see p27)* homes. Two commissions Frank Lloyd Wright undertook while working for Adler and Sullivan include the George W. Blossom House (4858 Kenwood Avenue) and the Warren McArthur House (4852 Kenwood Avenue).

Noteworthy are the mansions on Greenwood Avenue between 49th and 50th, in particular the elegant Prairie style of the Ernest J. Magerstadt House (4930 South Greenwood Avenue), designed in 1908 by George W. Maher, as well as the ornate houses lining South Kimbark Avenue.

Jackson Park ⓫

Bounded by 57th & 67th Sts, Stony Island Ave & Lake Michigan. **Map** 8 E5. Ⓡ *59th; 63rd.* 🗓 *call (312) 922-3432; bird walk, call (773) 493-7058.*

Jackson Park was designed by Frederick Law Olmsted and Calvert Vaux in 1871 as part of the unrealized South Park plan *(see p104).* Even though the park was redesigned after being chosen as the main site for the 1893 World's Fair, and again in 1895, its original aquatic theme is still evident.

Osaka Garden is a re-creation of the Japanese garden built for the fair. This serene spot on Wooded Island has a pavilion, waterfall, and gorgeous cherry trees. The island is considered the best place in Chicago for bird-watching: more than 120 species of birds have been sighted here.

In the center of the park, a smaller, gilded replica of the 65-ft- (20-m-) statue *The Republic* celebrates the fair's 25th anniversary. There are also two beaches and several sports facilities.

Jackson Park's "Golden Lady," a replica of Daniel Chester French's *The Republic*

The contemplative Osaka Garden in Jackson Park

Museum of Science and Industry ⑫

The Museum of Science and Industry celebrates the scientific and technological accomplishments of humankind, with an emphasis on achievements of the 20th century. Originally called the Rosenwald Industrial Museum, after the museum's benefactor, its name was soon changed at Julius Rosenwald's urging, who said that the museum belonged not to him but to the people. While the building, a monumental Neo-Classical structure dominating Jackson Park, is a nod to history *(see p109)*, the museum within has been the North American leader in modern, interactive displays, making the exploration of science and technology an accessible experience.

A carved stone figure over the north portal

Colleen Moore's Fairy Castle
This 9-sq-ft (0.8-sq-m) dollhouse is complete with miniature furniture and working electricity and plumbing.

Farm Tech
Showing how farmers are constantly developing cutting-edge techniques, this gallery explores the newest farming innovations.

Entrance to the U-505 Submarine exhibition which tells the story of a World War II U-Boat that sank eight allied ships before being captured by the US Navy in 1944.

Main Floor

Ground Floor

Apollo 8 Command Module
This historic spacecraft played an important role in early US lunar missions, which culminated in the landing on the moon.

Crown Entrance

Great Hall

STAR EXHIBITS

★ All Aboard the Silver Streak

★ Take Flight

★ Transportation Gallery

★ All Aboard the Silver Streak
Climb aboard the record-breaking 1930s train that revolutionized industrial design.

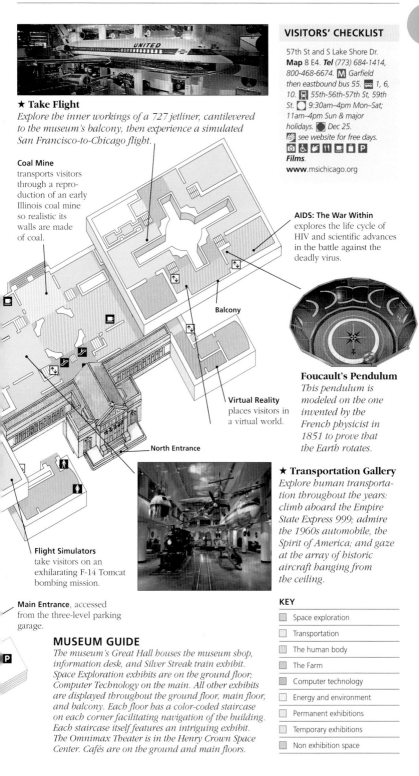

★ Take Flight
Explore the inner workings of a 727 jetliner, cantilevered to the museum's balcony, then experience a simulated San Francisco-to-Chicago flight.

Coal Mine transports visitors through a reproduction of an early Illinois coal mine so realistic its walls are made of coal.

Balcony

Virtual Reality places visitors in a virtual world.

North Entrance

Flight Simulators take visitors on an exhilarating F-14 Tomcat bombing mission.

Main Entrance, accessed from the three-level parking garage.

VISITORS' CHECKLIST

57th St and S Lake Shore Dr.
Map 8 E4. **Tel** (773) 684-1414,
800-468-6674. Garfield
then eastbound bus 55. 1, 6,
10. 55th-56th-57th St, 59th
St. 9:30am-4pm Mon-Sat;
11am-4pm Sun & major
holidays. Dec 25.
see website for free days.
Films.
www.msichicago.org

AIDS: The War Within explores the life cycle of HIV and scientific advances in the battle against the deadly virus.

Foucault's Pendulum
This pendulum is modeled on the one invented by the French physicist in 1851 to prove that the Earth rotates.

★ Transportation Gallery
Explore human transportation throughout the years: climb aboard the Empire State Express 999; admire the 1960s automobile, the Spirit of America; and gaze at the array of historic aircraft hanging from the ceiling.

KEY
- Space exploration
- Transportation
- The human body
- The Farm
- Computer technology
- Energy and environment
- Permanent exhibitions
- Temporary exhibitions
- Non exhibition space

MUSEUM GUIDE
The museum's Great Hall houses the museum shop, information desk, and Silver Streak train exhibit. Space Exploration exhibits are on the ground floor; Computer Technology on the main. All other exhibits are displayed throughout the ground floor, main floor, and balcony. Each floor has a color-coded staircase on each corner facilitating navigation of the building. Each staircase itself features an intriguing exhibit. The Omnimax Theater is in the Henry Crown Space Center. Cafés are on the ground and main floors.

Exploring the Museum of Science and Industry

Caryatids grace the museum's exterior

The Museum of Science and Industry has more than 35,000 artifacts, including 2,000 interactive displays, making it one of the largest science museums in the world. It encompasses everything from basic science to advanced technology. Space exploration, transportation, and human biology are particularly strong areas. With more than 350,000 sq ft (32,500 sq m) of exhibition space, there's more than enough to keep visitors of all ages engaged for a full day of investigation and discovery.

View of the Museum of Science and Industry from across Columbia Basin

SPACE EXPLORATION

The Henry Crown Space Center is the epicenter of the museum's display on space exploration. Here, you can view the Apollo 8 Command Module – the first manned spacecraft to circle the moon, orbiting ten times in December 1968. Less than 13 ft (4 m) in diameter and weighing 13,100 lb (6,000 kg), the vessel still bears the scars of its epic journey on its pitted exterior. The exhibit includes a replica of NASA's Apollo Lunar Module Trainer, used for astronaut training, and a 6.5-oz (185-g) piece of moon rock retrieved by the Apollo 17 mission.

The Space Center is also home to the Aurora 7 Mercury Space Capsule, one of the earliest manned spacecrafts to orbit the Earth – doing so four times in a row in May 1962.

Henry Crown Space Center, showcasing US space exploration

A 20-minute movie simulates for viewers the experience of blasting off in a space shuttle.

TRANSPORTATION

Pick a mode of transport – from train, plane, to automobile – and you can be sure the museum has an outstanding example.

Train-nostalgia buffs will enjoy the All Aboard the Silver Streak exhibit, which showcases the first diesel-electric, streamlined passenger train in America, the Pioneer Zephyr. Built in 1934, the Zephyr was the swiftest, sleekest train in the US, initiating the conversion from steam to diesel-electric locomotion and ushering in the era of luxury passenger rail travel. The Zephyr's interior was dramatically different from the opulent Pullman cars in use at the time (see p119) yet just as elegant in its simplicity. Visitors can get behind the controls and pretend to drive this historic train.

The museum also has one of the largest train models in the world. The 3,500-sq-ft (325-sq-m) model highlights the role of the railroad in the US economy.

The history of aviation is well represented in the museum's transportation zone. Look up to the balcony to see a rare Boeing 40B-2 airplane suspended from the ceiling.

Nearby is Take Flight, an exhibit explaining the scientific principles behind the wonder of flight, such as radar, aerodynamics, and engine and wing construction. This exhibit contains one of the museum's largest attractions, a cantilevered United Airlines Boeing 727. Visitors can board the aircraft to explore, and watch from the balcony its seven-minute simulated flight.

Adjacent to the Boeing 727 is Designed to Fly, an exhibit tracing the history of humans' efforts to fly, from the 15th century to the Wright Brothers' first successful powered flight, in 1903.

Another popular attraction is the restored U-505 Submarine, a World War II German U-Boat captured by US naval forces off the west coast of Africa in 1944. The submarine forms the centerpiece of a new 35,000-sq-ft (3,250-sq-m) climate-controlled exhibit which is located on the lower ground floor and tells the story of the search for and dramatic capture of the U-505.

Directly above, on the main floor, is the NAVY: Technology at Sea exhibit, where a high-tech flight simulator replicates a take-off and

The Great Hall, the popular Silver Streak train in the background

landing on the back of an aircraft carrier.

Closer to earth is the Auto Gallery's Spirit of America, the first car to break the 500 mph (800 kph) land speed barrier. On October 15, 1964, Craig Breedlove became the "fastest man on wheels" when he piloted this missile-like vehicle to spectacular speeds.

Fast machines in the museum's transportation zone

THE HUMAN BODY

Undoubtedly the weirdest exhibit in the museum is the Anatomical Slices, located on the blue staircase between the main floor and balcony. In the 1940s, the corpses of a man and woman who died of natural causes were frozen and then cut into 0.5-inch (1.25-cm) sections – the man, horizontally, and the woman, vertically – and preserved in fluid between glass. These unique displays allow you to look right inside the human body.

A large interactive exhibit, You! the Experience, showcases the connections between the human mind, body, and spirit. It examines and celebrates the experience of life, demonstrating the extraordinary complexity of the human body.

AIDS: The War Within is an exhibit on AIDS and HIV that explores the nine stages of the AIDS virus and ways to control it. Interactive displays cover viruses, the ecology of disease, and the immune system.

The Genetics: Decoding Life exhibit looks at the advancements in genetic engineering.

FARM TECH

This exhibit takes a look at modern technology on a 21st century farm. The Farm features a full-size tractor, a greenhouse, and replicas of a dairy barn and a cornfield.

FROM PLASTER TO STONE

Architect Charles B. Atwood *(see p30)* based his design of this majestic building – built as a temporary structure for the 1893 World's Fair and, today, the only surviving building from the fair – on classical Greek models. Over 270 columns and 24 caryatids, weighing 6 tons each, grace the exterior. Covered in plaster, with a roof of skylights, the building deteriorated badly after the fair. The Field Museum *(see pp86–9)* occupied it briefly, until 1920. The building then sat in a state of disrepair until the mid-1920s, when Julius Rosenwald, chairman of Sears, Roebuck and Co., campaigned to save it and founded the museum, donating millions of dollars to a massive reconstruction effort. Exterior plaster was replaced with 28,000 tons of limestone and marble in an 11-year renovation. The Museum of Science and Industry opened in 1933, in time for the Century of Progress World's Exposition.

Some of the original buildings during the 1893 World's Columbian Exposition

Through interactive exhibits, visitors can design their own cereal, "harvest" a field of corn or feel what it is like to milk a cow. They can also follow milk, corn and soybeans through a fascinating voyage from Midwest roots to a variety of everyday products.

COMPUTER TECHNOLOGY

Although effective use of computers is made in many of the interactive displays, relatively little space is devoted to the subject of computer technology. A fascinating exception is Imaging: The Tools of Science. This installation explores computer-imaging procedures such as MRIs (which produce the image of a cross-section of an object) and CT scans (soft-tissue X-rays). Visitors can delve into radiosurgery and forensic science through hands-on exhibits.

Don goggles in the main floor's Virtual Reality exhibit and become part of an environment created by computer technology. A video camera,

Bronze plaques on the main doors honor the sciences

real-time digitizer, and recorded images will place you in a virtual world, where you can "play" a drum or "bounce" a ball.

ENERGY AND ENVIRONMENT

One of the museum's most popular exhibits is Coal Mine. It is worth waiting for in the inevitable lineup. This re-creation of a 1933 Illinois coal mine is remarkably life-like. The 20-minute tour begins at the top of a mineshaft, where an elevator takes visitors down in semi-darkness to a bituminous coal seam and a fascinating demonstration of coal-mining machinery. A short ride on a mine train ends this unique, if a little claustrophobic, experience. Environmental issues are front and center at the Reusable City. Interactive displays encourage visitors to learn more about the Earth's ozone layer, climate change, and pollution. A periscope allows visitors to see inside a "landfill," down to its decades-old contents.

FARTHER AFIELD

Chicago's outlying areas offer a wealth of sight-seeing opportunities. For lovers of architecture, Oak Park is a must-see for its Frank Lloyd Wright designs. Other Chicago neighborhoods, such as Wicker Park and Lakeview, each with its own distinct character, are ideal day-trip destinations. Pullman is one of the US's best-preserved

Mexican sugar skull, Pilsen

19th-century neighborhoods. A little farther is Brookfield Zoo, renowned for its realistic animal habitats. Walking paths lead through varied landscapes at Morton Arboretum. Visitors with more time can traverse the canal corridor, which runs alongside the 1848 historic canal and encompasses extensive recreational trails and several fine museums.

SIGHTS AT A GLANCE

Historic Buildings, Districts Parks, and Canals
Jane Addams Hull-House Museum **7**
Illinois and Michigan Canal National Heritage Corridor **11**
Oak Park **5**
Pullman Historic District **12**

Neighborhoods
Lakeview and Wrigleyville **2**
Lower West Side **8**
Near West Side **6**
Wicker Park **3**

Zoos and Botanic Gardens
Brookfield Zoo **9**
Garfield Park Conservatory **4**
Lincoln Park Zoo (pp112–13) **1**
Morton Arboretum **10**

KEY

▦	Urban area
▬	Interstate highway
▬	State highway
═	Major road

5 miles = 8 km

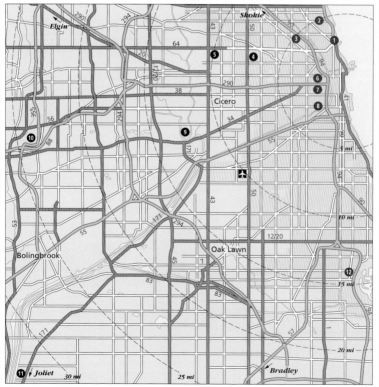

◁ Pink flamingos at Lincoln Park Zoo

Lincoln Park Zoo ●

Established in 1868 with the gift of two swans from New York's Central Park, Lincoln Park Zoo is the US's oldest free public zoo. Today, more than 1,000 mammals, reptiles, and birds from around the world live here, in realistic habitats. The zoo's status as a world leader in wildlife conservation is evident in its educational exhibits, as well as in its many international efforts to save endangered species. Although it is not Chicago's largest zoo *(see Brookfield Zoo p117)*, Lincoln Park Zoo, in the heart of Lincoln Park, is easily accessible from the Downtown Core. The park, Chicago's largest, offers walking and biking paths, paddle-boating ponds, lagoons, and sandy beaches.

Statue of Abraham Lincoln in Lincoln Park

Lincoln Park Conservatory
This stunning conservatory (1890–95), designed by architect Joseph L. Silsbee, houses many exotic plants, including orchids. Thousands of flowers grown here are for park use.

West Entrance

Pritzker Family Children's Zoo showcases wood-dwelling animals such as beavers, bears, and wolves.

★ Regenstein Small Mammal-Reptile House
This exhibit showcases 40 species, including African Dwarf crocodiles.

Waterfowl Lagoon
Flamingos and other waterfowl find refuge in this peaceful lagoon, one of the zoo's earliest features.

Café Brauer was designed in 1908 by Dwight Perkins, a leading architect of the Prairie School. The building was restored in 1989. Its Great Hall has spectacular chandeliers and a skylight.

STOCKTON DRIVE

STAR SIGHTS

- ★ Farm in the Zoo presented by John Deere

- ★ Regenstein Center for African Apes

- ★ Regenstein Small Mammal-Reptile House

★ Farm in the Zoo presented by John Deere
This working farm shelters cows, horses, chickens, and pigs. Children most enjoy watching the daily milking routine and horse grooming.

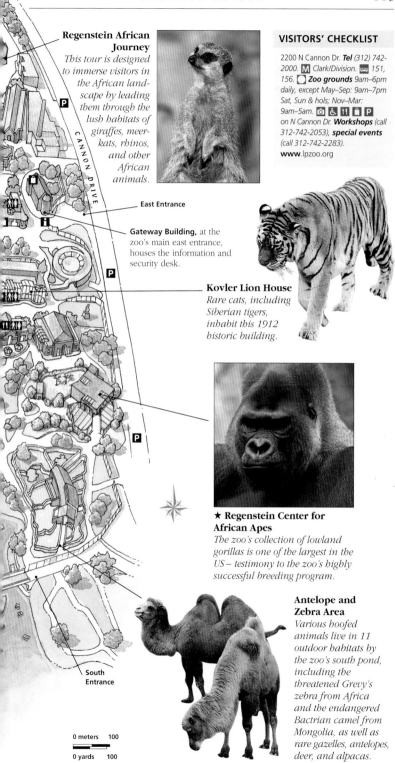

Regenstein African Journey
This tour is designed to immerse visitors in the African landscape by leading them through the lush habitats of giraffes, meerkats, rhinos, and other African animals.

East Entrance

Gateway Building, at the zoo's main east entrance, houses the information and security desk.

Kovler Lion House
Rare cats, including Siberian tigers, inhabit this 1912 historic building.

★ **Regenstein Center for African Apes**
The zoo's collection of lowland gorillas is one of the largest in the US – testimony to the zoo's highly successful breeding program.

Antelope and Zebra Area
Various hoofed animals live in 11 outdoor habitats by the zoo's south pond, including the threatened Grevy's zebra from Africa and the endangered Bactrian camel from Mongolia, as well as rare gazelles, antelopes, deer, and alpacas.

South Entrance

0 meters 100
0 yards 100

VISITORS' CHECKLIST

2200 N Cannon Dr. **Tel** (312) 742-2000. Ⓜ Clark/Division. 🚌 151, 156. Ⓞ **Zoo grounds** 9am–6pm daily, except May–Sep: 9am–7pm Sat, Sun & hols; Nov–Mar: 9am–5am. 🖼 ♿ 🏪 🛍 🅿 on N Cannon Dr. **Workshops** (call 312-742-2053), **special events** (call 312-742-2283).
www.lpzoo.org

Wrigley Field baseball stadium, home of the famous Chicago Cubs

Lakeview and Wrigleyville ❷

West of Lake Michigan to Ashland Ave, from Diversey Ave to W Irving Park Rd. Ⓜ *Belmont (red, brown, purple lines).* 🚌 *9, 22, 36.* 🎭 *See Entertainment p163.*

Lakeview and Wrigleyville are two of Chicago's most colorful neighborhoods. Now a cultural melting pot, the area was settled by German immigrants in the 1830s. Farms dotted the landscape until the mid-1800s, when the area began to develop as a residential neighborhood of working-class Swedish immigrants. After annexation by the City in 1889, a spurt of development established the area as one of the liveliest in Chicago – a distinction it continues to hold today.

Wrigleyville, the northern half of Lakeview, is named after Wrigley Field, home of the famous Chicago Cubs baseball team. This charming stadium, designed by Zachary Taylor Davis in 1914, is the oldest National League ballpark. The community resisted electric lighting of the stadium into the late 1980s.

Lakeview hosts a thriving theater scene as well as excellent restaurants, coffeehouses, bars, specialty shops, and bookshops. Trendy boutiques line Belmont Avenue between Halsted and Sheffield Streets. Lakeview is also the heart of Chicago's gay community.

To sample Lakeview's architectural heritage, visit

Alta Vista Terrace, between Grace and Byron Streets. This block of turn-of-the-century row houses was designed by Joseph C. Brompton in 1904 and was the first area in Chicago to be designated a historic district.

Hawthorne Place, north of Belmont Avenue, east of Broadway, is a rare surviving Victorian-era residential design that is typical of the area's early development.

Beautiful tombstones mark the resting places of Chicago's notables in **Graceland Cemetery** (4001 North Clark Street), just north of Lakeview. Buried here are Louis Sullivan (*see p30*) and George Pullman (*see p119*), among others. A site map is available at the cemetery's office.

Rapp House, one of Wicker Park's architectural gems

Wicker Park ❸

Bounded by North Ave, Milwaukee, Leavitt, and Division Sts. Ⓜ *Damen (blue line).* 🚌 *56.* 🎭 *Around the Coyote (Sep).*

If you are looking for the trendy area of Chicago, Wicker Park, brimming with galleries, boutiques, coffeehouses, restaurants, and nightclubs is it. In the late 1800s, Scandinavian and German immigrants built mansions here and many of them remain, making this a great area for an architectural tour. Of interest are John Rapp House (1407 North Hoyne Avenue) and Holy Trinity Cathedral (1121 Leavitt Street), designed by Louis Sullivan.

Garfield Park Conservatory ❹

300 North Central Park Ave. **Tel** *(312) 746-5100.* Ⓜ *Conservatory-Central Park Dr. (green line).* ⏰ *9am–5pm (to 8pm Wed) daily.* ♿ *available to members.* 🏛 ♿ 🅿 **www**.garfield-conservatory.org.

Designed by Jens Jensen, (who was known as "the dean of Prairie landscapes") in 1906, the spectacular Garfield Park Conservatory is a two-acre enclosed garden which houses the world's largest public horticultural collection under glass. Shows and events are held throughout the year. Children are well catered for, in particular with the Elizabeth Morse Genius Children's Garden, with exhibits showing how plants grow and reproduce.

Oak Park ❺

Bounded by N North Ave, S Roosevelt Rd, E Austin Blvd & W Harlem Ave. 🛈 *(708) 524-7800.* Ⓜ *Oak Park (green line); Harlem/Lake (green line).* 🚉 *Oak Park (Union Pacific/West line).* **Visitors' center***: 158 N Forest Ave.* ⏰ *10am–5pm daily.* 🚫 *Jan 1, Thanksgiving, Dec 25.* 🎫 🎦 **Frank Lloyd Wright Preservation Trust***: 931 Chicago Ave.* **Tel** *(708) 848-1976.* 🎫 **www**.gowright.org

In 1889, Frank Lloyd Wright moved to Oak Park, at the age of 22. During the next 20 years here, he created many groundbreaking buildings as his legendary Prairie School style evolved. This community is home to 25 Wright buildings – the largest grouping of his work anywhere. Oak Park is also known for its literary

Frank Lloyd Wright's Home and Studio, his residence for 20 years

Unity Temple, Frank Lloyd Wright's "little jewel"

association: famed American writer Ernest Hemingway *(see p31)* was born here in 1899.

The best place to feast on Wright's achievement is the **Frank Lloyd Wright Home and Studio**. Designed by Wright in 1889, the superbly restored residence and workspace is where the architect developed his influential Prairie style.

Nearby are two private homes that reveal Wright's versatility. The **Arthur Heurtley House** (1902: 318 Forest Ave) is typically Prairie style, with its row of windows spanning the low roofline and its simple but elegant entrance arch. The **Moore-Dugal House** (1895: 333 Forest Ave) is a hybrid of styles, with Tudor Revival and Gothic elements.

At the southern end of Oak Park is the masterful **Pleasant Home** (217 Home Ave), a 30-room Prairie-style mansion designed in 1897 by George W. Maher. The house contains extraordinary art glass (designed panels of leaded glass), intricate woodwork, and decorative motifs, as well as a display on the area's history.

Wright was particularly proud of **Unity Temple** (875 Lake St.), his design for the Unitarian Universalist Congregation. He called this church, one of his most important designs, his first expression of an "entirely new architecture." It was built between 1906 and 1908 using what was then an unusual technique of poured reinforced concrete, in part because of a budget of only $45,000. Unity Temple is a masterpiece of powerful simplicity wedded with functional ornamentation.

Ernest Hemingway lived in Oak Park until the age of 20. The **Ernest Hemingway Birthplace** (339 North Oak Park Ave) is a grand Victorian home with turn-of-the-century furnishings, and has displays on the life of this Nobel Prize winner. The **Ernest Hemingway Museum** (200 North Oak Park Ave) features artifacts from Hemingway's early life, including a childhood diary.

The Victorian house in which Ernest Hemingway was born

OAK PARK

0 meters   300

0 yards   300

Key to Symbols *see back flap*

Jane Addams Hull-House Museum, seen from the courtyard

Near West Side ❻

Bounded by Chicago River, 16th & Kinzie Sts, & Ogden Ave. **Map** 3 A1–A5. Ⓜ *UIC-Halsted.* 🚌 *8, 60.*

Over the years, Chicago's Near West Side has experienced waves of successive immigrant settlement. Today, it is one of the best places to experience the city's many ethnic communities.

It was settled in the 1840s and 1850s by working-class Irish immigrants. The Great Chicago Fire of 1871 began here, on DeKoven Street (No. 558), in the O'Leary barn. Appropriately (or ironically, depending on how you look at it), the **Chicago Fire Academy** is now located on the site. An arresting bronze sculpture of flames marks the spot where the devastating fire reportedly began.

Following the fire, Russian and Polish Jews settled the area in the 1890s, while to the north, a lively Greek Town developed, centered along Halsted Street, between Madison and Van Buren Streets. To the west, Little Italy, centered around Taylor Street at Halsted Street, flourished.

The **University of Illinois at Chicago** holds a prominent position in the area. Walter A. Netsch Jr. designed the university in the

Egon Weiner's sculpture at the Chicago Fire Academy

1960s, in the modern style known as Brutalism. The campus is characterized by unadorned concrete buildings with rows of narrow vertical windows.

Jane Addams Hull-House Museum ❼

800 S Halsted St. **Tel** *(312) 413-5353.* **Map** 3 A3. Ⓜ *UIC-Halsted.* 🚌 *7, 8, 60.* 🔴 *major public hols.* 🛇 🖾 *mandatory: 10am–4pm Tue–Fri, noon–4pm Sun.* 🅿

This museum, which is part of the University of Illinois campus, celebrates the work of Jane Addams *(see p29),* who won the 1931 Nobel Peace Prize for her social-justice work and advocacy and became perhaps the most famous woman in the US. In her pioneering work with the poor, Addams fought for child-labor laws, a minimum wage, and better public sanitation, among other social causes.

It was in this mansion in the then industrial center of Chicago that Addams and Ellen Gates Starr established, in 1889, a settlement house to provide social services to immigrants, the poor, and the dispossessed. The house's interior has been restored to look as it did in its early days. There are also settlement house exhibits.

Lower West Side ❽

Bounded by Chicago River, 16th St, & Pulaski Rd. Ⓜ *18th.* 🚌 *9, 18, 60.*

The Lower West Side, like the Near West Side, developed as an industrial, working-class neighborhood after the 1871 fire. Immigrants from Bohemia were the first to arrive, in the 1870s, followed in the early 20th century by Germans, Poles, and Yugoslavians. In the 1950s, an influx of Mexican and Puerto Rican immigrants brought a Hispanic flavor to the community.

Today, the neighborhood of Pilsen, centered along 18th Street between South Damen Avenue and South Halsted Street, is home to many fine Mexican restaurants, bakeries, and specialty shops. The sounds of salsa are everywhere, the inviting scent of corn tortillas emanates from tortillerias, and colorful murals brighten the streetscape. Artists, lured here by low rents in the 1980s, contribute a touch of eclecticism to the area.

The best way to experience this vibrant district is to stroll along 18th Street, admire the late-19th-century buildings – one of the most interesting is the Romanesque-style Thalia Hall at the corner of Allport Street – and perhaps stop at a street vendor for a tasty cob of roasted corn.

For more substantial fare, one of the best restaurants in Pilsen is Nuevo León (No. 1515), where the food is tasty and the portions huge. Café Jumping Bean (No. 1439) exhibits work by local artists

Café Jumping Bean on Chicago's Lower West Side

and serves up delicious snacks. Panaderia El Paraiso (No. 1156) is an excellent local bakery.

The cultural heart of Pilsen is the **National Museum of Mexican Art** (1852 West 19th Street; 312-738-1503; 10am–5pm Tue–Sun), the largest Mexican arts institution in the US. The museum rotates a broad range of exhibitions, covering subjects as diverse as ancient Mexico and young avant-garde artists. The more than 1,500 works in the permanent collection include Mexican masters such as Diego Rivera.

Signs for Mexican bakeries and eateries lining the streets of Pilsen

Brookfield Zoo ❾

First Ave & 31st St, Brookfield. *Tel* (708) 485-0263. Hollywood (Burlington Northern Santa Fe line). 304, 311. Memorial Day–Labor Day: 9:30am–6pm Mon–Sat; 9:30am–7:30pm Sun. Labor Day–Memorial Day: 10am–5pm daily. (free Jan–Feb: Tue, Thu, Sat, Sun; Oct–Dec: Tue, Thu; separate adm to some exhibits). P *Lectures, weekend special events*. www.brookfieldzoo.org

Brookfield Zoo, opened in 1934, is one of the largest zoos in the US. More than 5,900 animals representing approximately 440 species, gathered from around the world, roam realistic habitats.

Many of the animal exhibits are outdoors, along the zoo's 15 miles (24 km) of trails, but there are also a number of fascinating indoor displays, such as the Living Coast and Tropic World. The Fragile Kingdom comprises two

A Capuchin monkey at Tropic World watching visitors

indoor exhibits – an African desert and an Asian rainforest, with indigenous bats, squirrels, and foxes – and an outdoor display featuring large cats, including an Amur (Siberian) tiger. Nearby is the 2,000-seat Dolphinarium. Shows featuring Atlantic bottlenose dolphins are offered here daily. To the north of the Dolphinarium is Pinniped Point: outdoor pools containing sea lions, harbor seals, and walruses.

At the southeast corner of the grounds is the Children's Zoo, where kids can pet barnyard animals and watch cow and goat milking.

Another children's favorite is Tropic World, one of the largest indoor mixed-species exhibits in the world. Here, rainforest creatures and primates from South America, Asia, and Africa swing through trees and wander the forest floor while visitors watch from the observation deck. The Brazilian tapir, with a flexible snout; the giant anteater, with a 2-ft-(0.6-m-) long tongue; and Ramar, the 365-lb (165-kg) silverback gorilla, are particularly impressive.

Close by is the Swamp, an indoor re-created cypress swamp with egrets, storks, and a 10-ft- (3-m-) long American alligator, which sleeps with its eyes open.

The Living Coast features three habitats of South America's western coast: open ocean, near-shore waters, and rocky shores. Jellyfish, sharks, and penguins are just a few of the creatures to be found here.

At the interactive Be a Bird exhibit, visitors can learn about bird anatomy and behavior, and test their own ability to fly.

One of the most spectacular exhibits is Habitat Africa! This re-created savanna is complete with giraffes and wild dogs. A "danger game" trail allows visitors to pretend they're thirsty animals walking to a waterhole, their steps activating taped sounds of predators.

Along the zoo's northern boundary are enclosures for large animals, including the unusual Grevy's zebras. To the south, near Roosevelt Fountain, is Pachyderm House, home to elephants, rhinos, and hippos.

A hippopotamus grazing in the Pachyderm House

Morton Arboretum ❿

4100 Illinois Route 53, Lisle.
Tel (630) 719-2400. 🚉 *Lisle
(Burlington Northern Santa Fe line).*
⏰ *7am–7pm daily.* 💲 *(discount
Wed).* 🅿️ ♿ 🚻 🍴 📷 🅿️
Workshops, library.
www.mortonarb.org

Morton Arboretum is home
to more than 3,400 types of
trees, shrubs, and other plants
from around the world. Eight
lakes and ponds dot this 2.5-
sq-mile (6.5-sq-km) outdoor
museum, providing wonderful
picnic settings.
    Founded in 1922 by Joy
Morton of the Morton Salt
Company, the arboretum's
mission is educational. It
conducts scientific research as
well as providing informative
public displays. Collections
are grouped according to
plant families and habitats,
allowing visitors to learn
about each species' unique
features and to compare
related plants.
    The arboretum's Daffodil
Glade is particularly stunning
in spring. Its Schulenberg
Prairie, radiant in summer, is
a pioneering landscape restoration begun in the early
1960s by Ray Schulenberg.
The prairie is admired
throughout the Midwest as a
fine re-creation of this now-
endangered prairie that
covered the region before
settlement. The maples are
dramatic in the fall; the ever-
green trees striking in winter.

If you do not have time to
hike along any of the 14 miles
(23 km) of trails, you can drive
through the arboretum in about
50 minutes via 9 miles (15 km)
of one-way roads. Open-air
tram tours are offered daily
(weather permitting).
    Begin your visit at the new
visitors' center, located near
the entrance. The center lists
daily events and seasonal
bloom information. It also has
an excellent bookstore and a
dining area overlooking a
pond. The arboretum's
Thornhill Education Center
(open weekdays) houses
displays about Joy Morton
and the Morton family. The
Sterling Morton Library has a
wide range of publications on
plants, gardening and land-
scaping, and natural history.
It also holds rare botanical
books and prints.

Illinois and Michigan Canal National Heritage Corridor ⓫

From Chicago's south branch of
Chicago River to LaSalle-Peru.
Tel (815) 588-1100. *See* **The History
of Chicago** *p15.* www.canalcor.org

The first Europeans to
explore the Chicago region –
Louis Jolliet and Father
Jacques Marquette – urged, in
their 1673 expedition report,
the building of a canal to connect Lake Michigan to the Des
Plaines and Illinois Rivers.

St. James of the Sag, burial place
of many canal laborers

They believed that such a
transportation link would be
of great economic benefit to
the region. It took a century
and a half for their prediction
to come true, and the loss of
many – mostly Irish – canal
laborers to diseases such as
dysentery and cholera, but
when the Illinois and Michigan
(I&M) Canal opened in 1848, it
did indeed transform the area's
economy. It also established
Chicago as the transportation
center of the Midwest.
    As the use of rail to trans-
port freight became increasingly popular, however, canal
traffic declined. Carrying
waste away from Chicago
became the canal's primary
purpose, until the Sanitary
and Ship Canal took over this
function, in 1914. The I&M
Canal, with its 15 locks, was
abandoned entirely in 1933
when the Illinois Waterway
replaced it as a connection
between the Great Lakes and
Mississippi River.
    Fifty years later, in 1984,
the canal was designated a
national heritage corridor.
Today, with almost 100 miles
(160 km) of multiuse trails
running alongside the canal,
the canal route offers abun-
dant recreational opportunities, from bird-watching to
biking, hiking, and canoeing.
The route passes through
more than 40 towns and cities,
sites of historic buildings and
fascinating museums.
    A good place to begin your
exploration is the town of
Lockport, 30 miles (48 km)
southwest of Chicago. During

Lush trees reflected in one of Morton Arboretum's several lakes

the canal's heyday, this town thrived as the center of the boat-building and -repair trades. The visitors' center (200 West 8th Street) in Lockport's historic Gaylord Building, the oldest industrial structure along the waterway, offers maps and information. Adjacent to the center is a restored pioneer settlement, its buildings characteristic of those built during the development of the canal.

Will County Historical Society Museum is located in Lockport's scenic 1837 canal headquarters building. Tour guides tell stories of the canal and explain historic artifacts.

Pullman Historic District ⓬

Bounded by 111th & 115th Sts, Ellis & Cottage Grove Aves. Ⓜ 95/Dan Ryan then bus 111. 🚆 111th St (Electric District line). 🛈 11141 S Cottage Grove Ave. **Tel** (773) 785-8901. ◯ 11am–3pm Tue–Sun. 📷 May–Oct 12:30pm, 1:30pm 1st Sun of month; call (773) 785-8901. 🅿 www.pullmanil.org

Pullman Historic District, one of Chicago's best-preserved 19th-century communities, is the site of a fascinating – if ultimately unsuccessful – experiment. The town, the first of its kind in the US, was built by George M. Pullman, founder of the luxury rail-carriage manufacturer Pullman Palace Car Company, to house his employees. In 1879, Pullman purchased 6.25 sq miles

Interior of Hotel Florence, typical of the town's Queen Anne-style elegance

(16 sq km) of marshland in Chicago's far south side, 12 miles (19 km) south of downtown Chicago. He hired architect Solon S. Beman and landscape architect Nathan F. Barrett to plan the company town. Most of the more than 1,700 row houses and apartment units were constructed between 1880 and 1885.

Workers rented the living quarters from Pullman, who expected to realize a 6 percent profit by collecting rent on all the buildings, including the church and library. This was the first development to offer the working class indoor plumbing, gas, and recreational facilities.

The experiment ended in acrimony when Pullman laid off workers and cut wages without lowering rents during the 1894 depression. A huge strike, which eventually

Ornate west window of Greenstone Church

spread across the entire nation, ensued. The US government intervened, sending in federal troops. The workers lost the seven-week strike, but Pullman's experiment was tainted with failure. He died three years later, in 1897, still resentful. By 1907, all the houses in Pullman had been sold to private buyers.

Plans in 1960 to demolish the area's buildings and create an industrial park were defeated by residents. The district of Pullman was designated a national landmark in 1971. Today, many of the row houses have been restored and are individually owned. The town is easily explored in an afternoon; maps are available at the visitor center.

Hotel Florence (11111 S Forestville Ave), named for Pullman's favorite daughter, is a superb 1881 example of Queen Anne style. The hotel is now a museum, and is undergoing an extensive $3-million renovation.

The mansions lining 111th and 112th Streets were built for Pullman executives; the Pullman colors of maroon and green frame the windows and doors. The Greenstone Church (1882) and the curved Beman-designed Colonnade Apartments and Town Houses by Market Hall are also worth a look. The Market Circle apartments (1892) were bachelor units.

Building once housing several Pullman Palace Car Company workers

THREE GUIDED WALKS

With a rich architectural history that demands to be examined up close, Chicago is particularly rewarding to visitors exploring on foot. Three guided walks, two of which are on the city's North Side, and one in the Downtown Core, are described here.

The first, farther north in Lakeview, is a short urban stroll that takes in the eclectic shops of Belmont Avenue, the lively gay scene of Boystown, with its rainbow-colored pylons lining Halsted Street, and the American baseball shrine that is Wrigley Field. Also here you'll find the intriguing Alta Vista Terrace, a narrow street of 1904 rowhouses modeled after London's Mayfair, and the

fascinating Graceland Cemetery, where such Chicago luminaries as Marshall Field and Mies van der Rohe are laid to rest. The second walk, just to the north of the city's Downtown Core, explores Lincoln Park itself and the neighborhood to the park's west. This three-hour walk can include visits to the new Chicago History Museum and to several gems within the park, such as Lincoln Park Zoo with its child-friendly working farm, the beautiful Lincoln Park Conservatory, as well as the scenic path along Lake Michigan.

The third walk is a visual feast of outdoor art and architecture with the skyline of the Loop readily displaying its treasures in the background.

Frontage for the historic Mercury Theater ⑦

CHOOSING A WALK

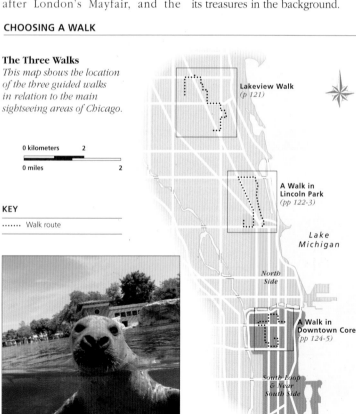

The Three Walks
This map shows the location of the three guided walks in relation to the main sightseeing areas of Chicago.

0 kilometers 2
0 miles 2

KEY
...... Walk route

Lakeview Walk *(p 121)*

A Walk in Lincoln Park *(pp 122-3)*

Lake Michigan

North Side

A Walk in Downtown Core *(pp 124-5)*

South Loop & Near South Side

Curious sea lion at Lincoln Park Zoo *(see p122)*

A 90-Minute Walk in Lakeview

Huge baseball,
Wrigleyville ④

From gray concrete streets to the gentle green slopes of Graceland Cemetery, this stroll through the north side of Lakeview is an urban adventure that reveals the charms – both historic and present-day – of one of Chicago's liveliest nooks. After taking in the sports-fanatic atmosphere of baseball's famous Wrigley Field and the colorful epicenter of Chicago's gay scene, meander your way past restaurants, eclectic boutiques, and cultural landmarks, joining the motley crowd of young and old.

Lifesize statue of 6-year-old Inez Clark, Graceland Cemetery ⑥

GRACELAND CEMETERY ⑥

WEST IRVING PARK RD

NORTH CLARK STREET

M Sheridan

0 meters 400
0 yards 400

W SHERIDAN ROAD

N SEMINARY AVE

WEST GRACE STREET

NORTH HALSTED ST

WEST

NORTH WILTON AVE

WAVELAND AVE

④

NORTH BROADWAY STREET

WEST ADDISON STREET

M Addison

NORTH WAYNE AVENUE
NORTH LAKEWOOD AVENUE
MAGNOLIA AVENUE

⑦
⑧

NORTH SOUTHPORT AVENUE

WEST EDDY ROAD
WEST CORNELIA ROAD
WEST NEWPORT ROAD

NORTH RACINE AVENUE

ELAINE PL
③

WEST ROSCOE RD

N CLIFTON AVE
NORTH SEMINARY AVENUE
N KENMORE AVE
NORTH SHEFFIELD AVE

NORTH CLARK STREET

WEST BUCKINGHAM PL
WEST ALDINE AVE
②
WEST MELROSE ST

①

WEST BELMONT AVENUE

M Belmont

KEY

••• Walk Route

M Metro station

Clark and Belmont/Boystown

Turn right out of the Belmont station and you soon hit Ann Sather's ①, a historic Swedish café at 909 W. Belmont Ave. famous for its cinnamon rolls. A few doors down is the lively intersection of N Clark

Baseball in Wrigley Field ballpark, home of the Chicago Cubs ④

Street and Belmont Ave. – a great spot for people-watching. Continue across N. Clark Street, once an Indian trail that ran 200 miles (322 km) north to Green Bay, Wisconsin, and you're in "Boystown," the gay pocket of Lakeview. At the next corner is Halsted Street ②, officially the country's first designated gay neighborhood, with its pairs of tall, rainbow-ringed pylons erected in 1999. Be sure to take a detour to Elaine Place ③ to see two giraffe sculptures made of car bumpers by John Kearney.

Wrigleyville

Back on Halsted Street, take a left at Addison Street, and you'll see the legendary Wrigley Field ④ *(see p114)* in the distance. Built in 1914, it's one of the oldest ballparks in the US, and home of the Chicago Cubs who, dubbed "lovable losers," haven't won a World Series in 100 years. Go north on Sheffield Ave., then a left turn on Grace Street. Here you will find an architectural gem, the Alta Vista Terrace District ⑤ *(see p114)*.

Graceland Cemetery

Head northwest up W. Irving Park Road, to see the lush Victorian-style Graceland Cemetery ⑥ *(see p114)*, the final resting place of some of Chicago's finest.

Southport Avenue

From here, stroll west on Irving Park Road to charming Southport Ave., with its pubs, boutiques, and restaurants. At 3745 N. Southport Ave. is the former silent movie house, the Mercury Theater ⑦, a 300-seat space hosting local and touring productions. Just south of this, you'll spot the old-time marquee of the Music Box Theatre ⑧, built in 1929 and still drawing crowds for obscure arthouse films.

TIPS FOR WALKERS

Starting point: Belmont El station.
Length: 3.5 miles (5.5 km).
Getting there: Take the Purple (rush hours only), Brown or Red Line train to Belmont, or the No. 22 bus to Clark and Belmont.

A Three-Hour Walk in Lincoln Park

One of Chicago's greatest treasures is its park system, and this leisurely walk is a lovely way to explore one of the quiet open spaces that lie within minutes of the skyscrapers of Downtown. Lincoln Park covers more than 1,200 acres (486 hectares) along Lake Michigan north of the Magnificent Mile, and offers diversions for strollers of all ages, including the nation's oldest free public zoo. Visitors can also visit the Chicago History Museum and an infamous site in gangster lore.

South Pond ④, with paddleboats for rental on fine days

Front of the newly renovated Chicago History Museum ①

Chicago History Museum

After expensive renovations, the once-modest Chicago Historical Society reopened in late 2006 as the sleek, airy, family-friendly Chicago History Museum ① (see p74), bringing the city's past to life with two floors of interactive exhibits. In the lobby a colorfully painted 1978 Chevy lowrider greets visitors; in the galleries beyond are permanent exhibits such as historical dioramas, one of the city's first El cars, and family-friendly displays. From the museum, take the path behind the building to admire one of

Chicago's most significant works of public art, Augustus Saint-Gaudens' 1887 bronze of President Abraham Lincoln ②, depicted deep in thought.

Lincoln Park Zoo and Beyond
Returning toward the museum, take the sidewalk path to the right and under the LaSalle Drive overpass, following the signs for the zoo. On a stretch of green to the west, on Wednesday and Saturday mornings from May to October, the organic Green City Market ③ has tempting displays of fresh cheeses, breads, and produce. A few minutes' walk farther up the path brings you to South Pond ④, a small haven for frogs, turtles, ducks, and geese. At the north end is the Café Brauer ⑤, a handsome red-brick, Prairie Style structure that bustles in summer. Stop for a beer or just to take in the fine views of the city skyline. Weather permitting, paddle-boats can also be hired from here. Just north of the café is the southern entrance to the Lincoln Park Zoo ⑥ (see pp112–113), one of the city's top attractions. Established in 1868, the zoo is free and

open daily, and despite its modest size of 35 acres (14 hectares) boasts more than 1,000 animals. Take the zoo's north exit and you're steps away from the lush, green Lincoln Park Conservatory ⑦, where a path leads through four glass display houses of towering palms, cycads, ferns,

Lincoln Park Conservatory ⑦, four glasshouses of tropical greenery

mosses, and fragrant orchids. North and just west of the Conservatory on Fullerton Parkway is another Chicago landmark, the lesser-known Alfred Caldwell Lily Pool ⑧, an intimate, serene garden designed in the Prairie School style with layered stone ledges and a waterfall.

Stroll across Fullerton Parkway to the Peggy

Peggy Notebaert Nature Museum ⑨, with child-friendly exhibits

observe 1,000 butterflies in the Judy Istock Butterfly Haven. This eco-friendly museum is "green" from its solar rooftop panels and rooftop gardens to the native prairie grasses that surround it.

The St. Valentine's Day Massacre
Just a few blocks away – but a world apart from the serenity of the park – is the site of one of the grisliest events in Chicago's history. Walk west on West Fullerton Parkway to North Clark Ave. Turning left here, make your way to 2122 N. Clark Ave. ⑩, where stands a vacant, fenced-in lawn with a few trees. You'll find no marker here, but this is one of the most infamous spots in the city. In a warehouse here on the morning of Valentine's Day 1929, seven of George "Bugs" Moran's men were gunned down by

thugs dressed as cops hired by Al Capone. The warehouse was torn down in 1967 but a central tree marks the spot where the men were killed.

Second City and St. Michael's Church
Continuing south on Clark Avenue, bear right onto North Wells Street (past Lincoln Ave.); on the northwest corner is the Piper's Alley center ⑪, home to one of the nation's legendary comedy theaters, Second City (see p173). Top comics such as John Belushi, Tina Fey, Bill Murray, Gilda Radner, and Mike Myers have appeared here, and newcomers still perform the company's signature blend of sketches, music, and improvisational comedy six nights a week.

Now head west on North Ave. four blocks to Cleveland Street; on your right you will see the majestic 1873 St. Michael's Church ⑫ (see p70), one of the city's oldest and grandest. The towering, airy interior features stained glass windows and five altars – one of which is Romanesque and made of silver, gold, and onyx.

Interior of St Michael's Church ⑫, with fine stained glass windows

TIPS FOR WALKERS

Starting point: *Chicago History Museum.*
Length: *3 miles (4.8 km).*
Getting there: *Take bus No. 22 or 36 to North Ave., or the Brown Line El to Sedgwick and walk east 5 mins to Clark Street.*
Stopping off points: *Café Brauer, 2201 N. Stockton Dr., has fast fare – bratwurst, burgers, beer – at an outdoor café. Mon Ami Gabi, 2300 N. Lincoln Park West, serves excellent French bistro food.*

Notebaert Nature Museum ⑨, a contemporary glass and stone structure housing child-friendly exhibits on regional plant and animal life. Visitors can build a dam at the River Works display; watch praying mantises feed at the Istock Family Look-In Lab; and

0 meters 300
0 yards 300

KEY

••• Walk Route

Ⓜ Metro station

A Three-Hour Walk in the Downtown Core

Dozens of works by world-renowned artists are on public display throughout Chicago's Downtown Core. This walk explores a selection from this huge outdoor art gallery and the buildings in the area, many of which are themselves works of art. The spectacular backdrop that the Loop's commanding architecture provides ensures excellent sights along the way.

South Michigan Avenue to South Dearborn Street

Start at the Adams CTA Station ① and walk east on Adams Street, turning right onto South Michigan Avenue and past the stately Art Institute of Chicago *(see p46–9)*. Lorado Taft's (1860–1936) *Fountain of the Great Lakes* (1913) ②, with its

View of buildings in the Loop look-ing west from Grant Park ③

five female figures, is at the south end of the main building. One block farther south is the main entrance of Grant Park ③, from where there is a good view of the buildings along Michigan Avenue, including the Santa Fe Building *(see p45)*. Walk

west along Van Buren Street, turning right at State. Continue north, bearing left at Jackson, to the Ralph Metcalfe Federal Building and the stainless steel and aluminium sculpture *The Town-Ho's Story* (1993) ④ by Frank Stella (b.1936).

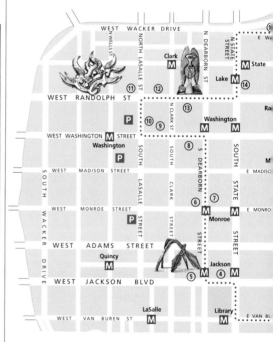

Dearborn Street to West Randolph Street

Cross Dearborn Street and enter the courtyard of the Federal Center *(see p43)* to see American sculptor Alexander Calder's (1898–1976) dramatic *Flamingo* (1974) ⑤. Retrace your steps to Dearborn Street.

The Four Seasons by Marc Chagall ⑥

Continue to walk north, passing the Marquette Building *(see p43)* on your left, to *The Four Seasons* (1974) ⑥ by Marc Chagall (1887–1985), at First National Plaza. This huge, four-sided mosaic consists of thousands of tiles in more than 250 colors that illustrate various Chicago scenes. Across the street is the ground-

Miró's Chicago

breaking Inland Steel Building ⑦. Steel pilings were driven 85 feet (26 m) down to the bedrock to support the building. Follow Dearborn Street to Washington, bearing left. On the left is Catalan artist Joan Miró's (1893–1983) *Chicago* (1981) ⑧, a surreal feminine figure made of plaster and bronze and studded with colorful ceramic tiles. County Building ⑨, with its 75-foot (23 m) Corinthian columns, can be seen at the corner of Washington and Clark. Continue along Washington Street, turning right onto LaSalle. Pass Chicago City Hall ⑩, the sister building of the County Building. On the northwest corner of Lasalle and Randolph is the Illinois State Office Building. On its exterior is *Freeform* (1993) ⑪, which Chicago sculptor Richard Hunt (b.1935)

Lantern on No. 35 East Wacker Drive ⑮

created to symbolize "a government supporting individual freedoms." Walk east on Randolph Street to the James R. Thompson Center *(see p56)* and French Art Brut artist Jean Dubuffet's (1901–1985) fiberglass sculpture *Monument with Standing Beast* (1984) ⑫. Just east, across the street in the Richard J. Daley Plaza, is the untitled sculpture by Pablo Picasso (1881–1973) ⑬.

TIPS FOR WALKERS

Starting point: Adams CTA station, at the corner of Wabash Avenue and East Adams Street.
Time: Three hours.
Getting there: Take the brown, green, orange, or purple line CTA train to Adams Station.
Stopping-off point: Numerous cafés and restaurants can be found along the route, though many may be open only during weekday business hours. Sopraffina Marketcaffe, at 10 North Dearborn Street, serves Italian fare, from biscotti to pizza. West Egg Cafe, at 66 East Washington Street, offers breakfast and lunch at modest prices.

features a miniature replica of Paris' Arc de Triomph. Turn right at Wacker Drive. At No. 35 ⑮ *(see p55)* is the former Jewelers Building, designed in 1926 and one of the last skyscrapers built in Chicago in the Beaux Artes style. Follow Wacker Drive east, turning right at Michigan Avenue, then left at Randolph Street to Prudential Plaza ⑯, consisting of two buildings. The Prudential Building, a towering limestone and aluminum structure built in 1952, was the first skyscraper to be built in the Loop since the 1930s. "Pru Two," with its chevron top, suggests New York's Chrysler Building.

KEY

- - - Suggested route
M CTA train station
R Metra train station
P Parking

The piece created a stir when first erected, as Chicagoans debated its merits.

State Street to East Randolph Street
One block east, on State Street, is the elegant Chicago Theatre ⑭ *(see p54)*. It was dubbed "the wonder theater of the world" when it opened in 1921. Its grand exterior

Façade of the Chicago Theatre ⑭

The two Prudential buildings, left; the AON Center, right ⑯

BEYOND
CHICAGO

Exploring Beyond Chicago

Visitors eager to discover more of Illinois won't be
disappointed by the rich mix of historical sights,
recreational activities, and picturesque countryside
Chicago's environs have to offer. Excursions to the
attractive North Shore towns of Evanston, Wilmette,
Glencoe, and Lake Forest will take you along the
shoreline of Lake Michigan, affording stunning views.

For those wishing to venture farther, the resort area
of Lake Geneva awaits just across the Wisconsin state
line. The delightful, historic town of Galena lies near
the Iowa border, a three-and-half hour drive west of
Chicago. The drive to both leads through rural
farmland dotted with small towns and state parks.
The typically flat Midwestern terrain gives way to
rolling hills just outside Galena.

Galena's Belvedere Mansion *(see p134)*

SIGHTS AT A GLANCE

Baha'i House of Worship **2**
Chicago Botanic Garden **3**
Evanston pp130–31 **1**
Galena pp134–5 **6**
Lake Forest **4**
Lake Geneva **5**

GETTING AROUND

Chicago has excellent Metra commuter rail links to
the northern suburbs. The Union Pacific/North line,
departing from the Ogilvie Transportation Center,
services Evanston, Wilmette, Glencoe, and Lake
Forest, with frequent trains during rush hour and
every one to three hours at other times. The CTA
purple line also services Evanston. You will need a
car to reach Lake Geneva and Galena. Highway I-94
leads north from Chicago; I-90 is the western route.

A picturesque circular barn near
Highway 20, West Galena

◁ A traditional farmhouse decked out with pumpkins

Rustic Road No. 29, on the outskirts of Lake Geneva

Francis Stupey Log Cabin in Highland Park, on Chicago's North Shore

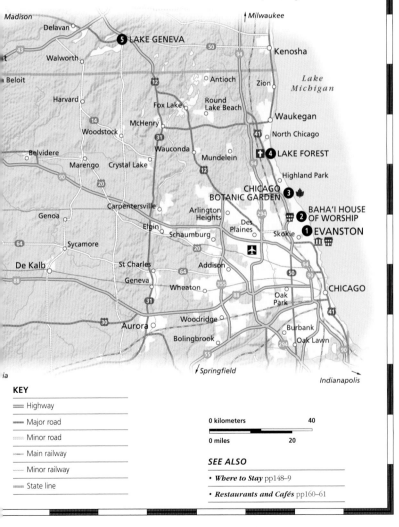

KEY

═══ Highway

━━━ Major road

┈┈┈ Minor road

╍╍╍ Main railway

─── Minor railway

═══ State line

0 kilometers   40

0 miles   20

SEE ALSO

• *Where to Stay* pp148–9

• *Restaurants and Cafés* pp160–61

Evanston ❶

Evanston, on the shores of Lake Michigan, 14 miles
(22 km) north of Chicago, offers stunning beaches,
charming boutiques and restaurants, and exciting
museums, art galleries, and theater. Originally known
as Ridgeville, it began as a community of farmers from
New England, and Irish and German immigrants. In
1850, a group of Chicago Methodists bought a large
tract of lakefront land, opening Northwestern University
five years later. Ridgeville changed its name to
Evanston in 1857 to honor John Evans, one of the
university's founders. By the 1870s, wealthy
Chicagoans, in search of cleaner neighborhoods, were
moving to Evanston. Many of their mansions still stand.

Charles Gates Dawes House, overlooking Lake Michigan

Exploring Evanston

Many of Evanston's attractions
are concentrated in the
historic downtown around
Grove Street and Sherman
Avenue, an area easily
explored on foot. Other
interesting districts include
those at Central Street, and
at Chicago Avenue and
Dempster Street. The large
lakefront university campus,
the buildings of which reflect
widely varied architectural
styles, provides greenspace
ideal for strolling. Or you can
saunter along Forest Avenue
to see the historic mansions
built for Chicago's wealthy.

🏛 Charles Gates Dawes House and Evanston History Center

225 Greenwood St. **Tel** *(847)
475-3410.* ◯ *1–4pm Thu–Sat.*
⬤ *major public hols.* 🎟 *(children
under 6 free).* 📷 *mandatory.* ♿
This massive Chateauesque
mansion was designed in
1894 by Henry Edwards-
Ficken for Robert Sheppard,
treasurer of Northwestern

University. Sheppard sold the
mansion in 1909 to Charles
Gates Dawes, who went on
to become US vice-president
under Calvin Coolidge. The
restored 25-room house,
home to the Evanston
Historical Society, showcases
the period 1925–9.

🏛 Frances Willard House

1730 Chicago Ave. **Tel** *(847) 328-
7500.* ◯ *1–4pm 1st & 3rd Sun of
month or by appt.* ⬤ *major hols.*
🎟 📷 *mandatory.* 🛈
Pioneering suffragist and
Woman's Christian Temp-
erance Union (WCTU)
activist Frances Willard
lived here from 1865 until
her death in 1898.
   This quaint, Gothic-style
(see p26) house, built by
Willard's father in 1865, is
now a museum devoted to
Willard's life and the history
of the WCTU. The world's
oldest voluntary, non-
sectarian women's organi-
zation, the WCTU is best
known for its campaign
against alcohol.

🏛 Block Sculpture Garden

40 Arts Circle. **Tel** *(847) 491-4000.*
◯ *daily.*
The Block Museum's
sculpture garden showcases
20th-century sculpture.
Among the garden's treasures
are two large, bronze abstract
sculptures by British artist
Barbara Hepworth (1903–1975)
and an intriguing movable
bronze sculpture by Spanish
artist Joan Miró (1893–1983).

🏛 Mary and Leigh Block Museum of Art

40 Arts Circle. **Tel** *(847) 491-4000.*
◯ *10am–5pm Tue–Sun, 10am–8pm
Fri.* ♿ 📷 *call for details.* **Lectures,
films, concerts. www.**
blockmuseum.northwestern.edu
Artwork from the 14th
century onward and thematic
historical displays are featured
at this art museum of Northwestern University, one of the
US's top university museums.
Major national exhibits
often stop here.

🏛 Grosse Point Light Station

2601 Sheridan Rd. **Tel** *(847) 328-6961.*
⬤ *hol weekends.* 🎟 📷 *mandatory:
Jun–Sep: 2, 3, 4pm Sat, Sun.*
www.grosspointlighthouse.net
This lighthouse was built in
1873 in response to one of
the worst maritime disasters
on the Great Lakes – the 1860
sinking of the paddle wheeler
Lady Elgin, in which nearly
300 people died.
   During the summer, visitors
can climb to the top of the
lighthouse for wonderful
views of the town and lake.
   A maritime museum is on
the lower floor. Plants native
to Illinois are grown in the
Wildflower Trail Garden, on
the grounds of the station.

**Grosse Point Light Station, guiding
ships since 1873**

Interior of the Mitchell Museum of the American Indian

🏛 Mitchell Museum of the American Indian

3001 Central Ave. **Tel** (847) 475-1030. ◯ 10am–5pm Tue, Wed, Fri, Sat; 10am–8pm Thu; noon–4pm Sun. ● major public hols, last two weeks Aug. 💰 by donation. 📷 ♿ 🛍
📽 Lectures, concerts, films.

The Mitchell Museum showcases North American Indian cultures from prehistoric to contemporary times. More than 6,000 domestic objects, including pottery, baskets, clothing, and textiles, are on display. The Mitchell is particularly rich in artifacts of Indians of the Midwest. Temporary exhibitions at the museum highlight ancient and present-day Native crafts.

🏛 Evanston Art Center

2603 Sheridan Rd. **Tel** (847) 475-5300. ◯ 10am–10pm Mon–Thu; 10am–4pm Fri & Sat; 1–4pm Sun. ● major public hols. 💰 by donation. 📷 ♿ 1st-floor gallery.
🛍 🅿 Lectures, workshops.

Housed in a 1926 mansion, the gallery of this community art center exhibits regional contemporary artwork by both established and emerging artists. Gallery talks by exhibiting artists are offered regularly. The center's annual spring art auction is a great opportunity to acquire work by Midwest artists.

The lovely grounds of the center were designed by the Prairie School-influenced landscape architect Jens Jensen, who is the designer of several parks in Chicago, including Columbus Park and the conservatory in Garfield Park, which is on Chicago's west side.

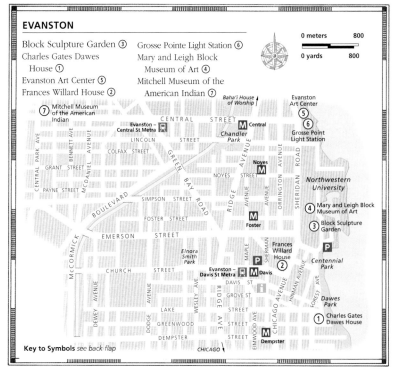

EVANSTON

Block Sculpture Garden ③
Charles Gates Dawes House ①
Evanston Art Center ⑤
Frances Willard House ②
Grosse Pointe Light Station ⑥
Mary and Leigh Block Museum of Art ④
Mitchell Museum of the American Indian ⑦

0 meters 800
0 yards 800

Key to Symbols see back flap

Baha'i House of Worship ❷

100 Linden Ave, Wilmette. *Tel (847)*
853-2300. Ⓜ *Linden.* 🚉 *Wilmette*
(Union Pacific/North line) then bus
421, 422. ⭕ *7am–10pm daily.*
Devotions*: 9:15am & 12:30pm.*
♿ 🅿 *www*.us.bahai.org

The Baha'i House of
Worship, gleaming like a
white beacon, is the North
Shore's most striking building.
There are seven major Baha'i
houses of worship in the
world; this is the only major
one in North America. The
Baha'i faith, based on the
teachings of the 19th-century
Persian prophet Baha'u'llah,
promotes unity among all
people and religions.

Construction of the house,
which began in 1920, wasn't
completed until 1953. Ad-
hering to Baha'i requirements,
there are nine sides to this
building designed by French-
Canadian architect Louis
Bourgeois. An entrance door
is on each side. Quotations
from Baha'u'llah are carved
into the stone, one above
each entrance and each of
the nine alcoves. Elaborate
filigree-like carvings adorn
the exterior. A dramatic dome
of quartz and white cement
rises 135 ft (41 m) above the
central auditorium, which can
seat almost 2,000 people.
It is lovely to take a stroll
in the colorful, yet sym-
metrical gardens.

A short video at the visitors'
center introduces the Baha'i
faith and the house's history.

The Baha'i House of Worship,
with its beautifully filigreed dome

Fountains and pools dot the serene grounds of
the Chicago Botanic Gardens

Chicago Botanic Garden ❸

1000 Lake Cook Rd, Glencoe.
Tel (847) 835-5440. 🚉 *Braeside;*
Glencoe (Union Pacific/North line)
then bus 213. ⭕ *8am–sunset daily.*
🌐 *Dec 25.* 📷 ♿ ✂ 🛍 🍴 🅿
Lectures, exhibits.
www.chicago-botanic.org

The Chicago Botanic
Garden, 25 miles (40 km)
north of downtown Chicago,
is dazzling with its 20 themed
gardens and 3 native habitats
of flowers, vines, shrubs, and
trees. Opened in 1972, the
Garden contains 2 million
specimens representing 8,000
plant families from around
the world. The
Garden's attrac-
tive grounds are
home to eight
lagoons and
nine islands.

The Gateway
Visitor Center, near
the entrance, leads
to the main island,
the site of the
majority of the
themed gardens.

The English Walled
Garden consists of a
secluded enclosure
with six garden "rooms," each
reflecting a different English
gardening style. The Heritage
Garden is modeled after

Chicago Botanic
Garden banners

Europe's first
botanical garden.
Intoxicating scents
of the Rose
Garden's 5,000 rose
bushes accompany
the colorful blooms.

Unsurprisingly,
the jewel of the
Waterfall Garden is
a 45-ft (14 m) water-
fall. Sansho-En, or
"garden of three
islands," reflects the
tranquil minimalism
of Japanese garden
design. One of the
islands is tantaliz-
ingly out of reach.

The Gardens of
the Great Basin
include Lakeside
Gardens, Evening
Island, and Water
Gardens. These
gardens, which
encircle the Botanic Garden's
central lake, extend into the
water and are linked by a
series of scenic pathways,
bridges, and terraces.

The Garden's three natural
habitat areas (an oak
woodland, a prairie, and a
riverscape) offer wonderful
walking trails through secluded
sections of the grounds.

Lake Forest ❹

🚉 *Lake Forest (Union Pacific/North*
line). 🚌 *472.* **Deer Path Golf**
Course *500 W Deerpath Rd.*
Tel (847) 234-4282.
www.lakeforestchamber.com

Lake Forest is one of Chicago's
most affluent suburbs, about
30 miles (48 km)
north of Chicago's
Downtown Core.

The town was
established in the
1850s by a group of
Presbyterians who
planned to build a
college. The St.
Louis landscape
architect hired to
plan the town
took advantage of the
area's beautiful prairie
lands, ravines, and
hills, designing streets
to follow the natural curves of
the landscape.

Presbyterian Lake Forest
College, established in 1857,

has many grand, late-1800 buildings. The Romanesque-style Hotchkiss Hall was designed by Henry Ives Cobb (see p26) in 1890 and named after the town's planner.

The First Presbyterian Church (700 N Sheridan Rd) was designed by Charles Frost in 1887. The church's unusual design is an adaptation of the New England cottage style, known as Shingle style.

Market Square, in downtown Lake Forest, is one of the first planned suburban shopping centers in the US. Designed in 1916 by Howard Van Doren Shaw, this pleasant town square has a quaint English character.

The charming Market Square in Lake Forest

The best way to experience Lake Forest is to drive on meandering Sheridan Road. Along the route are many beautiful homes on spacious, landscaped grounds.

Golfers can take advantage of Deer Path Golf Course, while at Forest Park Beach, beachgoers can enjoy the cooling waters of Lake Michigan during the summer heat.

Lady of the Lake, a reproduction of a Mississippi paddle wheeler

Lake Geneva ❺

🛈 201 Wrigley Dr, WI. *Tel* (262) 248-4416, 800-345-1020.
🕘 9am–5pm Mon–Fri; 10am–4pm Sat, Sun. 🚗 🍴 🛍
www.lakegenevawi.com

Lake Geneva, 70 miles (113 km) north of Chicago, nestles on the shores of a spring-fed lake of the same name. There is much to keep you occupied for a weekend in this picturesque resort town and its surrounding rural communities. Boating on the wide lake, hiking, and ballooning are just a few of the possibilities.

Lake Geneva is also a shopper's and diner's paradise. Many of the charming boutiques and antique stores are in turn-of-the-century buildings. Several of the town's restaurants, particularly those along Wrigley Drive, provide spectacular views of the lake.

In autumn, the countryside is ablaze with fall foliage. It is an ideal backdrop to the 21-mile (34-km) trail encircling the lake, a trail that once connected Indian camps. On the western edge of town is a state-designated "Rustic Road," an ideal route for a leisurely drive through the country. In winter, skiing and snowmobiling are popular activities. However, accommodations fill up quickly in summer and traffic is heavy.

Lake Geneva has a rich history. The Oneota tribes of the now-extinct Hopewell Culture Indians, an agricultural people, lived in the area as long ago as 1000 BC. In 1836, the local Potawatomi tribe was evicted from the area, and pioneer Christopher Payne built the first log cabin in town. The site is marked with a plaque on Center Street, north of White River.

The town, laid out in 1837, was originally a sawmill town. Following the Civil War, it became a resort for wealthy Chicagoans, who built their homes on the lakefront.

One of the best ways to see these mansions is by boat. Geneva Lake Cruise Line's fleet of ships includes replicas of a Southern paddle wheeler and a turn-of-the-century lake steamer. The *Walworth II* operates as a US mail boat, one of the last in service. A mail carrier delivers mail during the tour.

Geneva Lake Area Museum of History (255 Mill Street) displays interesting historical photographs and artifacts.

Riviera Docks, departure point for Lake Geneva boat cruises

Galena

A visit to Galena, "the town that time forgot," is like stepping into a bygone era. More than 85 percent of this town, in Jo Daviess County, is on the National Register of Historic Places. Its architectural gems, museums, and unique landscape make Galena a great weekend destination.

As early as the 1600s, Indians were mining the area's rich deposits of lead and ore. In the 1820s, as prospectors flocked to Galena, the town became one of the US's most important mining centers. By the mid-1800s, it was a major Mississippi River

Statue of Ulysses S. Grant

port. But as rail displaced shipping as the mode of freight transportation, the town went into decline. The expense of tearing down the old buildings ensured that its historic core remained intact.

The old town hall, built in 1872, in historic East Galena

Exploring Galena

The best way to explore Galena is on foot or by trolley tour. Downtown parking is limited; it is best to park at the lot by the visitors' center at the old railroad depot.

Galena has a number of noteworthy historic churches. The **Union Baptist Church** (1854) features a Romanesque Revival doorway, and the

A trolley tour is one of the best ways to explore Galena

enchanting **First Presbyterian Church** (1838) has a Georgian spire. The 1838 Erban organ is still played at the Gothic Revival-style *(see p26)* **Grace Episcopal Church**.

The **Galena post office** (1857–9) is the second-oldest continuously operating post office in the US.

🏛 Old Illinois Central Railroad Depot

101 Bouthillier St. *Tel (847) 464-2536.* ◯ *Memorial Day weekend–Oct: 9am–5pm Mon–Thu; 9am–7pm Fri, Sat; 10am–5pm Sun. Nov–Memorial Day weekend: 9am–5pm Mon–Sat; 10am–4pm Sun.* ♿
Originally Galena's station for passenger rail service, it was from here that former US president Ulysses S. Grant set off for war. The 1857 Italianate *(see p26)* building is now the Visitor Information Center.

🏛 Belvedere Mansion

1008 Park Ave. *Tel (815) 777-0747.* ◯ *11am–4pm Sun–Fri; 11am–5pm Sat.* ● *Nov–Memorial Day.* 🎫 🎫 *mandatory.*
Built in 1857 for J. Russell Jones, a steamship owner and US ambassador to Belgium, the Italianate-style Belvedere Mansion is the largest house in Galena.

Completely restored to its original condition, the 22 rooms contain Victorian furnishings. Pieces include furniture once belonging to former US president Theodore Roosevelt, and a gold-painted cabinet once owned by entertainer Liberace.

🏛 Washburne House

908 Third St. *Tel (815) 777-3310.* ◯ *10am–4pm Fri–Sun.* ● *Nov–Memorial Day weekend.* 🎫 🎫 *mandatory: on the hour and half-hour.* ♿
A stunning example of Greek Revival architecture, this house was built in 1843 for prominent Galena attorney

and later US congressman Elihu Washburne (1816–87). Washburne was a comrade of Abraham Lincoln and a strong supporter of the career of Ulysses S. Grant. It was in the library of Washburne's home that Grant first heard the news that he had won the 1868 US presidential election.

The restored interior of the house reflects Victorian middle-class elegance.

🏛 Ulysses S. Grant Home

500 Bouthillier St. *Tel (815) 777-3310.* ◯ *Apr–Oct: 9am–4:45pm Wed–Sun. Nov–Mar: 9am–4pm, Wed–Sun.* ● *public hols.* 🎫 🎫 *mandatory.* ♿
This two-story, brick Italianate *(see p26)* house designed by William Dennison was constructed in 1860. It was given to returning Civil War hero General Ulysses S. Grant by a group of prominent Galena citizens in 1865.

Even though Grant spent little time in the house after being elected US president in 1868, it has been restored to its 1870s appearance and contains furnishings used by the Grant family. Costumed guides lead visitors through the house while telling Grant's story.

The Old Illinois Central Railroad Depot now housing Galena's visitors' center

View of Galena looking northeast from the pedestrian bridge

VISITORS' CHECKLIST

Hwy 20. 🚌 Greyhound bus. 🛈
101 Bouthillier St. 🛈 (877) 464-
2536. 🚋 by trolley. 🎭 Irish
Heritage (Mar), Galena Arts
Festival (Jul), Fall Harvest (Sep–
Oct), County Fair (Oct).
www.galena.org

⊞ Dowling House

220 Diagonal St. **Tel** (815) 777-
1250. ◻ Jun–Oct: 10am–5pm
Sun–Fri; 10am–6pm Sat. Nov,
Dec: 10am–4pm Fri–Sun. 🚫
🛈 mandatory.

This 1826 example of
vernacular architecture is
Galena's oldest house. Built
of limestone, it originally
served as a miner's trading
post and rather crude residence. It has been restored
to reflect the era of Galena's
early pioneers.

⊞ DeSoto House Hotel

230 S Main St. **Tel** (815) 777-0090,
800-343-6562. 🚫 🛈 🍸 🅿
www.desotohouse.com

This hotel was considered the
largest, most luxurious hotel
west of New York City when
it opened its doors in 1855. It
was built by Galena mer-
chants in preparation for the
boom that accompanied the
1854 arrival of Illinois Central

Railroad service in Galena.
Many famous Americans,
including writer Mark Twain,
have stayed here. Abraham
Lincoln made a speech from
its balcony in 1856, and it was
from the DeSoto House Hotel
that Ulysses S. Grant ran his
1868 presidential campaign.

⊞ Old Market House

123 N Commerce St. **Tel** (815) 777-
2570. ◻ According to season; call
for details. ⬤ Thanksgiving, mid-
Dec–mid-Mar. 🚫 🛈 mandatory. 🚫

The handsome Greek
Revival-style Market House
was built by the City of
Galena in 1846. One of the
Midwest's oldest extant market houses, it was a hive of
activity until the early 1900s.
Farmers sold produce, city
offices were on the second
floor, and the basement was a
city jail. Today, an exhibition
space has displays of
historical interest.

🏛 Galena/Jo Daviess County Historical Society and Museum

211 S Bench St. **Tel** (815) 777-9129.
◻ 9am–4:30pm daily. ⬤ Jan 1,
Easter, Thanksgiving, Dec 24, 25.
🚫 (children under 10 free). 🛈
www.galenahistorymuseum.org

This 1858 Italianate mansion,
designed by William Dennison, was built for merchant
Daniel Barrows. It is now
occupied by a museum spe-
cializing in the area's history.

The creation of the stunning
geology of Jo Daviess County
– rugged hills, rocky bluffs,
and riveting vistas – is
depicted in a large landform
model, which shows how Ice
Age glaciers detoured around
the land, sparing this hilly
part of Illinois.

A display on the Galena
River tells the story of the
Army Corps of Engineers'
building of the town's flood
dike and massive gate.

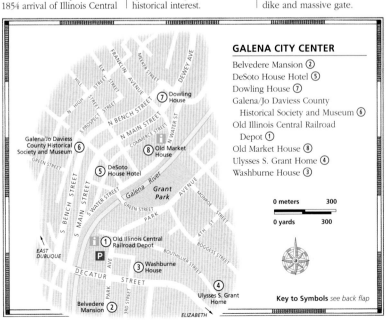

GALENA CITY CENTER

Belvedere Mansion ②
DeSoto House Hotel ⑤
Dowling House ⑦
Galena/Jo Daviess County
   Historical Society and Museum ⑥
Old Illinois Central Railroad
   Depot ①
Old Market House ⑧
Ulysses S. Grant Home ④
Washburne House ③

| 0 meters | 300 |
| 0 yards | 300 |

Key to Symbols see back flap

TRAVELERS' NEEDS

WHERE TO STAY

Chicago has a room for every taste and budget. The top hotels are good value by international standards. For those travelers on a budget, there are many inexpensive and comfortable hotels and youth hostels in the city. Two-room suites are suitable for families, and some have kitchenettes, for those visitors who want to do their

A friendly doorman

own cooking. Bed-and-breakfasts, often located in charming Victorian houses in residential areas, are also a good option for visitors to Chicago. The listings in *Choosing a Hotel,* on pages 140–49, will help you narrow down the numerous choices. We have selected over 100 places that represent the best of their kind, in all price ranges.

Hotel Burnham's lobby, modeled on the 1891 original *(see p140)*

WHERE TO LOOK

Most of Chicago's hotels are clustered in two areas: the Downtown Core and the North Side. Many are both good and moderately priced. Downtown hotels are particularly convenient for visitors interested in Chicago's cultural sights such as the Chicago Art Institute, the Museum Campus, and the theater district, as well as those attending conventions at McCormick Place. This area can become quiet at night, though. By contrast, hotels on the North Side, just north of the Loop, are in one of the liveliest areas of the city. Many of the city's finer hotels are on the Magnificent Mile and the Gold Coast.

Business travelers often favor the chain hotels near O'Hare and Midway airports. Bed-and-breakfasts are scattered throughout the city.

Contact the **Illinois Bureau of Tourism** or the **Chicago Convention and Tourism Bureau** for information.

FACILITIES

Air-conditioning and cable TV are both standard in Chicago hotels. Fax and photocopy service, computer modem hook-up, in-room speaker-phones, exercise facilities, and a swimming pool are amenities to inquire about. Be sure you understand the charges; some hotels offer these facilities for free, other hotels will charge handsomely for them.

The many conventions and trade shows held in the city provide Chicago's hotels with a major part of their business, so most hotels offer an array of business meeting rooms.

HOTEL RATES AND DISCOUNTS

Hotel prices in Chicago are competitive, but keep in mind when booking that hotels charge a steep 15.4 percent room tax.

Some hotels offer discounts to visitors attending a convention or major exhibition. Hotels may also offer corporate rates and discounts to persons in

the military, senior citizens, teachers, automobile-club members, and frequent flyers. Business travelers often leave the city on weekends, and hotels will offer special week-end rates to encourage more business. Be sure to ask.

Hotels in Chicago do not usually include meals in the room rate, though meal plans are sometimes available.

Two notable discount reservation agencies in Chicago are **Hot Rooms** and **Hotels.com**. Both charge a fee if you cancel for any reason.

HIDDEN COSTS

Room rates are usually quoted assuming double occupancy. But always ask; some hotels quote single-occupancy rates and charge as much as $35 per night for a second person.

Keep in mind, too, that a room with a view will likely come at a premium.

Convenience costs money. Parking at your hotel can add as much as $30 a day to your bill. You will also pay a steep

Guests relaxing in their suite at Palmer House Hilton *(see p140)*

◁ **The French Renaissance-style lobby of the Hilton Chicago**

Lobby of Hotel Allegro, inspired by the building's 1920 design *(see p140)*

premium for any drinks and snacks you take from the room's mini-bar.

A telephone call made from your room will cost substantially more than a telephone call made from the pay phone in the hotel lobby.

HOW TO RESERVE

If there is one secret to finding a good room, it is planning. Reserve as far in advance as possible. Hotels can fill up quickly when a convention is in town.

Reservations usually require a deposit by credit card. You will be given a confirmation or reservation number when you book. Always confirm your reservation before arriving at the hotel.

If you have special requirements, such as a quiet room away from busy streets, elevators, and ice machines, make these known when booking a room.

Notify the hotel if you expect to arrive later than 5 pm, or you may lose your reservation. If you need to cancel your reservation, it is advisable to record the cancelation number you are given, in case you are later charged for the room. Most hotels do not charge a cancelation fee if you give 24 or 48 hours' notice. Without sufficient notice, you may be charged for the room.

TRAVELERS WITH DISABILITIES

Hotels in the US are by law required to provide facilities for wheelchair-bound persons (some older properties are exempt). Most establishments are eager to provide rooms and assistance to travelers with disabilities. Persons with visual impairments may bring guide dogs into hotels.

TRAVELING WITH CHILDREN

Children are welcome in all Chicago hotels, and few charge extra when one or two children under 12 stay in their parent's room. Ask about family rates when making reservations, and make sure the room is suitable. The hotel may offer a room with two beds or a sofa that easily converts to a bed. Many hotels will provide a cot for an additional $15 to $35 a night. Suite hotel rooms are also a good option.

French Deco living room, Hotel Monaco *(see p140)*

BED-AND-BREAKFASTS

A bed-and-breakfast is a charming alternative to a hotel. Primarily in residential neighborhoods, such accommodations range from rooms in Victorian homes to rooms in high-rise buildings. Some have private bathrooms. In general, bed-and-breakfasts are reasonably priced. For information call **Illinois Bed and Breakfast Association**.

DIRECTORY

TOURIST OFFICES

Chicago Convention and Tourism Bureau
Tel (312) 567-8533, (877) 244-2246. **www**.choosechicago.com

Illinois Bureau of Tourism
Tel (800) 226-6632.
www.enjoyillinois.com

RESERVATION AGENCIES

Hot Rooms
Tel (773) 468-7666 or
(800) 468-3500.
www.hotrooms.com

Hotels.com
Tel (800) 246-8357.
www.hotels.com

BED-AND-BREAKFASTS

Illinois Bed and Breakfast Association
Tel (888) 523-2406.
www.illinoisbnb.com

YOUTH HOSTELS

Hostelling International Chicago
24 E Congress Pkwy, Chicago, IL 60605. *Tel* (312) 360-0300.
Fax 360-0313.
www.hichicago.org

Travelers Center
24 E Congress Pkwy, 1st Floor, Chicago, IL 60605.
Tel 360-0300 ext.1502.
⏰ *10am–6pm Tue–Sat*.

AIRPORT HOTELS

See page 185 for details.

Choosing a Hotel

The hotels in this guide have been selected across a wide price range for good value, facilities available, and location. All hotel rooms have air conditioning unless stated otherwise. The listings start with the central areas and continues with hotels outside the city center. For map references, see the street finder maps on *pp192–205*.

PRICE CATEGORIES
Prices categories are for a standard double room per night, including tax and service (prices will fluctuate depending on arrival date and availability):

ⓢ Under $100
ⓢⓢ $100–$180
ⓢⓢⓢ $180–$260
ⓢⓢⓢⓢ Over $260

DOWNTOWN CORE

Hotel Allegro
🏶 🎿 📺 &️ 🍸   ⓢⓢ

171 W Randolph St., Chicago, IL, 60601 **Tel** *236-0123/866-672-6143* **Fax** *236-0917* **Rooms** *483*   **Map** *3 C1*

Playful, colorful style meets Art Deco at this contemporary, pet-friendly hotel, which is popular for its location in the heart of the business and theater districts. The rooms offer serious amenities, from complimentary wireless Internet to down blankets and flat-screen TVs. **www.allegrochicago.com**

Crowne Plaza Hotel Chicago-Metro
🎿 📺 &️ 🍸   ⓢⓢⓢ

733 W Madison St., Chicago, IL, 60661 **Tel** *829-5000* or *800-972-2494* **Fax** *602-2199* **Rooms** *398*   **Map** *3 A1*

This upscale hotel sits among the warehouses and loft buildings of the trendy West Loop less than a mile west of the city center. Rooms are decorated in a bold, contemporary style with colorful bedspreads, sleek bathroom fixtures, and flat-screen TVs. An on-site restaurant serves comfort food like meatloaf. **www.ichotelsgroup.com**

Hard Rock Hotel Chicago
🎿 📺 &️ 🍸   ⓢⓢⓢ

230 N Michigan Ave., Chicago, IL, 60601 **Tel** *345-1000* or *866-966-5166* **Fax** *345-1012* **Rooms** *381*   **Map** *4 D1*

Based in the landmark Art Deco Carbide & Carbon Building, this uber-trendy new hotel has a prime location on Michigan Avenue and sleek, stylish rooms with state-of-the-art entertainment centers. China Grill, a pan-Asian restaurant offering tempting fare, is adjacent. **www.hardrockhotelchicago.com**

Hotel Burnham
📺 🏶 🎿 &️ 🍸   ⓢⓢⓢ

1 W Washington St., Chicago, IL, 60602 **Tel** *782-1111/877-294-9712* **Fax** *782-0899* **Rooms** *122*   **Map** *3 C1*

Set in the magnificent Daniel Burnham-designed Reliance Building, this stunningly refurbished hotel is both classic and cheerfully contemporary, with lovely touches like mosaic floors and metal elevator grills. Stylish, spacious rooms – many with great Loop views. A lobby-level café serves up modern American fare. **www.burnhamhotel.com**

Hotel Monaco
🏶 🎿 📺 &️ 🍸   ⓢⓢⓢ

225 N Wabash Ave., Chicago, IL, 60601 **Tel** *960-8500/866-610-0081* **Fax** *960-1883* **Rooms** *192*   **Map** *4 D1*

From its pet-friendly policy to "Tall Rooms" with 9-ft (2.5-m) beds and raised shower heads, this luxurious French Art Deco-style boutique hotel takes service seriously. A complimentary goldfish keeps guests company in the stylishly appointed rooms, which feature "meditation station" window nooks lined with pillows. **www.monaco-chicago.com**

Palmer House Hilton
🏊 🏶 🎿 📺 &️ 🍸   ⓢⓢⓢ

17 E Monroe St., Chicago, IL, 60603 **Tel** *726-7500/800-445-8667* **Fax** *917-1707* **Rooms** *1,639*   **Map** *3 C2*

An elegant, luxurious hotel in the heart of the Loop featuring classic antique furnishings, beds with 250 thread count linens and plush-top mattresses, and high-tech touches like iPod-compatible stereos and high-speed Internet access. Pets are welcome; an on-site pool and workout center are available for a nominal fee. **www.hilton.com**

Swissotel Chicago
🏊 🏶 🎿 📺 &️ 🍸   ⓢⓢⓢ

323 E Wacker Dr., Chicago, IL, 60601 **Tel** *565-0565/800-637-9477* **Fax** *312-565-0540* **Rooms** *632*   **Map** *4 E1*

Polished service, prime location, and comfortable rooms with stunning views of Lake Michigan and Grant Park make this luxury hotel a top Loop option. Rooms have workstations with Internet access. The penthouse workout center has a sauna and whirlpool. **www.swissotelchicago.com**

Travelodge Downtown Chicago
&️ 🍸   ⓢⓢⓢ

65 E Harrison St., Chicago, IL, 60605 **Tel** *312-427-8000/800-211-6706* **Fax** *312-427-8261* **Rooms** *235*   **Map** *4 D3*

This budget hotel offers small but comfortably furnished rooms at excellent rates in a convenient location just south of the Theater District and close to the Art Institute. Perks include free stays for children under 12, free high-speed Internet access, complimentary newspaper, and airport shuttle service. **www.travelodgehoteldowntown.com**

W Hotel Chicago City Center
🎿 📺 &️ 🍸   ⓢⓢⓢ

172 W Adams St., Chicago, IL, 60603 **Tel** *332-1200/888-625-5144* **Fax** *917-5771* **Rooms** *369*   **Map** *3 C2*

Part of the trendy W chain, this upscale, pet-friendly hotel in the Loop Theater District draws a stylish mix of business clients and tourists. "Wonderful" rooms are cool, but compact, with luxurious bed linen, robes, rainforest showers, and Bliss body products. The Whiskey Blue bar is an after-work hot spot. **www.starwoodhotels.com**

Key to Symbols *see back cover flap*

Amalfi Hotel   🛎️ 🛗 $$$$$

20 W Kinzie St., Chicago, IL, 60610 **Tel** *312-395-9000/877-262-5341* **Fax** *395-9001* **Rooms** *215*   **Map** *1 C5*

Personalized service is the focus of this River North luxury hotel, where guests are greeted by an "Experience Designer" and enjoy stylish contemporary rooms with deluxe amenities like Aveda spa products, pillow-top mattresses, and free high-speed Internet access. Complimentary 24-hour fitness center. **www.amalfihotelchicago.com**

Fairmont Hotel   🛏️ 🏋️ 🛎️ 🛗 🍸 $$$$$

200 N Columbus Dr., Chicago, IL, 60601 **Tel** *565-8000/800-257-7544* **Fax** *856-1032* **Rooms** *692*   **Map** *4 D1*

Roomy seating areas, dressing rooms with full-sized closets, and hand-drawn baths by a "Bath Sommelier" are among the pampering amenities at this sophisticated, centrally located luxury hotel. Guests may visit the adjacent Lakeshore Athletic Club or onsite Waves Spa; small pets (under 20 lb) are welcome. **www.fairmont.com**

Hotel 71   🏋️ 🛎️ 🛗 🍸 $$$$$

71 E Wacker Dr., Chicago, IL, 60601 **Tel** *312-346-7100/800-621-4005* **Fax** *312-346-4549* **Rooms** *439*   **Map** *4 D1*

Stunning views of the river or skyline plus optimal location a stone's throw from Michigan Avenue make this upscale boutique hotel a tempting downtown option. The spacious rooms are decorated in colorful, contemporary style; extras include bathroom phones, a gourmet minibar, and 24-hour complimentary gym. **www.hotel71.com**

Hyatt Regency Chicago   🏋️ 🛎️ 🛗 🍸 $$$$$

151 E Wacker Dr., Chicago, IL, 60601 **Tel** *565-1234/800-233-1234* **Fax** *239-4414* **Rooms** *2,019*   **Map** *4 D1*

Muted tones mix with bold splashes of color in the contemporary, comfortable rooms of this Loop chain hotel. Standard amenities include two-line phones, wireless Internet access, iPod clock radios, and a safe. Convenient to Navy Pier, Millennium Park, the Theater District, and Michigan Avenue shopping. **www.chicagoregencyhyatt.com**

Renaissance Chicago Hotel   🛏️ 🛎️ 🛗 🍸 $$$$$

1 W Wacker Dr., Chicago, IL, 60601 **Tel** *372-7200* **Fax** *372-0093* **Rooms** *553*   **Map** *3 C1*

A stylish lobby decked out with contemporary art and bold orange and green accents welcomes guests to this luxury hotel situated in the Loop on the Chicago River. The hotel's comfortable rooms boast high-speed Internet access, oversized bathrooms, premium bedding, and lovely views. There is a spa and a fitness center. **www.marriott.com**

Silversmith Hotel & Suites   🛎️ 🛗 🍸 $$$$$

10 S Wabash Ave., Chicago, IL, 60603 **Tel** *372-7696* **Fax** *372-7320* **Rooms** *143*   **Map** *4 D1*

Set in the landmark Silversmith building, this terra cotta-clad Arts and Crafts-style structure was designed by legendary Chicago architects D.H. Burnham and Co. The rooms are stylish, all muted tones and rich wood accents, with microwave, CD player, two-line phones, and high-speed Internet access. **www.silversmithchicagohotel.com**

NORTH SIDE

Ohio House Motel $

600 N LaSalle St., Chicago, IL, 60610 **Tel** *943-6000/866-601-6446* **Fax** *943-6063* **Rooms** *50*   **Map** *1 C5*

This throwback, 1950s-style hotel boasts great rates, modest accommodations, and prime location in the heart of the River North gallery district. You'll find no frills here – amenities include little more than cable TV, shower, and bath – but for exploring downtown on a budget, it doesn't get much more affordable. **www.ohiohousemotel.com**

Courtyard by Marriott Chicago Downtown   🛏️ 🏋️ 🛎️ 🛗 🍸 $

30 E Hubbard St., Chicago, IL, 60611 **Tel** *329-2500/800-321-2211* **Fax** *329-0293* **Rooms** *337*   **Map** *2 D5*

Within strolling distance of Michigan Avenue, the spacious rooms at this River North chain offer comfort and convenience at affordable rates. Rooms are spacious and pleasantly decorated; each includes a flat-screen TV and complimentary Internet access. An on-site fitness center has a spa and indoor pool. **www.marriott.com**

Dana Hotel and Spa   🏨 🛎️ 🛗 🍸 $$

660 N State St., Chicago, IL, 60654 **Tel** *888-301-3262* **Rooms** *216*   **Map** *1 C4*

Almost like a large, luxury-suites hotel whittled down to a manageable size, the Dana and its indulgent rooms master a delicate blend of upscale urban aesthetics with boutique homeliness. The spa and rooftop lounge – furnished like a chic patio – have become popular hot spots for locals. **www.danahotelandspa.com**

Doubletree Hotel Magnificent Mile   🛏️ 🏋️ 🛎️ 🛗 🍸 $$

300 E Ohio St., Chicago, IL, 60611 **Tel** *787-6100* **Fax** *787-6238* **Rooms** *495*   **Map** *2 E5*

This contemporary hotel offers great views and deluxe accommodations within walking distance of both Navy Pier and Michigan Avenue. Hotel guests enjoy free access to the attached Lakeshore Athletic Club, which houses tennis courts, weight and cardio rooms, and a full-service spa. **www.doubletreemagmile.com**

Flemish House $$

68 E Cedar St., Chicago, IL, 60611 **Tel** *312-664-9981* **Fax** *664-0387* **Rooms** *7*   **Map** *2 D3*

In the heart of the Gold Coast, this charming 19th-century Flemish Revival rowhouse boasts both vintage, turn-of-the-century charm and contemporary amenities, such as high-speed Wi-Fi and fully equipped kitchens. Within an easy stroll of Michigan Avenue shopping and the lake. **www.innchicago.com**

Gold Coast Guest House B&B
♿ $$

113 West Elm St., Chicago, IL, 60610 **Tel** *337-0361* **Fax** *337-0362* **Rooms** *4*   **Map** *1 C3*

Set in a quaint 1873 townhouse in the affluent Gold Coast neighborhood, this charming bed and breakfast is a block away from the upscale boutiques of Oak Street and a quick stroll from Michigan Avenue. Comfortable, contemporary rooms and a lush garden add to the appeal. **www.bbchicago.com**

Hilton Garden Inn Chicago Downtown North
📺 🚶 🛏 ♿ $$

10 E Grand Ave., Chicago, IL, 60611 **Tel** *595-0000/877-865-5298* **Fax** *527-1989* **Rooms** *357*   **Map** *2 D5*

Comfortable and spacious, friendly service, and deluxe perks for the business and leisure traveler keep this hotel bustling. It is close to great dining and shopping; a free trolley to Navy Pier stops out front. Rooms offer full-size refrigerator and microwave plus large TV; complimentary entry to nearby Fitness Center. **www.hiltongardeninn.com**

Howard Johnson Inn
♿ $$

720 N LaSalle St., Chicago, IL, 60610 **Tel** *664-8100/800-446-4656* **Fax** *664-2365* **Rooms** *71*   **Map** *1 C4*

For budget travelers who want to stay downtown in relative comfort, this two-story River North hotel is an excellent option. Rooms are spacious, pleasant, and clean; amenities include cable TV, dataport, refrigerator and microwave. Parking is free for guests, and pets are also welcome. **www.hojo.com**

Inn of Chicago
🛏 ♿ 🍾 $$

162 E Ohio St., Chicago, IL, 60611 **Tel** *595-787-3100/800-557-2378* **Fax** *573-3159* **Rooms** *357*   **Map** *2 D5*

Opened as the Hotel St. Clair in 1928, this newly renovated property sits a block east of the Magnificent Mile shopping district. It offers modest-sized, reasonably priced rooms that have spa bathrooms. Amenities include a fitness center and the hotel offers complimentary stays for children under 18. **www.innofchicago.com**

Ray's Bucktown B&B
$$

2144 N Leavitt St., Chicago, IL, 60647 **Tel** *773-384-3245/800-355-2324* **Rooms** *5*   **Map** *2 D4*

Inspired by cozy European spa hotels, this friendly, intimate bed and breakfast in the artsy Bucktown neighborhood offers surprising amenities like a steamroom and sauna plus high-tech toys like TiVo, and Wi-Fi Internet access. Breakfast is cooked to order and dietary restrictions can be accommodated. **www.raysbucktownbandb.com**

Red Roof Inn-Chicago Downtown
🚶 ♿ $$

162 E Ontario St., Chicago, IL, 60611 **Tel** *787-3580/800-733-7663* **Fax** *787-1299* **Rooms** *195*   **Map** *2 D4*

This good-value chain hotel offers comfortable accommodations in a prime Streeterville location. Within easy walking distance of restaurants, museums, Navy Pier, and the lake, rooms have Wi-Fi access for a daily fee. Children under 18 stay free with an adult; pets are welcome. **www.redroof-chicago-downtown.com**

Ruby Room
🛏 $$

1743–45 W Division St., Chicago, IL, 60622 **Tel** *773-235-2323* **Rooms** *8*

Adjacent to the holistic Ruby Room "spa for the spirit," this Wicker Park destination is not your typical B&B. No phones, no TV, no 24-hour reception – just the luxury of 500-thread-count sheets, marble and glass showers, and complimentary Wi-Fi, all in one of the city's hippest neighborhoods. **www.rubyroom.com**

Affinia Chicago
🛏 ♿ 🍾 $$$

166 E Superior St., Chicago, IL, 60611 **Tel** *787-6000/866-233-4642* **Fax** *787-6133* **Rooms** *216*   **Map** *2 D4*

This Streeterville hotel has up-to-the-minute amenities such as wireless Internet access, two-line phones, and ergonomic chairs. Rooms have classic furnishings and feature the plush, custom-designed "Affinia Bed," a choice of six pillows, and a triple-sheeted down comforter. **www.affinia.com/chicago-hotel**

Ambassador East
🚶 🛏 ♿ 🍾 $$$

1301 N State Prkwy, Chicago, IL, 60610 **Tel** *312-587-0660* **Fax** *312-587-0667* **Rooms** *283*   **Map** *1 C2*

At this elegant 1926 hotel in the heart of the Gold Coast, a recent makeover resulted in a more contemporary look and feel. Amenities include minibar, bathrobes, complimentary newspaper, and coffeemaker. The legendary Pump Room restaurant has hosted celebs from Lucille Ball to Richard Gere. **www.theambassadoreast.com**

Avenue Hotel Chicago
📺 🚶 🛏 ♿ 🍾 $$$

160 E Huron St., Chicago, IL, 60611 **Tel** *787-2900/888-201-1718* **Fax** *787-5158* **Rooms** *350*   **Map** *2 D4*

Less than a block from Michigan Avenue, this hotel boasts spacious, sleekly furnished guestrooms with free high-speed Internet access and refrigerator. On the 40th floor, an exercise room and outdoor heated seasonal pool have stunning views. The on-site Elephant & Castle Pub offers a comfort food menu. **www.avenuehotelchicago.com**

Best Western River North Hotel
📺 🚶 🛏 ♿ $$$

125 W Ohio St., Chicago, IL, 60610 **Tel** *467-0800/800-780-7234* **Fax** *467-1665* **Rooms** *150*   **Map** *2 D5*

Free guest parking, an indoor heated pool, and central location with easy access to museums, attractions, and Michigan Avenue shopping are a few of the perks of this reasonably priced downtown chain hotel. Spacious and comfortably furnished, rooms include free high-speed Internet access, cable TV, and safe. **www.rivernorthhotel.com**

Embassy Suites Chicago
📺 🚶 🛏 ♿ 🍾 $$$

600 N State St., Chicago, IL, 60610 **Tel** *312-943-3800/800-362-2776* **Fax** *312-943-7629* **Rooms** *365* **Map** *2 D4*

More than 300 rooms surround the 11-story atrium of this all-suite hotel in the heart of the River North district. Two TVs, refrigerator, microwave, sofa bed, and high-speed Internet access are standard; it also offers complimentary breakfasts, an indoor pool, and fitness center. Steps from free trolley to Navy Pier. **www.embassysuiteschicago.com**

Key to Price Guide *see p140* **Key to Symbols** *see back cover flap*

Embassy Suites Chicago – Downtown/Lakefront ⬜⬜⬜⬜⬜ $$$
511 N Columbus Dr., Chicago, IL, 60611 **Tel** *312-836-5900* **Fax** *312-836-5901* **Rooms** *455* **Map** *2 E4*

Located midway between Navy Pier and Michigan Avenue, this family-friendly, all-suite hotel features pleasantly furnished accommodations with private bedroom, living room, and kitchenette. Hotel amenities include fitness room, pool, business center, and special activities for children. **www.chicagoembassy.com**

Fairfield Inn & Suites ⬜⬜⬜ $$$
216 E Ontario St., Chicago, IL, 60611 **Tel** *312-787-3777* **Fax** *312-787-8714* **Rooms** *185* **Map** *2 D4*

A comfortable chain hotel with guestrooms featuring free high-speed Internet access, cable TV, microwave, and mini-fridge. Also "Wellness Suites" that offer organic bedding and purified air and water. Convenient location just east of the Magnificent Mile. **www.fairfieldsuiteschicago.com**

Holiday Inn Chicago Mart Plaza ⬜⬜⬜⬜⬜ $$$
350 W Mart Center Dr., Chicago, IL, 60654 **Tel** *312-836-5000/800-972-2494* **Rooms** *521* **Map** *1 B5*

Heated indoor pool, exercise facility, wireless Internet access, and free stays for kids are a few of the amenities provided by this large, family-friendly hotel situated on the Chicago River and connected to the Merchandise Mart. Its spacious rooms are comfortably furnished with workspaces and satellite TV. **www.martplaza.com**

Hotel Cass – A Holiday Inn Express Hotel ⬜⬜ $$$
640 N Wabash Ave., Chicago, IL, 60611 **Tel** *312-787-4030* **Fax** *312-787-8544* **Rooms** *175* **Map** *2 D4*

This smart hotel's reasonable rates and convenient location just off the Michigan Avenue shopping strip make it an appealingly affordable downtown option. It offers free Internet access and there is a complimentary full breakfast. **www.hotelcass.com**

Hotel Indigo ⬜⬜⬜⬜ $$$
1244 N Dearborn Prkwy, Chicago, IL, 60610 **Tel** *787-4980/866-521-6950* **Fax** *787-4069* **Rooms** *165* **Map** *1 C1*

Vibrant with tropical hues, this colorful boutique hotel is a sunny alternative to standard downtown accommodations. Whimsical touches include oversized Adirondack lobby chairs and photomurals in each room. All rooms have hardwood floors and free high-speed Internet access. **www.goldcoastchicagohotel.com**

Hotel Sax ⬜⬜⬜⬜ $$$
333 N Dearborn St., Chicago, IL, 60610 **Tel** *245-0333/877-569-3742* **Fax** *923-2458* **Rooms** *361* **Map** *1 C5*

Set among some of River North's top dining and nightlife spots, this trendy hotel – formerly the House of Blues Hotel – has had massive renovations and now boasts a "17th-century French salon with a 21st-century twist." That means small-but-chic rooms with exotic furnishings, luxury amenities, and excellent service. **www.hotelsaxchicago.com**

InterContinental Chicago ⬜⬜⬜⬜⬜ $$$
505 N Michigan Ave., Chicago, IL, 60611 **Tel** *944-4100/800-770-5675* **Fax** *944-1320* **Rooms** *792* **Map** *2 D5*

One of the city's grandest hotels, this 1929 beauty has been renovated to its former glory. A sweeping four-story lobby welcomes guests; the spacious, contemporary and classic rooms feature 27-inch TV, high-speed Internet access, and coffeemaker. Also has a junior Olympic-sized swimming pool. **icchicagohotel.com**

Marriott Residence Inn ⬜⬜⬜ $$$
201 E Walton Place, Chicago, IL, 60611 **Tel** *943-9800/800-331-3131* **Fax** *943-8579* **Rooms** *221* **Map** *2 D3*

Two blocks from the lake and one block from Michigan Avenue, this comfortable chain hotel offers oversized suites decked out with a full kitchen, free high-speed Internet access, and pull-out sofa beds. The on-site fitness center is open 24 hours. There is a complimentary daily breakfast buffet. Pets are welcome. **www.marriott.com**

Millennium Knickerbocker Hotel ⬜⬜⬜⬜ $$$
163 E Walton Place, Chicago, IL, 60611 **Tel** *751-8100/866-866-8086* **Fax** *751-9205* **Rooms** *305* **Map** *2 D3*

A Michigan Avenue fixture since 1927, after major renovations in 2008 this elegant hotel offers luxurious accommodations, and personalized service from babysitting to 24-hour front desk service. Asian-inspired rooms have 27-inch TVs, CD player, and dual-line phones. A short stroll from Oak Street shopping. **www.millenniumhotels.com**

Old Town Chicago Bed & Breakfast Inn ⬜ $$$
1442 N North Park Ave., Chicago, IL, 60610 **Tel** *440-9268* **Fax** *440-2378* **Rooms** *4* **Map** *1 C1*

Decked out with sumptuous Art Deco furnishings, this luxurious bed and breakfast features four suites with a queen-size bed and private bathroom, plus a common living/dining room with grand piano and extensive library. Free wireless Internet is available. Rooftop garden offers pleasant views. **www.oldtownchicago.com**

Raffaello Hotel ⬜⬜⬜⬜ $$$
201 E Delaware Place, Chicago, IL, 60611 **Tel** *943-5000/888-560-4977* **Fax** *924-9158* **Rooms** *175* **Map** *2 D3*

The former Raphael Hotel (just off N Michigan Ave.) has earth-toned suites with deluxe amenities such as 32-inch flat-screen TV, high thread-count bedding, rainforest showerheads, and more. Also features 24-hour room service, spa/fitness facilities, valet laundry, and limo/car service. **www.chicagoraffaello.com**

Seneca Hotel ⬜⬜⬜ $$$
200 E Chestnut St., Chicago, IL, 60611 **Tel** *787-8900/800-800-6261* **Fax** *988-4438* **Rooms** *130* **Map** *2 D4*

Intimate and quiet, yet just a block away from Michigan Ave., this European-style hotel is one of downtown's hidden gems. Rooms are tasteful with classic furnishings, jacuzzi bathtubs, and most rooms have kitchens with a microwave and dishwasher. The Saloon Steakhouse is known for its seafood and grilled meats. **www.senecahotel.com**

Sheraton Chicago Hotel and Towers
🏢 🚹 🛏 ✆ 🍴 $$$

301 E North Water St., Chicago, IL, 60611 **Tel** *464-1000/877-242-2558* **Fax** *464-9140* **Rooms** *1209*   **Map** *2 E5*

Perched just north of the Chicago River and a quick stroll from the lake, this 1,200-room chain hotel boasts a prime location and an upscale vibe. All rooms offer impressive views and the hotel's signature "Sweet Sleeper" beds. There's an on-site health club with indoor pool, sun deck and sauna, plus a business center. **www.sheratonchicago.com**

Sofitel Chicago Water Tower
🏢 🚹 🛏 ✆ 🍴 $$$

20 E Chestnut St., Chicago, IL, 60611 **Tel** *324-4000/877-813-7700* **Fax** *324-4026* **Rooms** *415*   **Map** *2 D4*

Architect Jean Paul Viguier's sleek, triangular structure slices dramatically into the skyline; inside, the airy, light-filled lobby gives way to luxurious and stylishly decorated rooms with good views of the Gold Coast and lake beyond. Cozy, cosmopolitan Le Bar and the upscale Café des Architectes restaurant are destinations in themselves. **www.sofitel.com**

Sutton Place Hotel Chicago
🚹 🛏 ✆ 🍴 $$$

21 E Bellevue Pl., Chicago, IL, 60611 **Tel** *266-2100/866-378-8866* **Fax** *266-2103* **Rooms** *246*   **Map** *2 D3*

This Gold Coast luxury hotel, whose Art Deco-meets-contemporary interior boasts original Robert Mapplethorpe floral photography, offers premium amenities: wireless Internet access, and entertainment center with flat-screen TV, DVD player and stereo. Close to Michigan Avenue and Oak Street shopping. **www.chicago.suttonplace.com**

Talbott Hotel
🛏 ✆ 🍴 $$$

20 E Delaware Pl., Chicgao, IL, 60611 **Tel** *944-4970/800-825-2688* **Fax** *944-7241* **Rooms** *149*   **Map** *2 D3*

One of the city's finest boutique hotels, this intimate, richly appointed Gold Coast destination is still gleaming from a 2005 renovation. Rooms have a classic look of muted tones and antique furnishings, while new high-tech touches include flat-screen TVs, and nifty electronic "do not disturb" panels outside each room. **www.talbotthotel.com**

The Allerton Hotel Chicago
🚹 🛏 ✆ 🍴 $$$

701 N Michigan Ave., Chicago, IL, 60611 **Tel** *440-1500/877-701-8111* **Fax** *440-1819* **Rooms** *443*   **Map** *2 D4*

Set in a landmark Italian Renaissance high-rise on Michigan Avenue, this completely renovated luxury hotel offers cheerful rooms and suites with marble bathrooms, plush bedding, dual-line phones, high-speed Internet access and cable TV with on-demand movies. A complimentary fitness center is open 24 hours. **www.theallertonhotel.com**

Whitehall Hotel
🚹 🛏 ✆ 🍴 $$$

105 E Delaware Pl., Chicago, IL, 60611 **Tel** *944-6300/800-555-7555* **Fax** *944-8552* **Rooms** *223*   **Map** *2 D3*

Conveniently located just steps from the Magnificent Mile, this boutique hotel offers comfortable, traditional rooms and suites at reasonable rates. Expect standard room amenities such as minibar, bathrobes, and safe. Downstairs, the atrium of Fornetto Mei restaurant is a popular after-work spot for cocktails and pizza. **www.hotelwhitehallchicago.com**

Wyndham Downtown Chicago
🏢 🚹 🛏 ✆ 🍴 $$$

633 N St. Clair St., Chicago, IL, 60611 **Tel** *573-0300* **Fax** *274-0164* **Rooms** *417*   **Map** *2 D4*

This upscale hotel is notable for its extensive list of guest services, from laundry and shoe shine to dry cleaning, computer rental and a full business center. Guestrooms offer lovely views, pillow-top mattresses, oversized desk and Aeron work chairs. Its restaurant Caliterra is one of the city's top hotel dining spots. **www.wyndham.com**

Chicago Marriott Downtown Magnificent Mile
🏢 🚹 🛏 ✆ 🍴 $$$$

540 N Michigan Ave., Chicago, IL, 60611 **Tel** *836-0100/800-228-9290* **Fax** *836-6139* **Rooms** *1198*   **Map** *2 D5*

This mammoth Michigan Avenue hotel scores with snazzy renovated rooms featuring stylish, contemporary decor and great downtown views, plus amenities such as flat-screen TVs, ergonomic chairs, and two-line phones. Conveniently located close to some of the area's top restaurants, boutiques, and attractions. **www.marriott.com**

Conrad Chicago
🚹 🛏 ✆ 🍴 $$$$

521 N Rush St., Chicago, IL, 60611 **Tel** *645-1500* **Fax** *645-1550* **Rooms** *311*   **Map** *2 D5*

This luxury hotel is connected to the upscale Westfield North Bridge shopping center and is within walking distance of Lake Michigan, Millennium Park, and Navy Pier. Guestrooms and suites are stylishly decorated in muted tones with contemporary decor and feature views of the skyline or lake. **www.conradhotels.com/chicago**

Four Seasons Hotel Chicago
🏢 🚹 🛏 ✆ 🍴 $$$$

120 E Delaware Pl., Chicago, IL, 60611 **Tel** *280-8800/800-819-5053* **Fax** *280-1748* **Rooms** *343*   **Map** *2 D3*

This elegant luxury hotel just off the Magnificent Mile now balances old-style glamour – crystal chandeliers, high ceilings, and marble galore – with contemporary additions such as flat-screen TVs and high-speed Internet access. Stunning views of the lake or city are an added bonus. **www.fourseasons.com/chicagofs**

Hilton Suites Chicago/Magnificent Mile
🏢 🚹 🛏 ✆ 🍴 $$$$

198 E Delaware Pl., Chicago, IL, 60611 **Tel** *664-1100* **Fax** *664-9881* **Rooms** *345*   **Map** *2 D3*

At a great location just off Michigan Ave., this all-suite hotel offers deluxe perks such as free Wi-Fi in the lobby, and a rooftop fitness center with indoor pool, sauna, whirlpool, and great views. Each two-room suite is furnished in colorful, contemporary style with Sweet Dreams beds. The on-site restaurant is Mrs. Park's Tavern. **www.hilton.com**

James Hotel
🛏 ✆ 🍴 $$$$

55 E Ontario St., Chicago, IL, 60611 **Tel** *877-JAMES-55/877-526-3755* **Fax** *337-7217* **Rooms** *297*   **Map** *2 D4*

A block west of the Magnificent Mile, this contemporary boutique hotel is a stylish oasis, with cool, minimalist rooms and deluxe amenities such as plasma screen TVs, free Wi-Fi, and custom robes/slippers. Other perks: acclaimed David Burke's Primehouse restaurant, a vast gym, and a new spa with a full menu of beauty services. **www.jameshotels.com**

Key to Price Guide *see p140* **Key to Symbols** *see back cover flap*

Park Hyatt Chicago
800 N Michigan Ave., Chicago, IL, 60611 **Tel** *335-1234/888-591-1234* **Fax** *239-4000* **Rooms** *198* **Map** *2 D4*

One of the best hotels in the city. Sophisticated and modern, this Magnificent Mile luxury property features stunning city views and premium amenities from 24-hour concierge and in-room wireless Internet to bathrooms with tub, walk-in shower, and TV. The 7th-floor restaurant NoMi is one of Chicago's top ten. **www.parkchicago.hyatt.com**

The Drake Chicago
140 E Walton Pl., Chicago, IL, 60611 **Tel** *787-2200/800-553-7253* **Fax** *787-1431* **Rooms** *535* **Map** *2 D4*

The grande dame of Chicago hotels, this luxurious Michigan Avenue destination still attracts celebrities from all over the world. Rooms boast stunning views of Lake Michigan or the Magnificent Mile. On-site dining includes the Cape Cod Room, for seafood, and the Palm Court, for sumptuous high tea. **www.thedrakehotel.com**

The Peninsula Chicago
108 E Superior St., Chicago, IL, 60611 **Tel** *337-2888/866-288-8889* **Fax** *751-2888* **Rooms** *339* **Map** *2 D4*

Continually named the finest hotel in North America. Rooms are spacious and lavishly appointed in muted colors, with superior service, outstanding views, and amenities such as in-tub TV and phone. The restaurant Avenues is among the city's best, while the Shanghai Terrace is perfect for cocktails. **chicago.peninsula.com**

The Ritz-Carlton Chicago
160 E Pearson St., Chicago, IL, 60611 **Tel** *266-1000/800-621-6906* **Fax** *266-1194* **Rooms** *435* **Map** *2 D4*

Perched above Water Tower Place on Michigan Ave., this grand luxury hotel is all about old-fashioned elegance, from the rooms' antique cherrywood furnishings and marble bathrooms to the famously service-oriented staff. All rooms have picture windows with views, and a full menu of in-room spa services. **www.fourseasons.com/chicagorc/**

Tremont Hotel
100 E Chestnut St., Chicago, IL, 60611 **Tel** *751-1900/800-621-8133* **Fax** *751-8691* **Rooms** *130* **Map** *2 D4*

With lots of dark wood accents and traditional furnishings, this charming hotel at the north end of Michigan Avenue has a classic American look and feel. Rooms boast marble bathrooms and amenities such as microwave, in-room safe, and city views; the hotel is also home to steakhouse Mike Ditka's Restaurant. **www.starwoodhotels.com**

Trump International Hotel & Tower
401 N Wabash Ave., Chicago, IL, 60611 **Tel** *312-588 8000* **Fax** *312-588-8001* **Rooms** *339* **Map** *1 D5*

This hotel has a superb location by the Chicago River between the Loop and N Michigan Avenue, within easy walking distance of the main shops and historic sights. The luxurious rooms and suites have floor-to-ceiling windows and there is a finess center and spa. The restaurant, Sixteen, offers innovative cuisine. **www.trumpchicagohotel.com**

W Hotel Chicago Lakeshore
644 N Lake Shore Dr., Chicago, IL, 60611 **Tel** *943-9200/888-627-9034* **Fax** *255-4411* **Rooms** *520* **Map** *2 E4*

This trendy hotel is just west of Lake Shore Drive and within walking distance of Navy Pier. The compact rooms boast truly stunning views. Other perks: enormous Bliss Spa, Mediterranean restaurant Wave, and the rooftop hipster lounge Whiskey Sky, featuring panoramic views of the city. **www.starwoodhotels.com**

Westin Michigan Avenue Chicago
909 N Michigan Ave., Chicago, IL, 60611 **Tel** *943-7200/888-627-8385* **Fax** *397-5580* **Rooms** *751* **Map** *2 D3*

Crisp, contemporary decor, marble bathrooms, and its signature 10-layer Heavenly Bed® make this upscale chain hotel at the north end of the Magnificent Mile an appealing option. It also has a business center, spa, gym, and 24-hour room service, the Grill on the Alley restaurant, and is a quick stroll from shops. **www.starwoodhotels.com**

SOUTH LOOP AND NEAR SOUTH SIDE

Essex Inn Chicago
800 S Michigan Ave., Chicago, IL, 60605 **Tel** *312-939-2800/800-621-6909* **Fax** *312-922-6153* **Rooms** *254* **Map** *4 D3*

This South Loop hotel across from Grant Park provides in-room wireless Internet access, 24-hour front desk service, and a free shuttle to North Michigan Avenue shopping district. Spacious rooms have floor-to-ceiling windows and are furnished in Art Deco style. The rooftop garden and swimming pool have stunning lake views. **www.essexinn.com**

The Congress Plaza Hotel
520 S Michigan Ave., Chicago, IL, 60605 **Tel** *427-3800/800-635-1666* **Fax** *427-2919* **Rooms** *870* **Map** *4 D3*

This hotel, originally built to house visitors to the "White City" of Chicago's 1893 World's Columbian Exposition, retains much of its original charm. Reasonably priced, it has spacious and comfortable rooms, many with excellent views of Grant Park. It has a 24-hour fitness center, and children under 17 stay free with an adult. **www.congressplazahotel.com**

Best Western Grant Park Hotel
1100 S Michigan Ave., Chicago, IL, 60605 **Tel** *922-2900/800-472-6875* **Fax** *922-8812* **Rooms** *172* **Map** *4 D4*

In the South Loop close to the Museum Campus, this pleasant affordable chain hotel offers clean rooms with some amenities not found in pricier properties, such as free in-room wireless Internet access and satellite TV. Other perks include an outdoor pool, exercise facility, dry-cleaning service, and 24-hour front desk. **www.bestwestern.com**

Hilton Chicago
🏢 🏃 📺 ♿ 🍸 $$$

720 S Michigan Ave., Chicago, IL, 60605 **Tel** *922-4400/800-445-8667* **Fax** *922-5240* **Rooms** *1,544*   **Map** *4 D3*

Overlooking Grant Park and the lake, this large hotel has a convenient location close to McCormick Place and the Museum Campus. It offers wireless Internet access and a huge health club. Rooms feature classic furnishings with dark wood accents, plus 27-inch flat-screen TVs and plush-top mattresses. **www.hilton.com**

Hyatt Regency McCormick Place
🏢 🏃 📺 ♿ 🍸 $$$

2233 S M. Luther King Jr. Dr., Chicago, IL, 60616 **Tel** *567-1234/888-591-1234* **Fax** *528-4000* **Rooms** *800*   **Map** *5 E2*

Connected to McCormick Place Convention Center with easy access to the lake, museums, and the Loop, this hotel is ideal for convention visitors. Spacious rooms look out onto Lake Michigan and the city, and have high-speed Internet access. Complimentary hotel shuttle to local attractions. **www.mccormickplace.hyatt.com**

The Wheeler Manion
$$$

2020 S Calumet Ave., Chicago, IL, 60616 **Tel** *312-945-2020* **Fax** *312-945-2021* **Rooms** *11*   **Map** *6 D1*

Set in an 1870 home on the near South Side that was one of the few buildings to survive the Great Chicago Fire, this beautifully restored hotel has 11 rooms and suites with antique furnishings and tapestries. Other amenities include complimentary gourmet breakfast, free parking, and high-speed Internet access. **www.wheelermansion.com**

Hotel Blake
📺 ♿ 🍸 $$$$

500 S Dearborn St., Chicago, IL, 60605 **Tel** *986-1234* **Fax** *939-2468* **Rooms** *162*   **Map** *3 C3*

Stylish and sophisticated, this boutique hotel is just south of the Loop in the historic Printer's Row district. Rooms are contemporary in design with dark woods and bold colors. Deluxe amenities include in-room spa treatments and free high-speed Internet access. It is adjacent to the renowned eaterie the Custom House. **www.hotelblake.com**

SOUTH SIDE

Benedictine B&B
$$

3111 S Aberdeen St., Chicago, IL, 60608 **Tel** *773-927-7424* **Fax** *773-927-5734* **Rooms** *2*

On the grounds of an active Benedictine monastery that dates to the late 19th century, this unique B&B in the South Side neighborhood of Bridgeport includes a spacious, private seven-room loft apartment with three bedrooms and a garden house with two bedrooms and a private deck. **www.chicagomonk.org**

Hutchins House Bed and Breakfast
🏃 $$

4810 S Ellis Ave., Chicago, IL, 60615 **Tel** *773-548-5534* **Rooms** *4*

Located in the Kenwood Landmark district near the University of Chicago campus, this hotel maintains the original woodwork and charm of the turn-of-the-century building in which it is housed. All rooms have modern amenities including wireless Internet and DVD players. **www.hutchinshouse.com**

Ramada Inn Lake Shore
🏢 🏃 ♿ 🍸 $$

4900 S Lake Shore Dr., Chicago, IL, 60615 **Tel** *773-288-5800* **Fax** *773-288-5819* **Rooms** *184*   **Map** *7 E1*

Basic comfort, reasonable rates, and convenient Hyde Park location are the draws of this South Side chain hotel. Rooms are modest but spacious, some with lake views; each has a refrigerator, free high-speed Internet, and coffeemaker. Extras include outdoor pool and free shuttle bus to local attractions. **www.ramada-chicago.com**

The Abode
🏢 $$

5412 S Blackstone Ave., Chicago, IL, 60615 **Tel** *773-955-4561* **Fax** *773-439-6901* **Rooms** *3*   **Map** *8 D3*

Within walking distance of Lake Michigan, the University of Chicago, and the Museum of Science and Industry, this pleasant home offers three fully furnished units with private entrance, dining area, kitchen, and a host of amenities such as Wi-Fi computer workstations, satellite TV, whirlpool or steam shower, and king size bed. **www.abodeltd.net**

University Quarters B&B
$$

6137 S Kimbark Ave., 1st Floor, Chicago, IL, 60637 **Tel** *773-855-8349* **Rooms** *3*   **Map** *8 D5*

Jacuzzi tubs, bathrobes, and free high-speed wireless Internet access are a few of the amenities at this intimate Hyde Park establishment located in a vintage greystone building less than a block from the University of Chicago campus. The three rooms here (two with shared bath) boast contemporary decor. **www.universityquarters.net**

FARTHER AFIELD

EDGEWATER The Ardmore House
$$

1248 W Ardmore Ave., Chicago, IL, 60660 **Tel** *773-728-5414* **Rooms** *3*

In a Victorian house in the Edgewater neighborhood on the city's far north side, this tastefully furnished guesthouse caters to a mostly gay clientele. Its three rooms include satellite TV, robe and beach towels, and free Wi-Fi. Guests have access to a full kitchen at all times, as well as a spacious patio, hot tub, and sundeck. **www.ardmorehousebb.com**

Key to Price Guide *see p140* **Key to Symbols** *see back cover flap*

ITASCA Eaglewood Resort & Spa

1401 Nordic Rd., Itasca, IL, 60143 **Tel** *630-773-1400/877-285-6150* **Fax** *630-773-1709* **Rooms** *295*

From a championship-level 18-hole golf course to a full-service spa, heated indoor pool, private bowling alley, and kids activities galore, this resort offers deluxe, yet-reasonably priced, accommodations. Guestrooms feature pillow-top mattresses, Internet access, and lovely views. **www.eaglewoodresort.com**

LAKEVIEW Best Western Hawthorne Terrace

3434 North Broadway St., Chicago, IL, 60657 **Tel** *773-244-3434/888-860-3400* **Fax** *773-244-3435* **Rooms** *59*

Prime location in the heart of Boystown makes this comfortable chain hotel a solid North Side option. Rooms are small but comfortable; amenities include complimentary breakfast, in-room refrigerators and microwaves, and a workout room with whirlpool and sauna. Children 12 and under stay free. **www.hawthorneterrace.com**

LAKEVIEW City Suites Hotel

933 West Belmont Ave., Chicago, IL, 60657 **Tel** *773-404-3400/800-248-9108* **Fax** *773-404-3405* **Rooms** *45*

Another of the Neighborhood Inns of Chicago, this hotel is in the heart of Lakeview on the buzzing Belmont strip. Considering the busy surroundings and proximity to the El train platform, rooms are surprisingly quiet and have Art Deco furnishings, plus fridge, robes, iron, and TV. **www.cityinns.com/citysuites**

LAKEVIEW Majestic Hotel

528 West Brompton Ave., Chicago, IL, 60657 **Tel** *773-404-3499/800-727-5108* **Fax** *773-404-3495* **Rooms** *52*

The most regal of the Neighborhood Inns of Chicago, this intimate boutique hotel in Lakeview is quite close to the lake and an easy walk away from Wrigley Field. A spacious lobby area welcomes with rich wood features, and a wood-burning fireplace; rooms have a classic feel, with gold, green, or violet accents. **www.cityinns.com/majestic**

LAKEVIEW The Willows Hotel

555 West Surf St., Chicago, IL, 60657 **Tel** *773-528-8400/800-787-3108* **Fax** *773-528-8483* **Rooms** *55*

Part of the Neighborhood Inns of Chicago, this charming boutique hotel sits on a quiet residential street in a stately 1920s building. Done up in French Countryside style, it is an intimate refuge with tasteful rooms. Free coffee and tea are available 24 hours, and free Wi-Fi; also access to Bally's fitness facility, a block away. **www.cityinns.com/willows**

LINCOLN PARK Arlington House International Hostel and Hotel

616 West Arlington Place, Chicago, IL, 60614 **Tel** *773-929-5380/800-467-8355* **Fax** *773-665-5485* **Rooms** *250*

On a quiet street in residential Lincoln Park, this pleasant hostel offers clean dormitory and private rooms close to dining and nightlife and a walk away from Lake Michigan. Amenities include self-service laundry, 24-hour check-in, vending machines, TV room, and wireless Internet access (lobby). There is no curfew. **www.arlingtonhouse.com**

LINCOLN PARK City Scene Bed and Breakfast

2101 North Clifton Ave., Chicago, IL, 60614 **Tel** *773-549-1743* **Fax** *773-549-1763* **Rooms** *2*

Set in a charming Victorian home, this intimate Lincoln Park guesthouse offers private suites decorated comfortably with classic American furnishings. Amenities include steam shower, fireplace, and full kitchen. Its location provides easy access to downtown, Lake Michigan, and the campus of DePaul University. **www.cityscenebb.com**

LINCOLN PARK Days ınn Lincoln Park North

644 W Diversey Prkwy, Chicago, IL, 60614 **Tel** *773-525-7010/888-576-3297* **Fax** *773-525-6998* **Rooms** *133*

Easily one of the best-value hotels in the city, this award-winning place offers comfortable, clean rooms and deluxe amenities such as valet parking, complimentary gym passes, guest laundry services, and complimentary breakfast. Executive rooms include a spacious workstation area with extra phone jacks. **www.lpndaysinn.com**

LINCOLN PARK Inn at Lincoln Park

601 W Diversey Prkwy, Chicago, IL, 60614 **Tel** *773-348-2810/866-774-7275* **Fax** *773-348-1912* **Rooms** *74*

Rooms are modest and on the small side, but this hotel's reasonable rates and proximity to Lake Michigan as well as to Lincoln Park and Lakeview restaurants, shops, and bars more than make up for that. Amenities provided in the rooms include coffeemaker and microwave; on-site parking is available. **www.innlp.com**

LINCOLN PARK Villa D'Druse

2230 N Halsted Ave., Chicago, IL, 60654 **Tel** *312-771-0696* **Rooms** *5*

Inspired by a modern Tuscan villa, this unique B&B is housed in a quintessential greystone mansion typical of late 19th-century Chicago architecture. The mansion has undergone extensive renovation and now oozes luxury and old world comfort. Located a short walk from Lincoln Park. **www.villaddruse.com**

LINCOLN PARK Windy City Urban ınn

607 West Deming Place, Chicago, IL, 60614 **Tel** *773-248-7091/877-897-7091* **Fax** *773-529-4183* **Rooms** *8*

Set in a cozy red brick Victorian home, this Lincoln Park B&B offers comfortably appointed guestrooms and apartments named after famous Chicago writers such as Mike Royko and Studs Terkel. Some rooms include jacuzzi tub; common areas feature fireplace and TV/VCR. Room price includes buffet breakfast. **www.windycityinn.com**

LINCOLN PARK Belden-Stratford Hotel

2300 Lincoln Park West, Chicago, IL, 60614 **Tel** *773-281-2900/800-800-8301* **Fax** *773-880-2039* **Rooms** *60*

Looking out over Lincoln Park five minutes north of downtown, this elegant, landmark apartment building and hotel boasts a stunning lobby with grand piano, painted sky ceiling, and two upscale restaurants. Guestrooms and suites are decorated sumptuously and have free satellite TV and high-speed Internet access. **www.beldenstratfordhotel.com**

LINCOLN PARK Windy City Sailing B&B $$$$
3851 N Leavitt St., Chicago, IL, 60618 **Tel** *773-868-0096* **Fax** *270-778-2377* **Rooms** *1*

One of the city's most unique B&B experiences can be had aboard this sailboat. Deluxe accomodations are available in the owner's stateroom with feather beds and down comforters, a full-service galley kitchen, and a flat-screen TV/DVD player. Along with breakfast, a two-hour morning sail is also included. **www.windycitysailing.com**

OAK BROOK Hyatt Lodge at McDonald's Campus $$$
2815 Jorie Blvd., Oak Brook, IL, 60523 **Tel** *630-990-5800* **Fax** *630-990-8287* **Rooms** *217*

On the landscaped 88-acre grounds of the world headquarters of McDonald's, this hotel boasts recently renovated rooms with granite bath, 27-inch flat-screen TV, wireless Internet access, and Hyatt's "Grand Bed". The hotel also features a private lake and four miles of trails for hiking, biking, and running. **www.thelodge.hyatt.com**

OAK PARK Carleton of Oak Park Hotel $$
1110 Pleasant St., Oak Park, IL, 60302 **Tel** *708-848-5000/888-227-5386* **Fax** *708-848-0537* **Rooms** *153*

In a historic 1928 brick building, this boutique hotel is a short stroll from Frank Lloyd Wright's Unity Temple. Most of the comfortably furnished rooms have a kitchen with microwave and refrigerator as well as in-room wireless Internet access. Classic American restaurant Philander's features live jazz nightly. **www.carletonhotel.com**

OAK PARK Harvey House Bed & Breakfast $$
107 S Scoville Ave., Oak Park, IL, 60302 **Tel** *708-848-6810* **Rooms** *5*

Set in a charming red brick Victorian-style home in the heart of Oak Park's historical district, this pleasant B&B offers gourmet breakfasts, Wi-Fi, and a lovely common area with fireplace and grand piano. Suites are furnished with antique furniture and include such amenities as a jacuzzi and flat-screen TV. **www.harveyhousebb.com**

ROSEMONT Sofitel O'Hare $$
5550 N River Rd., Rosemont, IL, 60018 **Tel** *847-678-4488* **Fax** *847-678-4244* **Rooms** *312*

Close to O'Hare and within easy access of downtown, this luxury hotel attracts mostly corporate guests, and offers business-related services and a fully staffed business center. The tastefully furnished rooms feature standard amenities like satellite TV and 24-hour room service. The restaurant Colette serves up French bistro fare. **www.sofitel.com**

ROSEMONT Hyatt Regency O'Hare $$$
9300 W Bryn Mawr Ave., Rosemont, IL, 60018 **Tel** *847-696-1234* **Fax** *847-698-0139* **Rooms** *1,096*

Conveniently located adjacent to O'Hare International Airport, this newly renovated hotel is suited to the business traveler, with extensive meeting facilities and a business center. The spacious guestrooms offer king-size beds, Portico bath products, pillow-top mattresses, and oversized television. **www.ohare.hyatt.com**

WHEELING Westin Chicago North Shore $$$$
601 N Milwaukee Ave., Wheeling, IL, 60090 **Tel** *847-777-6500* **Fax** *847-777-6510* **Rooms** *412*

This new luxury hotel on the North Shore boasts not only deluxe amenities like the Westin "Heavenly Bed" and workout facilities, but also the restaurants Osteria di Tramonto and Tramonto's Steak and Seafood from esteemed chefs Rick Tramonto and Gale Gand. Guestrooms are stylishly decorated. **www.starwoodhotels.com**

WICKER PARK House of Two Urns $$
1239 N Greenview Ave., Chicago, IL, 60622 **Tel** *773-235-1408/877-896-8767* **Fax** *773-235-1410* **Rooms** *6*

This charming B&B set in a 1912 brownstone in the trendy Wicker Park neighborhood boasts eclectic decor and antique furnishings in its four guestrooms and three apartments. Full hot breakfast is served each morning; other amenities include rooftop deck and garden, free Internet access, and in-room TV and DVD players. **www.twourns.com**

BEYOND CHICAGO

EVANSTON Homestead Hotel $$
1625 Hinman Ave., Evanston, IL, 60201 **Tel** *847-475-3300* **Fax** *847-570-8100* **Rooms** *90*

On a residential street near Northwestern University, this 1927 Williamsburg-style building has a wide front porch and pleasant salon area decorated with antiques. It offers rooms, suites, and apartments for overnight and extended stays; amenities include cable TV and self-service laundry. Close to restaurants. **www.thehomestead.net**

EVANSTON Margarita European inn $$
1566 Oak Ave., Evanston, IL, 60201 **Tel** *847-869-2273* **Fax** *847-869-2353* **Rooms** *42*

Built in 1915 to house working women, this elegant inn is furnished with antiques and has a welcoming atmosphere. Rooms are quiet and comfortable; amenities include continental breakfast, evening room service, wireless Internet access in the common areas, and fine dining at Va Pensiero for Italian fare. **www.margaritainn.com**

EVANSTON Hotel Orrington $$$
1710 Orrington Ave., Evanston, IL, 60201 **Tel** *847-866-8700/888-677-4648* **Fax** *847-866-8724* **Rooms** *277*

Close to Northwestern University, this downtown hotel has had a $34 million renovation; rooms are freshly decorated with improved amenities such as power showerheads, and free high-speed internet access. A fitness center and business center are open 24 hours. Globe Café and Bar is popular for cocktails. **www.hotelorrington.com**

Key to Price Guide *see p140* **Key to Symbols** *see back cover flap*

GALENA Best Western Quiet House and Suites ⬛🚻📺♿ $$

9923 W US Route 20 Galena, IL, 61036 **Tel** *815-777-2577/800-528-1234* **Fax** *815-777-0584* **Rooms** *42*

Spacious rooms and a location close to Galena attractions draw visitors to this chain hotel. Rooms are large and comfortably and colorfully furnished; all rooms have living room, microwave and refrigerator, while some luxury suites include a whirlpool. Hotel amenities include swim-through pools and a fitness facility. **www.quiethouse.com**

GALENA Chestnut Mountain Resort ⬛🚻♿📺 $$

8700 West Chestnut Rd., Galena, IL, 61036 **Tel** *815-777-1320/800-397-1320* **Fax** *815-777-1068* **Rooms** *120*

Set above the Mississippi River, this ski resort lodge offers pleasant, spacious rooms with excellent views. During the winter, the place buzzes with skiers heading for the resort's 19 runs and snowboard terrain. In summer, guests can ride the resort's Alpine Slide. Resort amenities include indoor pool, sauna, and whirlpool. **www.chestnutmtn.com**

GALENA Eagle Ridge Resort and Spa ⬛🚻📺♿📺 $$

444 Eagle Ridge Dr., Galena, IL, 61036 **Tel** *815-777-5000/800-240-1681* **Fax** *815-777-4502* **Rooms** *450*

Ideal for sportsmen and families alike, this sprawling resort six miles (10 km) from Galena boasts four award-winning golf courses, a full-service spa, plus facilities for fishing, boating, and more. Accommodations include an inn, villas, and fully furnished private homes of up to eight bedrooms. **www.eagleridgeresortonline.com**

GALENA Galena Log Cabin Getaway and Adventure Creek Alpaca Farm 🚻♿ $$

9401 W Hart John Rd., Galena, IL, 61036 **Tel** *815-777-4200* **Rooms** *12*

A truly charming haven south of Galena, this rustic property offers genuine log cabins that have been fully renovated for modern comfort. Each cabin features new beds, gas fireplace, refrigerator, microwave, and satellite TV with 250 channels. The site is also a working alpaca farm, and guests can interact with the animals. **www.galenalogcabins.com**

GALENA Stoney Creek Inn ⬛🚻📺♿📺 $$

940 Galena Square Dr., Galena, IL, 61036 **Tel** *815-777-2223/800-659-2220* **Fax** *815-777-6762* **Rooms** *75*

This family-friendly chain hotel is all about rustic charm, from log furniture to theme suites with murals. Rooms include color TV, iron and ironing board, and wireless internet access. Also offers continental breakfast, gift shop, indoor heated pool, whirlpool, and sauna. Children under 17 stay free with adult. **www.stoneycreekinn.com**

LAKE GENEVA Budget Host Diplomat Motel ⬛🚻♿ $

1060 Wells St. Lake Geneva, WI, 53147 **Tel** *262-248-1809/800-264-5678* **Fax** *262-248-2455* **Rooms** *23*

This good-value motel east of Lake Geneva features a large heated outdoor pool plus an expansive recreation area for badminton, volleyball, and picnicking. Comfortably furnished rooms include amenities such as cable TV, microwave, and refrigerator, and pillow-top beds. Small pets are allowed. **www.budgethost-lakegeneva.com**

LAKE GENEVA French Country Inn on the Lake 🚻♿📺 $$

W4190 West End Rd., Lake Geneva, WI, 53147 **Tel** *262-245-5220* **Rooms** *33*

True to its name, this full-service inn is typical of the French country style popular in the area at the turn of the 19th century. With beautifully restored parquet floors, hand-carved staircases and rooms appointed with fireplaces and whirlpool tubs, the inn is a popular destination for Chicagoans on holiday. **www.frenchcountryinn.com**

LAKE GENEVA T.C. Smith Inn Bed and Breakfast 🚻 $$

834 Dodge St., Lake Geneva, WI, 53147 **Tel** *262-248-1097/800-423-0233* **Fax** *262-248-6395* **Rooms** *3*

Within strolling distance of downtown Lake Geneva, this historic, quaint 1865 home offers three comfortable suites elegantly furnished with antiques as well as premium amenities like private bath and whirlpool. Guests enjoy a full breakfast buffet (breakfast in bed is available). **www.tcsmithinn.com**

LAKE GENEVA Best Western Harbor Shores ⬛🚻📺♿📺 $$$

300 Wrigley Dr., Lake Geneva, WI, 53147 **Tel** *262-248-9181/888-746-7371* **Fax** *262-248-1885* **Rooms** *108*

By Lake Geneva, this hotel offers spacious accommodations, indoor/outdoor pools and whirlpool, workout room, and great lake views. Rooms include cable TV, VCR, fridge, microwave, high-speed Internet access, and work area. Includes breakfast. The on-site restaurant Gina's East of Chicago serves deep dish pizza. **www.bestwestern.com**

LAKE GENEVA Geneva Inn on the Lake 🚻📺♿📺 $$$

N2009 S. Lake Shore Dr., Lake Geneva, WI, 53147 **Tel** *262-248-5680/800-441-5881* **Fax** *262-248-5685* **Rooms** *37*

On the site of a former historic lodge and restaurant, this charming inn offers furnished luxury suites and guestrooms, many with excellent lake views. Room amenities can include private balcony or whirlpool tub; wireless Internet access is standard. Coffee and continental buffet breakfast are also included. **www.genevainn.com**

LAKE GENEVA Lake Lawn Resort ⬛🚻📺♿📺 $$$

2400 E Geneva St. Delavan, WI, 53115 **Tel** *262-728-7950/800-338-5253* **Fax** *262-728-2347* **Rooms** *284*

On Delavan Lake shore 12 miles (19 km) west of Lake Geneva, this deluxe, family-friendly resort has an 18-hole golf course, a full-service spa, and indoor/outdoor swimming pools. For kids, there's a video arcade and supervised activities. Cozy, spacious rooms or suites have flat-screen TVs and private balcony. **www.lakelawnresort.com**

LAKE GENEVA Grand Geneva Resort and Spa ⬛🚻📺♿📺 $$$$

7036 Grand Geneva Way, Lake Geneva, WI, 53147 **Tel** *262-248-8811* **Fax** *262-249-4763* **Rooms** *355*

With two championship golf courses, indoor and outdoor swimming pools, tennis courts, an indoor/outdoor water park, and full-service spa, this resort is Lake Geneva at its most luxurious. Comfortable, modern rooms and suites are furnished in rich colors, with private patio/balcony and wireless Internet access. **www.grandgeneva.com**

RESTAURANTS AND CAFES

C hicago is a big city and many establishments, from coffee shops to four-star restaurants, ask big-city prices. However, with thousands of places to eat and drink in Chicago, competition between restaurants is fierce, and visitors can find great food at reasonable prices. The city's immigrant roots mean you can sample dishes

from around the world, from Greek and Italian dishes to Vietnamese and Korean specialties. If you're in Chicago during the annual Taste of Chicago festival *(see p33)*, you will be able to sample cuisine from dozens of Chicago's restaurants. Those in our listings, *Choosing a Restaurant* (pages 152–61), have been selected as among the best Chicago offers.

A waiter serving champagne

CHICAGO'S RESTAURANTS

Chicago restaurants represent the many cultures that make up the city. Some ethnic restaurants are clustered together, such as those in Chinatown *(see p94)* or on Greek Town's Halsted Street. Italian eateries abound on Taylor Street between Halsted and Western Avenues.

However, restaurants on the city's major streets offer a broad range of cuisine. Those in the Loop tend to cater to office workers, though many are staying open later as the area's theater district blossoms. River North is home to many of the city's premier restaurants. Numerous restaurants are situated farther north along Wells Street in Old Town and along nearby Lincoln and Halsted Avenues.

Although there are few strictly vegetarian restaurants in Chicago, most establishments offer vegetarian dishes. The menus at Amitabul and Chicago Diner *(see p159)*,

however, exclusively focus on vegetarian dishes.

Many restaurants are wheelchair accessible *(see p177)*.

RESTAURANT MENUS

Most menus offer three courses: appetizer (starter), entrée (main course), and dessert. Almost all restaurants, except fast-food, serve bread and butter at no charge. Water glasses are filled with (free) tap water; bottled water is usually available.

Most Italian menus list pasta as a first course before a main course of meat or fish, but many restaurants also treat pasta as an entrée.

Coffee and dessert conclude the meal. If you have coffee, your cup may be refilled until you refuse any more.

OTHER PLACES TO EAT

Delicatessens offering soups, salads, and sandwiches are mostly found downtown. Hotdog stands and no-frills

The handsome bar in the Omni Hotel Chicago *(see p144)*

lunch counters are a quick, inexpensive alternative to restaurants.

Most malls have food courts, selling a variety of dishes. Some don't rise above fast-food fare, but a few are excellent, notably Foodlife at Water Tower Place, and 7 on Seven at Marshall Field's.

Brew pubs are popular in Chicago. They serve beer brewed on site, as well as "pub grub" such as hamburgers or fish and chips. Many taverns that appear to be only bars serve steaks, pasta, fish, and sandwiches.

ALCOHOL

The legal drinking age in Chicago is 21 and is strictly enforced. Alcohol is served until 2am most days. Some bars have late-night licenses and pour until 4am. On Sunday, alcohol is not served before 11am.

The grand mahogany and crystal Pump Room *(see p156)*

The welcoming interior of Venus restaurant, Greektown *(see p158)*

HOURS AND PRICES

The city opens early: coffee shops and diners at 6am. Coffee and a roll costs about $3.50. A breakfast of bacon and eggs is about $5 in diners and twice that in hotel restaurants. Sunday brunch, served between 11am and 2pm, costs about $20 per person.

Lunch is offered between 11am and 2pm. Restaurants catering to office workers may offer weekday lunch specials in the $5 to $8 range.

Most restaurants open for dinner at 5:30pm. Kitchens close once business tapers, around 10pm on weekdays, later on weekends. The most difficult time to secure a table is from 7:30pm to 9:30pm.

Salads and appetizers generally cost between $5 and $8 each, entrées between $9 and $25. Many restaurants offer superb wines by the glass for between $5 and $9.

Ethnic restaurants offer good value for the money. Mexican and Thai restaurants are always a good bet, as are pizzerias. Indian and Greek food is often a good bargain.

Some restaurants, especially Thai ones, let you "B.Y.O.B" ("bring your own bottle") of wine. A corkage fee is unlikely unless the restaurant has a bar.

Valet parking, offered by many restaurants, costs between $6 and $8.

PAYING AND TIPPING

The check will be brought to the table after you have finished eating. This is not meant to hurry you. Nearly all restaurants accept major credit cards. Traveler's checks are accepted with appropriate identification. Personal checks are not welcome. *(see p172.)*

A sales tax of 9.75 percent will be added to meal checks in downtown Chicago; 8.75 percent in surrounding areas.

Sign for a Mexican restaurant specializing in seafood

You are expected to tip servers 15 percent for average service, 18 to 20 percent for excellent service. Calculate the tip before tax. The gratuity is usually added to the check for parties of six or more.

An especially helpful wine steward may be tipped $2 or $3. There is no need to tip the host or hostess. Nor will slipping him or her money get you a better table or position on the waiting list.

DRESS CODES

Few restaurants have dress codes. Some hotel and country-club establishments expect men to wear a jacket and tie, and women to be dressed-up. At trendier spots, diners are expected to be fashionably attired. Inquire when making reservations.

RESERVATIONS

Try to make a reservation at any restaurant you plan to eat at unless it's fast-food. If booking more than a day in advance, confirm the booking on the day of your reservation. Some restaurants will not accept reservations for parties of less than six.

Even with a reservation, expect to wait up to an hour at the bar for your table at the most popular restaurants. You may be seated sooner by accepting a table in the bar or kitchen area.

CHILDREN

All restaurants in the city are happy to serve well-behaved children. Many are particularly kid-friendly, supplying high chairs and offering children's portions or menus. However, you may feel uncomfortable bringing children to some of the more fashionable spots. In general, Italian, Greek, Mexican, and chain restaurants are more family-oriented. Children may accompany adults to taverns and pubs if food is ordered.

Goose Island Brewpub, brewing beer on the premises *(see p172)*

Choosing a Restaurant

These restaurants have been selected across a wide price range for their good value, exceptional food, and location. They are listed by area and within these by price, starting with Chicago's Downtown Core and moving on to those farther outside the center. Map references refer to the Street Finder on *pp198–205*.

PRICE CATEGORIES
Prices categories include a three-course meal for one, a glass of house wine, tax, and a 15–20% tip:
$ Under $30
$$ $30–$45
$$$ $45–$65
$$$$ $65–$90
$$$$$ Over $90

DOWNTOWN CORE

Hannah's Bretzel $
180 W Washington St., Chicago, IL, 60602 **Tel** *312-621-1111*   **Map** 3 C1

A popular lunch spot for Loop workers, this sleek, modern storefront specializes in pretzel-like German "bretzels" made into sandwiches with toppings like prosciutto, gruyere cheese, vegetables, and more. The store also offers over 20 different brands of gourmet chocolates from all over the world.

Heaven on Seven $
Garland Building, 111 N Wabash Ave (7th Floor), Chicago, IL, 60602 **Tel** *312-263-6443*   **Map** 4 D1

Gregarious chef/owner Jimmy Bannos has been serving spicy Cajun and Creole fare for lunches and breakfasts here for more than 25 years. Loop breakfast regulars enjoy bananas Foster french toast and sausage omelets; lunch highlights are jambalaya, Louisiana crab cakes, and po'boys. Dinner served every third Friday of the month.

Lou Mitchell's $
565 W Jackson Blvd., Chicago, IL, 60661 **Tel** *312-939-3111*   **Map** 3 B2

One of the city's top breakfast spots, this super-casual, always-buzzing diner has been a Loop staple since 1923. Close to the Sears Tower and the Union Station commuter hub, the place gets packed for its fluffy, stuffed omelets, french toast, hash browns, and lunchtime soups, salads, and sandwiches.

Miller's Pub $
134 Wabash Ave., Chicago, IL, 60603 **Tel** *312-263-4988/312-645-5377*   **Map** 3 C2

Under the El tracks in the heart of the Loop, this classy tavern and restaurant was established in 1935 and has been a favorite with celebrities from Jay Leno to Lou Rawls. The space has oodles of character, with ornate chandeliers and accents of dark wood in a spacious bar and dining room. Classic American menu of ribs, steak, seafood, and spaghetti.

Potbelly Sandwich Works $
190 N State St., Chicago, IL, 60601 **Tel** *312-683-1234*   **Map** 3 C1

Fresh-made sandwiches and salads, hand-dipped shakes and malts, and a relaxed setting filled with antiques has made this growing cheap-eats spot one of the city's most popular. Go for the Wreck, a meat-lover's delight of salami, roast beef, turkey, ham, and Swiss cheese on a chewy Italian roll.

Avec $$
615 W Randolph St., Chicago, IL, 60606 **Tel** *312-377-2002*   **Map** 3 A1

This Randolph Street hot spot is long, tight, and narrow with communal tables, cedar walls, and ceiling, and accents of stainless steel and glass, giving it a chic, spa-like feel. The food is just as cool – a rustic Mediterranean menu of nibbles such as chorizo-stuffed dates and prosciuto di parma. A great wine list.

Italian Village $$
71 W Monroe St., Chicago, IL, 60603 **Tel** *312-332-7005*   **Map** 3 C2

For old-school Chicago Italian, this is the place to go. This complex houses three restaurants: The second-floor Village specializing in big bowls of pasta; the lower-level Cantina Enoteca, for steak and seafood; and the contemporary Vivere, a modern space with dishes such as pappardelle with rabbit and fennel.

Park Grill $$
11 N Michigan Ave., Chicago, IL, 60602 **Tel** *312-521-7275*   **Map** 4 D1

Prime location in the heart of Millennium Park has made this comfortable American spot one of the Loop's most buzzing restaurants. Front windows offer great views of the park's plaza. The creative menu features favorite dishes like thyme-roasted sea scallops, slow-roasted suckling pig, and one of the best burgers in the city.

Atwood Café $$$
1 W Washington St., Chicago, IL, 60602 **Tel** *312-368-1900*   **Map** 3 C1

In the landmark, Daniel Burnham-designed Reliance Building, this relaxed Hotel Burnham restaurant features whimsical decor and playful American fare from chef Heather Terhune. Menu favorites include graham cracker fried calamari, chicken pot pie, and pan-seared scallops with pumpkin risotto.

Key to Symbols *see back cover flap*

Red Light

🧒 ♿ 🍴 V 🍷 $$$

820 W Randolph St., Chicago, IL, 60607 **Tel** *312-733-8880*   **Map** *3 B1*

Creative pan-Asian fare stars at this wildly colorful Randolph Street favorite, whose wide-open dining room is richly decked out. Veteran chef Jackie Shen turns out signature dishes like Jonah crab cake with sweet corn-leek hash, Shanghai-style catfish served whole, and Shen's "chocolate bag" dessert.

Rhapsody

🧒 ♿ 🍴 V 🍷 $$$

65 E Adams St., Chicago, IL, 60603 **Tel** *312-786-9911*   **Map** *4 D2*

For pre-concert dining, this sunny Loop restaurant is the place. A well-heeled crowd gathers for American fare; dishes on the seasonal menu might include blackened short ribs with bamboo shoots or mahi-mahi with dried winter fruit couscous. Lovely outdoor garden is lush and – with the El train overhead – urban.

The Gage

♿ 🍴 $$$

24 S Michigan Ave., Chicago, IL, 60603 **Tel** *312-372-4243*   **Map** *4 D2*

This upscale tavern is a fine destination for a casual lunch of burgers or fish and chips or a special occasion meal of bone-in filet mignon or seared bigeye tuna. Settle in for a drink at the handsome mahogany front bar or grab a table in one of the stylish, intimate dining rooms, which features sage subway tiles and plush, leather booths.

Trattoria No. 10

🧒 ♿ V 🍷 $$$

10 N Dearborn St., Chicago, IL, 60602 **Tel** *312-984-1718*   **Map** *3 C1*

Rich wood accents and warm colors give this contemporary Italian spot a masculine feel. Close to the downtown Theater District, the restaurant is popular as a pre-show destination – and for its weeknight $12 appetizer buffet. Expect a modern take on Italian classics such as pasta with duck *confit* and asparagus.

Blackbird

♿ 🍴 V 🍷 $$$$

619 W Randolph St., Chicago, IL, 60661 **Tel** *312-715-0708*   **Map** *3 A1*

James Beard Award-winning chef and Chicago native Paul Kahan heads up the kitchen at this sleek, minimalist American spot on Randolph Street's Restaurant Row. Pork belly is one of the specialties – try it in a delectable lunch sandwich topped with slaw, or with knackwurst, potatoes, and sauerkraut at dinner.

Marche

🧒 ♿ 🍴 V 🍷 $$$$

833 W Randolph St., Chicago, IL, 60607 **Tel** *312-226-8399*   **Map** *3 B1*

Owned by the Red Light folks, this restaurant boasts similar circus-type decor and a squad of tattooed and pierced servers. All eyes are on the bright, buzzing open kitchen, where executive chef Paul Wildermuth turns out spot-on French bistro fare: escargots, succulent duck *confit* salad, and grilled quail and duck.

Russian Tea Time

🧒 ♿ V $$$$

77 E Adams St., Chicago, IL, 60603 **Tel** *312-360-0000*   **Map** *4 D2*

With its Old World ambiance and elegant red decor, dining at this Loop restaurant can feel like being in a Moscow tea room. Dig into cold borscht and warm potato pancakes with sour cream and applesauce, as well as meat-stuffed *pelmeni* (dumplings) and chicken kebobs. Afternoon tea is served daily 2:30–4:30pm.

Everest

🧒 ♿ V 🍴 🍷 $$$$$

Chicago Stock Exchange, 440 S LaSalle St., 40th Floor, Chicago, IL, 60605 **Tel** *312-663-8920*   **Map** *3 C2*

Forty floors above the city, this exquisite French restaurant is considered one of the world's finest dining experiences. This is special-occasion dining: tuxedoed staff, hushed atmosphere, crystal chandeliers, and a strict jacket-required policy. You can try Master chef Jean Joho's artful cuisine from a choice of tasting menus.

NORTH SIDE

FAR NORTH SIDE M. Henry

🧒 ♿ V $

5707 N Clark St., Chicago, IL, 60660 **Tel** *773-561-1600*

In the blossoming north side neighborhood of Edgewater, this charming storefront restaurant is decked out with painted hanging window frames as cheeky room dividers. The new American menu is just as whimsical, with such items as birds in a basket (two eggs cooked inside bread slices) and blackberry bliss cakes.

FAR NORTH SIDE Hopleaf Bar

♿ V $$$

5148 N Clark St., Chicago, IL, 60640 **Tel** *773-334-9851*

In the airy back dining room of this cozy hangout in Andersonville, a relaxed crowd digs into the celebrated mussels, steamed in white Belgian ale and served in a big kettle with crispy *frites* on the side. Another tempting option is the toasted Nueske ham sandwich with gruyere cheese and apple-tarragon coleslaw. Hundreds of beers on offer, too.

Ed Debevic's

🧒 ♿ V $

640 N Wells St., Chicago, IL, 60620 **Tel** *312-664-1707*   **Map** *1 C4*

One part diner, one part theme restaurant, this '50s-style hangout is all about sassy, entertaining service – your waiter may suddenly hop up on the counter and do a dance routine – offered up with a menu of classic American favorites like hamburgers, nachos, chili, hot dogs, and milkshakes.

Edwardo's Natural Pizza   🚹 ♿ Ⅴ   ⑤
1212 N Dearborn St., Chicago, IL, 60610 **Tel** *312-337-4490*   **Map** 1 C3

This cozy, casual Gold Coast restaurant is worth a visit for the impossibly cheesy stuffed spinach pie flecked with greens and oozing with mozzarella. Other menu offerings include calzones, Italian beef sandwiches, and plates of lasagna, mostaccioli, and spaghetti with pesto sauce.

Giordano's   🚹 ♿ Ⅴ   ⑤
730 N Rush St., Chicago, IL, 60611 **Tel** *312-951-0747*   **Map** 2 D4

Just off the Mag Mile, this spacious, buzzing joint is the city's top destination for "stuffed" pizza, with spinach, sausage, and mushrooms actually stuffed between top and bottom crusts. Aside from pizza, the menu offers fried treats – cheese sticks, mushrooms, zucchini – plus salads, pasta, and sandwiches. Attracts a local crowd.

Goose Island Brewery   🍴🚹♿   ⑤
1800 N Clybourn Ave., Chicago, IL, 60614 **Tel** *312-915-0071*   **Map** 1 A1

Chicago's brewery scene is on the rise, and this award-winning outfit is the leader of the pack. This comfortable, capacious pub offers up signature brews like 312 and Honker's Ale along with a satisfying menu of pub grub – think burgers and wings, *quesadillas,* and chopped salads.

Mr. Beef   🍴🚹♿   ⑤
666 N Orleans St., Chicago, IL, 60610 **Tel** *312-337-8500*   **Map** 1 B3

The city's best Italian beef sandwich can be found at this unassuming River North shack. Step up to the counter and place your order, then head to the "dining room," where blue-collar workers rub elbows with CEOs at long, institutional tables. The beef sandwich is sublime – wet, sloppy, and perfect with a bag of skinny, crispy fries.

Nookies   🚹 ♿ 🍴   ⑤
1746 N Wells St., Chicago, IL, 60614 **Tel** *312-337-2454*   **Map** 1 C1

From Greek omelets to banana nut pancakes, from grilled salmon salads to turkey burgers, plus meatloaf, macaroni and cheese, wraps, pastas and more, this casual, cozy Old Town hangout has long been a neighborhood favorite for reasonably priced breakfasts, lunches, and dinners. Expect a wait for weekend brunch. It's bring your own beer/wine.

Pizza Metro   🚹 ♿ 🍴 Ⅴ   ⑤
1707 W Division St., Chicago, IL, 60622 **Tel** *773-278-1753*

A favorite for late-night, post-bar cravings in Wicker Park, this casual counter provides some great people-watching along with custom-made, by-the-slice thin-crust pizza with creative toppings such as potato rosemary, blue cheese, and zucchini. Also on the menu: pasta dishes such as penne arrabiata and Caesar salads.

Old Jerusalem   🚹 ♿ 🍴 Ⅴ   ⑤
1411 N Wells St., Chicago, IL, 60610 **Tel** *312-944-0459*   **Map** 1 C2

Middle Eastern fare is done well – and cheaply – at this modest storefront restaurant in Old Town. From starters of stuffed grape leaves and creamy hummus with pitta to platters of shwarma and one of the city's finest falafel, the menu has tempting choices, most of which are well under $10.

Pizzeria Uno   🚹 🍴 Ⅴ   ⑤
29 East Ohio St., Chicago, IL, 60611 **Tel** *312-321-1000*   **Map** 2 D4

Set on the garden level of a red brick River North townhouse, the dining room is low-ceilinged, loud, and intimate. Waiting up to two hours for a table is all part of the experience of dining at this legendary restaurant, where Chicago-style deep-dish pizza was born back in 1943.

Twisted Spoke   🍴 Ⅴ   ⑤
501 N Ogden Ave., Chicago, IL, 60622 **Tel** *312-666-1500*

Cheeky biker-bar attitude and surprisingly good comfort food keep the crowds coming to this casual hangout west of downtown. The "Fatboy" burgers are a must-try; other popular items include meatloaf and barbecue pork sandwiches. There is a great rooftop deck in summer, too.

Bandera   ♿ 🎵   ⑤⑤
535 N Michigan Ave., Chicago, IL, 60611 **Tel** *312-644-3524*   **Map** 2 D5

Overlooking Michigan Ave., this second floor hidden gem draws crowds of business folk for relaxed sophistication at lunch and dinner with a simple, comforting menu of traditional American fare. Favorites include rotisserie chicken, fresh-from-the-skillet cornbread, and a "macho" salad with greens, goat cheese, dates, and shredded chicken.

Café Iberico   Ⅴ 🍴   ⑤⑤
737 N LaSalle Dr., 60610 **Tel** *312-573-1510*   **Map** 1 C4

Filled with a lively Spanish-speaking crowd, this traditional tapas restaurant is group-friendly, with large communal tables in several dining rooms. Pitchers of red sangria are the drink of choice; the menu is full of Spanish favorites like potatoes with garlic mayo, baked goat cheese, and grilled shrimp with garlic.

Carmine's   🚹♿🎵🍴Ⅴ🍴   ⑤⑤
1043 North Rush St., Chicago, IL, 60611 **Tel** *312-988-7676*   **Map** 2 D3

This popular Gold Coast spot attracts thirty- and forty-something high rollers with a taste for steak, seafood, and stiff drinks. The main dining room gets loud and boisterous with live entertainment and chatty bar patrons; the upstairs is a mellower scene. Highlights include chicken Vesuvio with garlic.

Key to Price Guide *see p152* **Key to Symbols** *see back cover flap*

Carson's The Place for Ribs ⚐ & ♀ $$

612 N Wells St., Chicago, IL, 60610 **Tel** *312-280-9200* **Map** *1 C4*

Chicago's most famous barbecue restaurant, this legendary River North spot has been serving up plates of sauce-slicked baby back ribs and barbecued pork chops, chicken, and shrimp since 1976. The room has a slightly dated supper club feel, but that has not kept the crowds away.

Fireplace Inn ⚐ & 🔲 $$

1448 N Wells St., Chicago, IL, 60610 **Tel** *312-664-5264* **Map** *1 C2*

An Old Town institution since 1969, this comfy, low-lit dining room is famous for its barbecued baby back ribs. The menu offers plenty of other hearty fare as well – fried calamari, broiled chicken, cheeseburgers, chili, and mashed potatoes with gravy. For a more casual experience, sit on the bright all-weather patio.

Mity Nice Grill ⚐ & Ⅴ $$

835 N Michigan Ave., Water Tower Place, Mezzanine Level, Chicago, IL, 60611 **Tel** *312-335-4745* **Map** *2 D4*

A fine, family-friendly spot in Water Tower Place, this 1940s-style restaurant provides a relaxed alternative to the frenetic shopping center's food court (grab one of the comfy, oversized leather booths). Serves smart updates of classic American fare from Asian tuna nachos to turkey burgers, and classic meatloaf.

Twin Anchors ⚐ 🔲 $$

1655 N Sedgwick St., Chicago, IL, 60614 **Tel** *312-266-1616* **Map** *1 B1*

Tender baby back ribs are the draw at this convivial Old Town tavern, here since 1932. Christmas lights twinkle year-round, and the walls are covered with rave reviews (Frank Sinatra was a fan). The menu offers burgers, chicken sandwiches, and steak, but everybody orders the ribs – with zesty or mild sauce.

Bistro 110 ⚐ & 🎵 🔲 Ⅴ ♀ $$$

110 East Pearson St., Chicago, IL, 60611 **Tel** *312-266-3110* **Map** *2 D4*

Steps from Michigan Avenue is this lively French bistro, where local ladies lunch side-by-side with tourists laden with shopping. Chef Dominique Tougne's cuisine is authentic and reliably good. Signature dishes include artichoke baked with brie, and rich, hearty chicken and morels "Paul Bocuse."

Brasserie Jo ⚐ & 🎵 🔲 Ⅴ ♀ $$$

59 W Hubbard St., Chicago, IL, 60610 **Tel** *312-595-0800* **Map** *1 C5*

With its high ceilings, mosaic tile floor, and gleaming zinc bar, this big, bustling bistro feels like a bit of Paris in the middle of River North. The menu is classic French with an emphasis on the Alsace region: steak *frites*, frog legs Provençal, and coq au vin. Huge profiteroles are worth saving room for. Pets welcome on the outdoor terrace.

Café Spiaggia & Ⅴ ♀ $$$

980 N Michigan Ave., Level 2, Chicago, IL, 60611 **Tel** *312-280-2750* **Map** *2 D3*

Adjacent to four-star Spiaggia, this more casual sibling restaurant offers equally excellent cuisine at reasonable prices. Copies of 15th-century Italian murals; window tables offer pleasant views. Dishes might include Tuscan bean soup; slow-roasted pork with creamy polenta; and gnocchi with wild boar *ragu*.

Cyrano's Bistrot ⚐ & 🎵 🔲 Ⅴ ♀ $$$

546 N Wells St., Chicago, IL, 60610 **Tel** *312-467-0546* **Map** *1 C4*

Decorated in charming country French style with cheerful yellow walls and shelves full of knick-knacks, this rustic River North spot is a cozy, romantic date destination. The menu offers traditional dishes like *vichyssoise* and *confit* of duck leg; the downstairs Café Simone features regular cabaret acts and a special menu.

Frontera Grill ⚐ & 🔲 Ⅴ ♀ $$$

445 N Clark St., Chicago, IL, 60610 **Tel** *312-661-1434* **Map** *1 C5*

One of the nation's most acclaimed Mexican restaurants, this art-filled room is the brainchild of star chef Rick Bayless, who crafts fine regional fare such as duck *enchiladas* and skatewing with cilantro sauce. The packed bar is a great place for margaritas and fresh, chunky *guacamole*.

Le Colonial & 🔲 Ⅴ $$$

937 N Rush St., Chicago, IL, 60611 **Tel** *312-255-0088* **Map** *2 D3*

Rattan chairs, ceiling fans, and lush foliage transport diners to 1920s-era Southeast Asia at this elegant, upscale French-Vietnamese hot spot. Delicate nibbles like *chao tom* (shrimp wrapped around sugar cane) and grilled sesame beef rolls are on offer. Try the chic upstairs lounge for the mango martinis.

Rosebud on Rush 🎵 🔲 Ⅴ ♀ $$$

720 N Rush St., Chicago, IL, 60611 **Tel** *312-266-6444* **Map** *2 D4*

A Chicago classic for traditional Italian fare, this River North restaurant boasts a cozy atmosphere and quality food. Generous starters such as sausage and peppers, and stuffed mushrooms lead into plates of spaghetti with meatballs or *rigatoni alla vodka*; the menu also offers lamb or veal chops and several prime steaks.

Salpicon & 🔲 Ⅴ ♀ $$$

1252 N Wells St., Chicago, IL, 60610 **Tel** *312-988-7811* **Map** *1 C2*

On a quiet strip of Wells Street in Old Town sits this whimsical, upscale Mexican restaurant with bold, colorful decor. Amiable husband-and-wife team Priscila and Vincent Satkoff (she's the chef, he's the wine director) offer flavorful fare, from blue marlin *ceviche* to pork tenderloin with roasted tomato-*chipotle* sauce.

Shaw's Crab House   🚶 ♿ 🎵 Ⓥ 🍷 $$$

21 E Hubbard St., Chicago, IL, 60611 **Tel** *312-527-2722*   **Map** *1 C5*

This sophisticated seafood parlor in River North offers reliably excellent seasonal fare in a loud, buzzing space. Servers hustle between tables in the open room, which is handsomely furnished with red leather booths and rich, dark wood accents. The menu offers sushi plus dozens of other seasonal seafood specials.

West Town Tavern   ♿ 🍷 $$$

1329 W Chicago Ave., Chicago, IL, 60622 **Tel** *312-666-6175*   **Map** *1 A4*

In the up-and-coming area of West Town, this charming neighborhood restaurant showcases chef Susan Goss's contemporary comfort food. There's skillet-roasted mussels with bay leaf, garlic and chilies, farm-raised chicken with fontina, spinach and mushrooms, and slow-cooked duck leg *confit* with saffron rice.

Coco Pazzo   🚶 ♿ Ⓥ 🍷 $$$$

300 W Hubbard St., Chicago, IL, 60610 **Tel** *312-836-0900*   **Map** *1 C5*

River North restaurant's urban, loft-like setting is a perfect pairing with chef Tony Priolo's contemporary Italian fare. Try the *antipasti* – a specialty – with such temptations as wood-roasted oyster mushrooms, fried squash blossoms, and fresh buffalo mozzarella. Entrées include risotto of the day and *osso buco*.

Gibsons Steakhouse   🚶 ♿ 🎵 � Ⓥ 🍷 $$$$

1028 N Rush St., Chicago, IL, 60611 **Tel** *312-266-8999*   **Map** *1 C3*

Autographed photos of rock stars, politicians, and local athletes line the walls here, and with its country-club feel it is considered one of the city's finest steakhouses. The bar is a popular spot for the local martini crowd. Career waiters effortlessly dole out chops and steaks with mammoth baked potatoes and side orders of creamed spinach.

Morton's Steakhouse   ♿ 🍷 $$$$

1050 N State St., Chicago, IL, 60610 **Tel** *312-266-4820*   **Map** *1 C3*

The original location of the legendary chain, this subterranean restaurant is the epitome of the Chicago steakhouse: low light, a buzzing bar scene, leather and dark wood accents, and impeccable service. Everything is enormous – and delicious – from succulent shrimp cocktail to massive beefsteak tomato salads to the steaks. **www.mortons.com**

Pump Room   🚶 ♿ 🎵 🍷 $$$$

1301 N State Pkwy, Chicago, IL, 60610 **Tel** *312-266-0360*   **Map** *1 C2*

Once the ultimate see-and-be-seen restaurant in Chicago, the famed Booth One has seated everyone from Bette Davis to Eddie Murphy. The contemporary American menu offers updated classics such as lobster club sandwich with avocado mayo and beef tartare with crispy capers. At the weekends there is live music and dancing.

Signature Room at the 95th   🚶 ♿ 🎵 Ⓥ 🍷 $$$$

875 N Michigan Ave., John Hancock Center, 95th Floor, Chicago, IL, 60611 **Tel** *312-787-9596*   **Map** *1 C2*

At the top of the John Hancock Center, 1,000 ft (305 m) above ground, this contemporary American restaurant draws in crowds of people for its stunning views. The food is overpriced and mostly so-so, with entrees costing in the $30–$44 range. Best value is the weekday lunch buffet.

Spiaggia   ♿ Ⓥ 🍷 $$$$$

980 N Michigan Ave., Level 2, Chicago, IL, 60611 **Tel** *312-280-2750*   **Map** *2 D3*

The finest Italian restaurant in the city, and a favorite with President Obama, this special-occasion spot offers chef Tony Mantuano's award-winning cuisine, impeccable service, and lovely lake views in a hushed atmosphere. Choose a multiple-course tasting menu (around $135) or dishes such as wood-roasted sea scallops. Strict dress code.

Tru   ♿ Ⓥ 🍷 $$$$$

676 N St. Clair St., Chicago, IL, 60611 **Tel** *312-202-0001*   **Map** *2 D4*

Style meets substance at this playful, pricey Streeterville restaurant from top chefs Gale Gand and Rick Tramonto. Works of modern art – including one of Warhol's "Marilyn" pieces – hang on the stark white walls. Food presentation is intricate – caviar on a mini glass staircase – and service is immaculate.

SOUTH LOOP AND NEAR SOUTH SIDE

Eleven City Diner   🚶 ♿ 🚑 Ⓥ $

1112 S Wabash Ave., Chicago, IL, 60605 **Tel** *312-212-1112*   **Map** *4 D4*

In a surprisingly classy, comfortable space, this Jewish-style deli and restaurant has high ceilings, mirrors, and supple leather booths. All-day breakfast features lox and bagels, omelets, and Belgian waffles; the kitchen also whips up burgers, big salads, pasta, steaks, and mixes classic shakes, malts, and egg creams.

Manny's Cafeteria and Delicatessen   🚶 ♿ Ⓥ $

1141 S Jefferson St., Chicago, IL, 60607 **Tel** *312-939-2855*   **Map** *3 A4*

A favorite for off-duty police officers and neighborhood old-timers, this old-fashioned cafeteria has been a South Side staple since 1942 and serves up what is widely considered the best corned beef sandwich in the city. Other popular plates include breakfasts of omelets and pancakes plus lunch items like chicken salad, burgers, and daily specials.

Orange 🚶 ♿ Ⓥ ⑤

75 W Harrison St., Chicago, IL, 60605 **Tel** *312-447-1000*   **Map** *3 C3*

Breakfast food gets creative at this sunny South Loop restaurant. Start off with orange-infused coffee or a fruit and vegetable juice offering, then progress to "frushi" (fruit rolled *maki*-style) or fun plates of "green eggs and ham" (basil-flecked scrambled eggs with roasted tomatoes, mozzarella, and diced pancetta). Waits are long on weekends.

Zapatista ♿ 🍴 Ⓨ ⑤⑤

1307 S Wabash Ave., Chicago, IL, 60605 **Tel** *312-435-1307*   **Map** *4 D4*

Sea scallops with tomatillo-avocado salsa; grilled *tilapia tacos* with purple pickle relish; and sides of creamy *chipotle* spinach are a few of the creative Mexican plates that highlight the menu at this rustic South Loop restaurant. The dining room features warm tones of gold and burnt orange and accents of stone and dark wood.

Custom House ♿ Ⓨ ⑤⑤⑤

500 S Dearborn St., Chicago, IL, 60605 **Tel** *312-523-0200*   **Map** *3 C3*

Award-winning chef Shawn McClain has won raves for his subdued yet stylish take on the Chicago steakhouse. The dining room is decorated in muted reds and ivory tones; the meat-focused menu offers elegant dishes such as roasted quail with onion beignet, shiitake mushroom soup with parmesan gnocchi.

Opera ♿ Ⓥ Ⓨ ⑤⑤⑤

1301 S Wabash Ave., Chicago, IL, 60605 **Tel** *312-461-0161*   **Map** *4 D4*

Chinese fare gets a funky, modern treatment at this bold, colorful restaurant from the owners of Marché, Gioco, and Red Light. Walls are papered with Chinese-language news clippings. The dynamic menu pops with flavor, from crisp Maine lobster spring roll to steamed cod with sesame oil and zippy firecracker chicken.

Gioco ♿ 🍴 Ⓥ Ⓨ ⑤⑤⑤⑤

1312 S Wabash Ave., Chicago, IL, 60605 **Tel** *312-939-3870*   **Map** *4 D4*

One of the city's hippest Italian spots, Gioco has a loud, trendy crowd enjoying the modern Tuscan- and Umbrian-inspired fare. Think octopus *carpaccio*; pappardelle with red wine-braised wild boar; truffle-scented scallops with white polenta and wild mushroom sauce, and flourless chocolate cake.

Emperor's Choice 🚶 ♿ Ⓥ ⑤

2238 S Wentworth Ave., Chicago, IL, 60616 **Tel** *312-225-8800*   **Map** *5 C2*

Adventurous appetites can go for shark's fin soup, marinated jellyfish or cuttlefish at this modest Cantonese place in Chinatown, but the menu also has Americanized staples such as egg *foo yung* and General Tso's chicken and shrimp fried rice. Try the lunch (a great deal at under $10) of soup, fried or steamed rice, entrée, hot tea, and almond cookie.

Lao Sze Chuan 🚶 ♿ ⑤

2172 S Archer Ave., Chicago, IL, 60616 **Tel** *312-326-5040*   **Map** *5 B2*

In the Chinatown Square shopping center, this popular Szechuan storefront restaurant of chef Tony Hu's, host of a local Chinese-language TV cooking show, is locally renowned for the authenticity of its cuisine. Try the ginger-spiked calamari, spicy pan-fried sliced pork, and tender smoked tea duck. (Hu has two other restaurants in the same shopping center.)

The Phoenix 🚶 ♿ Ⓥ ⑤

2131 S Archer Ave., Chicago, IL, 60616 **Tel** *312-328-0848*   **Map** *5 B2*

The place for *dim sum* in Chinatown, on weekends from 8am this big, banquet hall of a dining room is packed, when carts laden with dishes like dumplings, spareribs, salt and pepper calamari and more start rolling through. Other favorites include "bird's nest" shrimp and steamed sea bass. Downstairs, there's the more casual Dumpling House.

South Coast ♿ ⑤⑤

1700 South Michigan Ave., Chicago, IL, 60616 **Tel** *312-662-1700*   **Map** *4 D5*

The second outpost of a popular Bucktown restaurant, this minimalist BYOB sushi spot boasts a dynamic menu of small plates and specialty *maki* and *nigiri*. Signature dishes include the sunrise *maki* with ginger-seared tuna and mint wrapped with mango, and the Maine, with cooked lobster, ginger mayo and salmon roe topped with cucumber.

Chicago Firehouse 🚶 ♿ 🎵 🍴 Ⓨ ⑤⑤⑤

1401 South Michigan Ave., Chicago, IL, 60605 **Tel** *312-786-1401*   **Map** *4 D5*

Once the home of Chicago Firehouse Engine Co. 104, this South Loop building has been transformed into one of the area's more handsome restaurants. Guests can stand at the bar or head into the comfortable dining room for dynamic takes on classic American fare: Oysters Rockefeller, blackened catfish, and slow-cooked pot roast.

Mulan ⑤⑤⑤

2017 S Wells St., Chicago, IL, 60616 **Tel** *312-842-8282*   **Map** *5 C1*

A recent arrival to the Chinatown dining scene, this contemporary, stylish space boasts chocolate-colored banquettes, mosaic tile accents, and an undulating ceiling panel. The Asian-inspired menu includes dishes like grilled Wagyu beef with lemongrass marinade, wasabi pea-crusted salmon, and seafood bouillabaisse served on glass noodles.

Room 21 ♿ 🍴 Ⓨ ⑤⑤⑤⑤

2110 S Wabash Ave., Chicago, IL, 60616 **Tel** *312-328-1198*   **Map** *6 D1*

This plush, contemporary supper club has a bordello-esque feel, with heavy velvet curtains, hand-painted wall coverings, and rich, dark wood, and wrought-iron accents. The menu offers hearty, updated American classics, from mini burgers made with barbecued short ribs to roasted halibut with corn puree and mushrooms.

SOUTH SIDE

Caffe Florian   🏃 ♿ Ⓥ   Ⓢ
1450 E 57th St., Chicago, IL, 60637 **Tel** *773-752-4100*   **Map** *8 D2*

Popular with a budget-conscious university crowd, this super-casual Hyde Park spot serves up hearty, reasonably priced salads, sandwiches, pasta, and pizza. Popular menu items include chicken *quesadillas*, vegetarian garden wraps, Italian beef sandwiches, and thin-crust or pan pizza. Bring your own wine or beer with no corkage fee.

Dixie Kitchen and Bait Shop   🏃 ♿   Ⓢ
5225 S Harper Ave., Chicago, IL, 60615 **Tel** *773-363-4943*   **Map** *8 D2*

From fried green tomatoes and meaty, rich gumbo to fried oyster po'boys, crawfish *étouffée* and jambalaya, this quirky Hyde Park spot offers an authentic taste of southern US cooking. The space is a comfortable hodgepodge of petrol station signs and other Americana, service is leisurely, and there is often a wait at lunch.

Medici on 57th   🏃 ♿ 🍴 Ⓥ   Ⓢ
1327 E 57th St., Chicago, IL, 60637 **Tel** *773-667-7394*   **Map** *8 D4*

Bring your own beer or wine to this University of Chicago student hangout, which has cheap prices and a low-key atmosphere, including cozy, graffiti-covered wooden booths and a leafy rooftop deck that is perfect for lounging. Pizza is the specialty, available pan-style or thin-crust. Their bakery next door whips up sandwiches and coffee to go.

Valois   🏃 ♿ Ⓥ   Ⓢ
1518 E 53rd St., Chicago, IL, 60615 **Tel** *773-667-0647*   **Map** *8 E2*

A bustling, super-casual restaurant popular with Hyde Park families and University of Chicago faculty and students. This cheerful cafeteria offers comfort foods served up in hearty portions like French toast, omelets, and other breakfast fare, popular all day long, as well as mac and cheese, deli sandwiches, ribs and baked chicken.

La Petite Folie   ♿ Ⓥ 🍴   ⓈⓈⓈ
1504 East 55th St., Chicago, IL, 60615 **Tel** *773-493-1394*   **Map** *7 B3*

Hyde Park's best fine dining, this intimate French restaurant is in the courtyard of the Hyde Park Shopping Center, close to the University of Chicago and the Museum of Science and Industry. Dishes on the classic menu include wild mushroom crepes and beef bourguignon. Three-course fixed-price menu nightly from 5–6:30pm.

FARTHER AFIELD

BUCKTOWN/WICKER PARK Rodan   ♿ Ⓥ   Ⓢ
1530 N Milwaukee Ave., Chicago, IL, 60622 **Tel** *773-276-7036*

Rodan buzzes with lounge-goers late into the night, but the secret here is its surprisingly unique pan-Asian dinner and brunch menus. Japanese-style curry entrées, spicy maki rolls and wasabi fries are as inviting as the hip sound-track and seductive, dimly-lit teakwood dining booths.

BUCKTOWN/WICKER PARK Café Bolero   🎵 Ⓥ   ⓈⓈ
2252 N Western Ave., Chicago, IL, 60647 **Tel** *773-227-9000*

This rollicking Cuban restaurant is a good, cheap place for tasty tapas. The front room has a casual diner feel; for a more intimate vibe, move to the low-lit back area, which hosts regular live Cuban jazz and salsa. The menu offers Latin favorites *empanadillas*, ham *croquetas*, *ropa vieja* sandwiches, stuffed peppers, and more.

BUCKTOWN/WICKER PARK Spring   ♿ Ⓥ 🍴   ⓈⓈⓈⓈ
2039 W North Ave., Chicago, IL, 60647 **Tel** *773-395-7100*

Set in a former Wicker Park bathhouse, this cool, contemporary fine dining spot features the cuisine of award-winning chef Shawn McClain in a soothing space done up in mellow tones with organic materials and a Zen garden. The Asian-influenced American menu has a particular emphasis on seafood.

GREEKTOWN Venus   ♿ 🎵 Ⓥ 🍴   ⓈⓈ
820 W Jackson St., Chicago, IL, 60607 **Tel** *312-714-1001*   **Map** *3 A2*

Just off Halsted Street, this addition to the Greektown dining scene specializes in both Greek and Cypriot food. The space is warm and welcoming, with a bar designed to look like an ancient warship. Don't miss signature dishes *afelia* (red wine-marinated pork) and *kleftiko* (slow-baked lamb). Live music on weekend evenings.

LAKEVIEW Ann Sather   🏃 ♿ Ⓥ   Ⓢ
929 W Belmont Ave., Chicago, IL, 60657 **Tel** *773-348-2378*

Famous for its sweet cinnamon rolls, this laid-back diner has been a Lakeview favorite since 1945. Originally a Swedish café, the menu still offers Scandinavian specialties such as pancakes with lingonberries, pickled herring, limpa bread, and Swedish meatballs. These days it is more American classics: omelets, burgers, and salads.

Key to Price Guide *see p152* **Key to Symbols** *see back cover flap*

LAKEVIEW Chicago Diner 🏃 �️ Ⓥ ⑤

3411 N Halsted St., Chicago, IL, 60657 **Tel** *773-935-6696*

Vegetarians and vegans flock to this casual storefront in the heart of Boystown for filling, meat- and dairy-free fare. Plates of potstickers, hummus, and spinach portabella *quesadillas* are popular, as are "meat" dishes like lasagna bolognese with tofu-basil ricotta, chili mac with spicy *seitan*, and "chickin" parmigiana.

LAKEVIEW erwin 🏃 ♿ ♟ ⑤⑤

2925 N Halsted St., Chicago, IL, 60657 **Tel** *773-528-7200*

Regional American cuisine with a focus on seasonal ingredients is the mantra at this intimate but bustling room from Chef Erwin Dreschler and his wife Cathy. Offerings are creative but unpretentious: onion tart with caramelized onions and blue cheese, Nova Scotia salmon with Brussels sprouts and prosciutto. Excellent Sunday brunch, too.

LAKEVIEW Mia Francesca 🏃 ♿ 🚍 Ⓥ ♟ ⑤⑤

3311 N Clark St., Chicago, IL, 60657 **Tel** *773-281-3310*

Rustic fare and casual, contemporary ambiance have made this Lakeview spot one of the city's most popular Italian joints. The menu is basic but well executed: bruschetta, fried calamari and *carpaccio*, four-cheese pizzas, goat cheese salads, homemade pastas, and entrées such as veal medallions with wild mushrooms.

LAKEVIEW Kit Kat Lounge & Supper Club ♿ 🎵 🚍 Ⓥ ⑤⑤⑤

3700 N Halsted St., Chicago, IL, 60613 **Tel** *773-525-1111*

An eclectic comfort food menu and sleek, South Beach-inspired atmosphere draws a mixed gay-straight crowd of Boystown professionals. Female impersonators strut and lip-synch during regular numbers throughout the evening while guests nosh on signature dishes like coconut crab cakes and ginger-rubbed tuna.

LINCOLN PARK Café Ba-Ba-Reeba! 🏃 ♿ 🎵 🚍 Ⓥ ♟ ⑤

2024 N Halsted St., Chicago, IL, 60614 **Tel** *773-935-5000*

Perfect for group dining, this colorful Lincoln Park restaurant is known for its good Spanish tapas and large outdoor patio. In addition to traditional tapas items like beef *empanadas*, and goat cheese in tomato sauce, the menu offers skewers of shrimp, chicken, pork, or beef, five kinds of paella, and six types of sangria.

LINCOLN PARK Dunlays on Clark ♿ Ⓥ ⑤

2600 N Clark St., Chicago, IL, 60614 **Tel** *773-883-6000*

One in a small empire of dining establishments, Dunlays serves casual modern American fare in a laid-back, pub atmosphere. Chicken and fish dishes are the specialties here, though the pork and beef are good too. The veggie burgers are among the best in town.

LINCOLN PARK R.J. Grunts 🏃 Ⓥ ⑤

2056 N Lincoln Park West, Chicago, IL, 60614 **Tel** *773-929-5363*

Close to the Lincoln Park Zoo, this comfortable family restaurant is a tempting spot to stop for a casual meal. The atmosphere is a throwback to the 1960s and 1970s with weathered wooden booths. The menu is just as classic, with a big salad bar and an extensive selection of burgers, chicken sandwiches, and shakes and malts.

LINCOLN PARK The Wieners Circle 🍽 🚍 ♿ ⑤

2622 N Clark St., Chicago, IL, 60614 **Tel** *773-477-7444*

This late-night classic is one of the best places to get a Chicago-style hot dog with all the toppings. It is little more than a shack – no seating aside from a few counter stools – but it is worth a visit for the hot dogs and gooey cheese fries, not to mention the comically belligerent staff, famous for engaging in verbal warfare with the clientele.

LINCOLN PARK Vinci 🏃 ♿ Ⓥ ♟ ⑤⑤

1732 N Halsted St., Chicago, IL, 60614 **Tel** *312-266-1199*

There is a warm, inviting vibe at this popular pre-theater destination down the street from several theaters. Chef Paul LoDuca's rustic Italian menu includes baked artichoke with tomato-basil sauce, grilled calamari, handmade pastas, and mains such as veal saltimbocca and rosemary-skewered shrimp.

LINCOLN PARK Geja's Café ♿ 🎵 Ⓥ ♟ ⑤⑤⑤

340 W Armitage Ave., Chicago, IL, 60614 **Tel** *773-281-9101*

The site of countless special occasion dinners, this subterranean fondue spot is one of the city's most romantic restaurants. The space is low-lit and low-ceilinged; live flamenco guitar adds to the ambiance. Choose from different fondue combos, dipping skewers of meat, vegetables, or fruit into pots of hot oil, cheese or chocolate.

LINCOLN PARK Sweets & Savories ♿ ♟ ⑤⑤⑤

1534 W Fullerton Ave., Chicago, IL, 60614 **Tel** *773-281-6778*

Chef/owner David Richards tweaks traditional French cuisine with delicious results in this homey, stylish space. The intimate dining room is decorated simply; the menu offers delights such as *salade lyonnaise*, pan-roasted grouper with black truffle butter, and pumpkin cake with white chocolate ice cream.

LINCOLN PARK North Pond 🏃 ♿ 🚍 ♟ ⑤⑤⑤⑤

2610 N Cannon Dr., Chicago, IL, 60614 **Tel** *773-477-5845*

In the middle of Lincoln Park, this contemporary restaurant is in one of the loveliest settings in the city. The airy, light space is decorated in Arts and Crafts style. Award-winning chef Bruce Sherman uses fresh, seasonal ingredients in dishes such as apple-leek soup, gingerbread-crusted venison, and wine-poached turbot.

LINCOLN PARK Alinea ♿ V ♨ ⑤⑤⑤⑤⑤
1723 N Halsted St., Chicago, IL, 60614 **Tel** *312-867-0110*   **Map** *1 A1*

Named the best restaurant in the nation by *Gourmet* magazine, this inconspicuous place showcases the cuisine of chef Grant Achatz. Dishes here engage all the senses, from the smell of juniper that accompanies the duck to the white truffle ravioli that explodes in the mouth. Tasting menu of 12 or 24 courses only.

LINCOLN PARK Charlie Trotter's ♿ V ♨ ⑤⑤⑤⑤⑤
816 West Armitage Ave., Chicago, IL, 60614 **Tel** *773-248-6228*

Elegant atmosphere, impeccable service, and chef Charlie Trotter's cuisine have made this one of the world's most celebrated restaurants. Daily-changing tasting menus might include butternut squash soup with kaffir lime, roasted monkfish tail with yellowfoot mushrooms. Atmosphere friendly but formal; jacket required.

NEAR WEST SIDE Francesca's On Taylor ♿ ♿ V ♨ ⑤⑤
1400 W Taylor St., Chicago, IL, 60607 **Tel** *312-829-2828*

A sibling of Lakeview's Mia Francesca, this restaurant scores with the same formula: Hearty Northern Italian fare in a warm, welcoming environment. Dishes include calamari, four-cheese pizza, linguine *primavera*, and veal medallions with wild mushrooms. A children's menu offers basic pasta, pizza, and chicken plates.

NEAR WEST SIDE Greek Islands ♿ ♿ ♨ V ♨ ⑤⑤
200 S Halsted St., Chicago, IL, 60661 **Tel** *312-782-9855*

This always-buzzing, upscale but casual Greektown favorite draws crowds of local businessmen, families, and neighborhood loft-dwellers. The menu is classic Greek: Plates of tangy feta cheese, grilled octopus, stuffed grape leaves, and *moussaka*. Set-price family-style menus are the best value here.

NEAR WEST SIDE The Parthenon ♿ ♿ V ⑤⑤
314 S Halsted St., Chicago, IL, 60661 **Tel** *312-726-2407*

A Greektown institution since 1968, this convivial, sprawling restaurant was the birthplace of flaming *saganaki*, fried cheese that is flambéed tableside with a shout of "Opa!" Other favorites on the menu include spinach-cheese pies, house-made sausage, roast leg of lamb, shishkabob, and tiramisu.

NEAR WEST SIDE The Rosebud ♿ ♨ V ♨ ⑤⑤
1500 W Taylor St., Chicago, IL, 60607 **Tel** *312-942-1117*

This Little Italy joint boasts the same top-notch Italian cuisine as Rosebud on Rush, but with a dash more sophistication. Dark woods and leather accents set an upscale, supper-club scene. The menu offers hearty signature dishes such as baked clams, *panzanella* salad, and chicken Vesuvio with roasted potatoes and peas.

NORTHWEST SIDE Eli's Cheesecake World ♿ ♿ ⑤
6701 W Forest Preserve Dr., Chicago, IL, 60634 **Tel** *773-736-3417*

Eli's Cheesecake has been a Chicago tradition for more than 60 years. Visitors can tour the bakery (weekdays, by reservation only), grab a quick lunch in the on-site Cheesecake Café, or purchase cakes – from plain to chocolate chip, Key lime to white chocolate raspberry – and other baked goods in the retail store.

NORTHWEST SIDE Arun's ♿ V ♨ ⑤⑤⑤⑤
4156 N Kedzie Ave., Chicago, IL, 60618 **Tel** *773-539-1909*

This intimate Thai restaurant is worth the trek to the far northwest side. The elegant space is divided into cozy alcoves. Servers quiz guests on their spice tolerance and dietary restrictions; the result is a customized tasting menu of 12 delectable courses, from delicate spring rolls to fried walleye pike with sweet-and-sour rhubarb.

OAK PARK Café Winberie ♿ ♿ V ♨ ⑤
151 N Oak Park Ave., Oak Park, IL, 60301 **Tel** *708-386-2600*

A bright, busy restaurant and wine bar on Oak Park's main strip, this is one of Oak Park's top dining options. Antiques give the space a charming feel; the eclectic menu is casual but creative, with fried calamari, niçoise salads and parmesan shrimp po'boys, plus seafood, steak, pasta. Extensive wine list.

BEYOND CHICAGO

EVANSTON Blind Faith Café ♿ ♿ V ⑤
525 Dempster St., Evanston, IL, 60201 **Tel** *847-328-6875*

Spacious wooden booths, large picture windows, and walls hung with colorful quilts make this casual vegetarian restaurant pleasant. The menu features breakfast, lunch, and dinner, with items like tofu scrambled eggs, pear and goat cheese salad, *seitan fajitas*, veggie burgers, and more. A self-service café sells food to go.

EVANSTON Dave's Italian Kitchen ♿ ♿ V ⑤
1635 Chicago Ave., Evanston, 60201 **Tel** *847-864-6000*

Checkered tablecloths and beat-up wooden booths are enjoyed by a budget-conscious crowd of students and families in this subterranean dining room. Prices are cheap, and portions are huge. Start with garlic bread or a Caesar salad, then move on to pizza, a *calzone*, or pasta dishes like *fettucine alfredo*.

Key to Price Guide *see p152* **Key to Symbols** *see back cover flap*

EVANSTON Lucky Platter
514 Main St., Evanston, IL, 60202 **Tel** *847-869-4064*

The menu at this quirky, casual café is charmingly chaotic, offering everything from breakfast omelets and apple ricotta blintzes to fried green tomatoes, horseradish crusted tilapia, tandoori chicken sandwiches, burgers and salads. Reasonable prices and relaxed ambiance, making this a favorite hangout for students.

EVANSTON Tommy Nevin's Pub
1454 Sherman Ave., Evanston, IL, 60201 **Tel** *847-869-0450*

Live music, reliably good pub grub, and a convivial Irish pub atmosphere draw a casual mix of college students and locals to this popular tavern and eatery. Behind a bold red facade, the multi-room space is decked out with dark wood accents and exposed brick walls dotted with photos and Guinness posters.

EVANSTON Davis Street Fishmarket
501 Davis St., Evanston, IL, 60201 **Tel** *847-869-3474*

This bustling family restaurant is a top spot for seafood in Evanston. A raw bar offers fresh oysters, clams, and peel-and-eat shrimp. The menu features blackened calamari, Chesapeake Bay crab cakes, and daily flown-in fish, from king salmon to Lake Superior whitefish. For kids, there is fried shrimp and fish and chips.

EVANSTON Koi
624 Davis St., Evanston, IL, 60201 **Tel** *847-866-6969*

This sophisticated pan-Asian spot has exposed brick walls and lush foliage, and a candlelit *sake* lounge. The menu ranges from Chinese to sushi, with classic starters like springrolls, dumplings, and wonton soup, plus main dishes of Mongolian chicken, Peking duck, and sesame shrimp along with a full sushi menu of *maki* rolls and *nigiri*.

EVANSTON The Stained Glass
1735 Benson Ave., Evanston, IL, 60201 **Tel** *847-864-8600*

An upscale, but casual, wine-centric destination, with a seasonal contemporary American menu and an expansive wine list, including 32 selections by the glass. There are wine-friendly nibbles plus hearty dishes, such as pork chops with savory brioche and date bread pudding, and Atlantic salmon with potato and horseradish croquettes.

EVANSTON Va Pensiero
1566 Oak Ave., Evanston, IL, 60201 **Tel** *847-475-7779*

One of Evanston's most elegant restaurants, this hushed, upscale Italian spot on the lower level of the Margarita inn boasts an award-winning, all-Italian wine list that complements chef Eric Hammond's fine, seasonal fare; from lamb tartare with quail egg to hand-rolled *cavatelli* with tuna, and polenta-crusted sea scallops.

GALENA One Eleven Main
111 N Main St., Galena, IL, 61036 **Tel** *815-777-8030*

This restaurant offers big portions of local fare using recipes inspired by the heartland: beef, pork, fish, and veggie dishes are served with a smile. Among the traditional Midwest favorites are chicken and mashed potatoes, meatloaf, stroganoff, mac 'n' cheese, and goulash, all made using the finest regional produce.

GALENA Vinny Vanucchi's Little Italy
201 S Main St., Galena, IL, 61036 **Tel** *815-777-8100*

Checkered tablecloths and Italian signs on the walls sets an Old World scene at this restaurant, which sprawls over several rooms and an outdoor patio. Dishes include fried ravioli, and Italian meatballs, also burgers, pasta dishes like fettucine carbonara and stuffed shells, and entrées chicken parmigiano and veal marsala.

GALENA Fried Green Tomatoes
213 N Main St., Galena, IL, 61036 **Tel** *815-777-3938*

Set in an historic 1838 building, this charming storefront on Galena's Main Street is now an upscale-casual, Italian-inspired restaurant popular for special-occasion dining. Must-try dishes include the namesake appetizer, plus pasta such as fettucine alfredo, chicken or veal marsala, and lobster ravioli. Award-winning wine list.

LAKE GENEVA The Cactus Club
430 Broad St., Lake Geneva, WI, 53147 **Tel** *262-248-1999*

A wooden bridge leads to this festive, colorful restaurant with an expansive menu of Mexican and American dishes making it a favorite in downtown Lake Geneva. Expect Mexican standards like *quesadillas, nachos, enchiladas,* and *fajitas.* Weekdays 3–7pm: Drink specials and half-price appetizers in the bar.

LAKE GENEVA Kirch's at the French Country Inn
Highway 50 West, W4190 West End Road, Lake Geneva, WI, 53147 **Tel** *262-245-5756*

On the south shore of Lake Como north of Lake Geneva, this fine restaurant has lovely panoramic lake views and features upscale, eclectic cuisine. The pricey menu might include starters of escargots with garlic butter or bacon-wrapped lobster tail, plus entrées such as Cajun-seared salmon filet, and parmesan-crusted veal.

LAKE GENEVA The Grandview at the Geneva Inn
N2009 S Lake Shore Drive, Lake Geneva, WI, 53147 **Tel** *262-248-5690*

This special-occasion restaurant on the shores of Lake Geneva offers creative, upscale American fare and a sophisticated atmosphere. Jumbo crab cakes, grilled beef tenderloin, and pan-roasted Alaskan halibut are on the menu. Half-price wine and tempting appetizers are served daily from 4–6pm.

SHOPS AND MARKETS

Shopping, rather than sports, may well be the major pastime of Chicagoans. The sheer number of shops in the small area around Michigan Avenue alone makes Chicago a world-class shopping destination. Everything from basic necessities to outrageous luxuries can be found at

Clock at Macy's, a favorite meeting spot

Chicago's boutiques, specialty shops, and legendary department stores. No matter what your passion, you will find a merchant in Chicago who shares it. Many of the shops listed on pages 164–7 will take you off the beaten track into the city's many distinct and charming neighborhoods.

Ghirardelli Chocolate Shop and Soda Fountain

WHEN TO SHOP

Most chain stores are open seven days a week, from 10am to 6pm. Some shops open an hour later and close an hour earlier on Sundays. Malls and shopping centers usually stay open evenings as well as on Sundays.

Neighborhood shops, antique dealers, vintage-clothing stores, and galleries keep more relaxed hours. Many are closed on Mondays and Tuesdays and may not open until noon on other days.

Shops are blissfully empty on weekday mornings, gradually becoming crowded as the evening approaches. On the weekends, downtown shops and malls are packed.

SALES

Pre-season sales, end-of-season sales, 13-hour sales, Mother's Day sales – it is easy to find some kind of sale each day of the year.

Many sales, especially when shops want to clear their racks to make way for the next season's merchandise, offer great bargains.

Be wary of "going out of business" sales – some have been going on for years. However, some are legitimate sales; ask at nearby stores.

TAXES

Sales tax in Chicago is 10.25 percent and is added to everything except newspapers, magazines, and groceries. Sales tax is not refundable to visitors from overseas. However, if the shop ships your purchase to an address outside Chicago or Illinois,

you can avoid city and/or state sales tax. Foreign visitors may be required to pay duty on the purchase once they arrive home.

PAYMENT

Major credit cards are accepted in most Chicago stores, as are bank debit cards, though small businesses may have a minimum-price policy (usually a $10 minimum) for purchases paid for this way. Traveler's checks must be accompanied by identification. Personal checks are discouraged; foreign currency is never accepted. A few smaller shops are still run on a cash-only basis.

RETURNS

Be sure you understand the shop's return policy before you make an important purchase. Keep your receipt as a proof of purchase.

Each store sets its own return-and-exchange policies; they are generally posted at the cash register. Some shops will give a full refund with no

Vibrant window signs brightening a storefront in Chinatown

Sunday morning in the busy Maxwell Street Market *(see p165)*

Water Tower Place, with eight levels of boutiques and stores

questions asked, whereas other shops maintain an all-sales-are-final policy. Some places offer an in-shop credit rather than a refund. Sale items are often not returnable.

MALLS AND SHOPPING CENTERS

Chicago's malls come in two varieties. Suburban malls resemble small cities surrounded by vast parking lots. City malls tend to rise upward from the ground. The most notable of these vertical malls are on the Magnificent Mile (see pp60–61).

Water Tower Place contains major department stores, eight levels with more than 100 boutiques and specialty shops, and a movie theater.

Across the street is **The 900 Shops**, an elegant mall on seven levels with over 70 luxury shops and boutiques, including Gucci,

MaxMara, Montblanc, and Bloomingdale's, as well as numerous restaurants and cafés.

Westfield North Bridge has world-class specialty shops, more than twenty restaurants and five hotels.

A block south of these three powerhouse malls is **Chicago Place**, home to the flagship Midwest location of Saks Fifth Avenue, among other stylish shops.

DEPARTMENT STORES

Many department stores have a prominent street location. **Macy's** (formerly Marshall Field's; see pp50–51) is the benchmark for luxurious department stores across the country. Don't leave Chicago without a box of its Frango mints.

Seattle-based **Nordstrom**, which is known for its quality clothing and shoes for men, women, and children, has its flagship Midwest store on the Magnificent Mile.

Posh **Neiman Marcus** bills itself as a world-famous specialty store and prides itself on its personal service and exclusivity. The store specializes in clothing and accessories by many top fashion designers. Its epicurean shop offers delectable items, including caviar and wine.

Saks Fifth Avenue attracts a ritzy clientele with its selection of designer and private-label clothing.

Bloomingdale's is also stylish but less pricey. It has a great selection of fashionable clothing and shoes, and a floor devoted to housewares. Watch for its sales, which are legendary.

PARKING

Downtown parking lots are expensive, and street parking is almost nonexistent (see p189). Many department stores offer discounted parking in their lots, but the few dollars saved are rarely worth the time spent in the parking maze. The CTA (Chicago Transit Authority) offers convenient public transit (see p189).

An interior-furnishings shop on the street level of the historic Santa Fe Building (see p45)

DIRECTORY

MALLS AND SHOPPING CENTERS

Chicago Place
700 N Michigan Ave.
Map 2 D4.
Tel 266-7710.
www.chicago-place.com

The 900 Shops
900 N Michigan Ave.
Map 2 D4.
Tel 915-3916.
www.shop900.com

Water Tower Place
835 N Michigan Ave.
Map 2 D4.
Tel 440-3166.
www.shopwatertower.com

Westfield North Bridge
520 N Michigan Ave.
Map 2 D5. **Tel** 327-2300.

DEPARTMENT STORES

Bloomingdale's
The 900 Shops,
900 N Michigan Ave.

Map 2 D4.
Tel 440-4887.
www. bloomingdales.com

Macy's
(formerly Marshall Field's)
111 N State St.
Map 4 D1.
Tel 781-1000.
Water Tower Place,
835 N Michigan Ave.
Map 2 D4.
Tel 335-7700.
www.macys.com

Neiman Marcus
737 N Michigan Ave.
Map 2 D4. **Tel** 642-5900.
www.neimanmarcus.com

Nordstrom
55 E Grand Ave.
Map 2 D5.
Tel 464-1515.
www.nordstrom.com

Saks Fifth Avenue
700 N Michigan Ave.
Map 2 D4.
Tel 944-6500.
www.saxfifthavenue.com

Where to Shop

Chicago is a shopper's paradise. The city's many neighborhoods attract locals and tourists alike with ethnic and one-of-a-kind shops. Visitors looking for fine and unusual artwork are sure to find a treasure in the River North Gallery District. Furnishing shops are clustered at Clybourn Corridor, while Oak Street is home to top fashion boutiques. Myriad shops, including chain and department stores, line the Magnificent Mile.

ART

River North Gallery District has Chicago's highest concentration of art galleries, though there are several good galleries outside its traditional boundaries. **Stephen Daiter Gallery** offers vintage 20th-century and experimental photography. **Carl Hammer Gallery** is known for its collection of "outsider art." Art with an emphasis on realism by emerging local artists can be found at a gallery called **gescheidle**. **Zolla/Lieberman Gallery** specializes in contemporary painting, sculpture, drawings, and photographs. **Mongerson Galleries** showcases Western art: paintings, sculpture, and photographs from the 18th to 20th centuries.

The collection of original European advertising posters dating from the late 1800s on display at **Spencer Weisz Galleries** is really marvelous. **Posters Plus** specializes in aviation, circus, food, and wine posters.

ANTIQUES

Most of the antique shops in the former antique district at West Belmont and North Lincoln Avenues have dispersed to other areas. Some of the shops remaining are still worth visiting, but many resemble thrift shops rather than authentic antique shops. For genuine antiques, go to **Jay Robert's Antique Warehouse** or visit **Salvage One** if you are looking for the likes of an antique doorknob or leaded stained glass. **Architectural Artifacts** has a great selection of salvaged pieces, and stocks everything from wooden desks to original church pews.

ART AND CRAFT SUPPLIES

Pearl Art & Craft Supplies stocks drafting, etching, and silk-screening supplies, in addition to paints, papers, and brushes. **Paper Source** sells specialized papers and the city's largest assortment of rubber stamps.

International Importing Bead & Novelty Co. is known for handmade beads, pearls, crystals, and trim. **Tom Thumb Hobby & Crafts** offers a great selection of beads and craft materials.

BOOKS

Local bookshops abound in Chicago. **Barbara's Bookstore** specializes in small- and alternative-press titles. The **Chicago Architecture Foundation Shop** has an excellent selection of books dedicated to the city's architecture.

Afrocentric Bookstore stocks books by African-American writers, from mysteries to histories. **Europa Books** stocks a broad range of foreign-language books, magazines, calendars, and language-instruction materials.

The top bookshop for gay and lesbian literature in Chicago is **Unabridged Books**. **57th Street Books** has a great general selection of books but specializes in cookbooks, mysteries, and film, computer, and especially in children's books.

Women & Children First is one of the largest feminist bookstores in the country, stocking more than 30,000 books by and about women. **Powell's Bookstore** buys and sells used books, specializing in rare, out-of-print, and scholarly titles.

BUTTONS AND FABRICS

Everything from reams of fabric to craft materials and seasonal holiday supplies line the generous aisles at **JoAnn Fabric**.

From decorator fabrics to bridal finery, try the dizzying selection at **Vogue Fabrics**. **Fishman's Fabrics** carries a range of theatrical fabrics, laces, and decorative trims as well as silks, woolens, and cottons.

CAMERAS AND ELECTRONICS

Camera buffs will want to visit **Central Camera**, an old-world shop crammed with cameras of every make and model. **Helix Camera & Video** carries underwater equipment and used cameras.

Visit **Bang & Olufsen** for high-quality Danish entertainment centers. **The Apple Store** is a wonderland of high-tech gadgets and electronics, while **Best Buy** has superb home and car stereo systems and knowledgeable staff.

COINS

The full-service coin dealer **Harlan J. Berk** buys and sells all currencies of coins. It also deals in paper money and rare and ancient coins. Another respected dealer is **Chicago Coin Company**, located near Midway Airport.

DISCOUNT CLOTHING

Discount clothing stores are plentiful in Chicago. **Marshall's, TJ Maxx**, and **Filene's Basement** all have great selections.

Many department stores (*see p163*) also have discount outlets scattered throughout the suburbs.

DESIGNER CLOTHING

For hip men's and women's fashions by designers such as Gucci and Fendi, **Ultimo** is a must-visit. **Giorgio Armani** stocks the designer's entire collection, including eyewear and fragrances. Italian design house **Prada** sells its fashions from a sleek and ultra-hip Oak Street shop. **Barneys New York** has an excellent selection of designer clothing.

For the more adventurous, there's New Yorker **Betsey Johnson**'s shop, and **Sugar Magnolia**, for fashions from European and US designers.

SHOES

Stocking stylish women's shoes, purses, and accessories, **Lori's Designer Shoes** is a treasure. The somewhat hectic store is self-serve. **Altman's Men's Shoes**, a Chicago mainstay since 1932, offers current men's styles and specialty sizes.

FURS AND LEATHERS

The midwest's largest fur importer and wholesaler is **Chicago Fur Mart**. A large selection of furs at reasonable prices is also available at **Chicago Fur Outlet**. Chic furs and leathers by top designers are sold at **Elán Furs**. **Glove Me Tender** has a vast array of gloves for men, women, and children.

JEWELRY

The gems of the jewelry district are clustered along Wabash Avenue between Madison and Washington Streets. Some are open only to the trade, but several open to the public. **Harold Burland & Son** sells diamonds and other precious stones. **Tiffany & Co**. sells designer jewelry, crystal, and clocks.

FOOD AND WINE SHOPS

Visiting the **Spice House** is an aromatic adventure. Its proprietors will gladly discuss the differences between the several varieties of cinnamon or basil they sell. **Treasure Island** carries hard-to-find imports and the city's best selection of gourmet foodstuffs. The organic food at **Whole Foods** is delicious.

For a rare Bordeaux or obscure Puerto Rican rum, visit **Sam's Wines & Spirits**.

House of Glunz carries wines in vintages as early as 1804. It also has a tasting room and wine museum.

MARKETS

From June to October, Midwest farmers come to sell their produce at Chicago's 30 or so markets. Some markets are on weekdays, but Saturday is the main market day. Hours are usually from 7am to 1pm. **Near North Market** is held Saturdays, as is **Lincoln Park Market**. **Evanston Farmers' Market**, on Saturday mornings, has wonderful organic produce. The fabulous **Daley Plaza Market** is alternate Thursdays.

Chicago's famous **New Mawell Street Market** (now on Roosevelt Rd) has been around since 1871. Up to 400 vendors sell new and used items, from power tools to fresh delicacies. The market runs Sundays, April to October.

Be prepared to pay with cash at the markets. Prices are generally not negotiable. Call the **Farmers' Market Information Line** for details and to confirm locations.

GIFTS AND SOUVENIRS

For a piece – literally – of Chicago, visit the **City of Chicago Store**. It sells fragments of Chicago landmarks, such as bricks from the old Comiskey Park, as well as other, more commonplace, souvenirs. The **Chicago Architecture Foundation Shop** has a good selection of souvenir books, posters, and Chicago memorabilia.

Purchase hats, shirts, mugs, and other items at the **Navy Pier Store**. The **Illinois Artisans Shop** is an excellent source of affordable crafts by local artisans, while the **Gallery 37 Store** sells a wide range of artwork by teenagers enrolled in its nonprofit art program.

HOME AND GARDEN FURNISHINGS

Upscale reproductions of vintage furniture and fixtures are the specialties of **Restoration Hardware**.

Jayson Home & Garden carries unusual furnishings and garden pots. **Williams-Sonoma** sells all kinds of homewares and gifts, including garden gadgets. **Smith & Hawken** offers pricey but alluring garden supplies and accessories. Its discount outlet is next door.

MEMORABILIA

You will find a fascinating, and broad, collection of political, sports, and movie memorabilia at **Yesterday**.

MUSIC

A vast classical-music collection, as well as folk, jazz, rock, pop, and show tunes, is to be found at **Best Buy**.

What is arguably the world's best collection of jazz recordings is found at **Jazz Record Mart**. Staff here are extremely knowledgeable. **Dr. Wax Records** is a fun place to browse through secondhand CDs.

SPORTING GOODS

Everything the company manufactures can be found at **Nike Town**, while **Vertel's Authentic Running & Fitness** is serious about athletic shoes. If outdoor equipment is an interest, an expedition to **The North Face** is worthwhile.

TOYS, GADGETS, AND SPECIALTY SHOPS

Useful gadgets are stocked at **Sharper Image**, while **Chicago Kite/Kite Harbor** entices with an astonishing selection of kites and radio-controlled toys. Extraordinary miniature dollhouse furniture and figures are offered at **Think Small By Rosebud**. Everything from chemistry kits to telescopes is sold at **American Science and Surplus**.

For children, a firm favorite is **The Disney Store**, which is filled with trinkets, costumes, and stuffed toys. The popular **American Girl Place** sells historic and contemporary dolls and doll accessories.

DIRECTORY

ART

Carl Hammer Gallery
740 N Wells St.
Map 1 C4.
Tel 266-8512.

gescheidle
118 N Peoria,
Near West Side.
Tel 925-5570.

Mongerson Galleries
704 N Wells St.
Map 1 C4.
Tel 943-2354.

Posters Plus
200 S Michigan Ave.
Map 4 D4.
Tel 312-461-9277.

Spencer Weisz Galleries
843 W Chicago Ave (near West Side).
Map 1 A4.
Tel 527-9420.

Stephen Daiter Gallery
311 W Superior St.
Map 2 D4.
Tel 787-3350.

Zolla/Lieberman Gallery
325 W Huron St.
Map 1 B4.
Tel 944-1990.

ANTIQUES

Architectural Artifacts
4325 N Ravenswood Ave,
North Center.
Tel (773) 348-0622.

Jay Robert's Antique Warehouse
149 W Kinzie St.
Map 1 C5.
Tel 222-0167.

Salvage One
1840 W Hubbard St.
Wicker Park.
Tel 733-0098.

ART AND CRAFT SUPPLIES

International Importing Bead & Novelty Co.
111 N Wabash Ave,
7th floor.
Map 4 D1.
Tel 332-0061.

Paper Source
232 W Chicago Ave.
Map 1 C4.
Tel 337-0798.

Pearl Art & Craft Supplies
225 W Chicago Ave.
Map 1 C4.
Tel 915-0200.

Tom Thumb Hobby & Crafts
1026 Davis St, Evanston.
Tel (847) 869-9575.

BOOKS

Afrocentric Bookstore
4655 S Martin Luther King Jr. Dr.
Map 7 A1.
Tel (773) 924-3966.

Barbara's Bookstore
233 S Wacker Dr,
Willis Tower. **Map** 3 B2.
Tel 466-0223.
One of several locations.

Chicago Architecture Foundation Shop
224 S Michigan Ave.
Map 4 D2.
Tel 922-3432.

Europa Books
832 N State St.
Map 1 C3.
Tel 335-9677.

57th Street Books
1301 E 57th St.
Map 8 D4.
Tel (773) 684-1300.

Powell's Bookstore
1501 E 57th St.
Map 8 D4.
Tel (773) 955-7780.
One of three locations.

Unabridged Books
3251 N Broadway,
Lakeview.
Tel (773) 883-9119.

Women & Children First
5223 N Clark St.
Map 3 B2.
Tel (773) 769-9299.

BUTTONS AND FABRICS

Fishman's Fabrics
1101 S Des Plaines St.
Map 3 A4.
Tel 922-7250.

JoAnn Fabric
2639 N Elston Ave.,
Logan Sq.
Tel 773-227-7874.

Vogue Fabrics
718 Main St, **Evanston.**
Tel (847) 864-9600.
One of three locations.

CAMERAS AND ELECTRONICS

Bang & Olufsen
609 N State St.
Map 2 D3. **Tel** 787-6006.
One of two locations.

Best Buy
See Music, p167.

Central Camera
230 S Wabash Ave.
Map 4 D3.
Tel 427-5580.

Helix Camera & Video
310 Racine Ave,
Near West Side.
Tel 421-6000.

The Apple Store
679 N Michigan Ave.
Map 2 D4.
Tel 981-4104.

COINS

Chicago Coin Company
6455 W Archer Ave,
Garfield Ridge.
Tel (773) 586-7666.

Harlan J. Berk
31 N Clark St.
Map 3 C1.
Tel 609-0016.

DISCOUNT CLOTHING

Filene's Basement
830 N Michigan Ave.
Map 2 D4.
Tel 482-8918.
One of two locations.

Marshall's
600 N Michigan Ave.
Map 2 D4.
Tel 280-7506.
One of several locations.

TJ Maxx
11 N State St. **Map** 3 C1.
Tel 553-0515.
One of three locations.

DESIGNER CLOTHING

Barneys New York
15 E Oak St. **Map** 2 D3.
Tel 587-1700.
One of two locations.

Betsey Johnson
835 N Michigan Ave,
Tel 312-280-6964.

Giorgio Armani
800 N Michigan Ave.
Map 2 D4.
Tel 751-2244.

Prada
30 E Oak St. **Map** 2 D3.
Tel 951-1113.

Sugar Magnolia
34 E Oak St. **Map** 2 D3.
Tel 944-0885.

DIRECTORY

Ultimo
116 E Oak St. **Map** 2 D3.
Tel 787-1171.

SHOES

Altman's Men's Shoes
120 W Monroe St.
Map 3 C2.
Tel 332-0667.

Lori's Designer Shoes
824 W Armitage Ave,
Lincoln Park.
Tel (773) 281-5655.

FURS AND LEATHERS

Chicago Fur Mart
645 N Michigan Ave.
Map 2 D4.
Tel 951-5000.
One of two locations.

Chicago Fur Outlet
777 W Diversey Pkwy.
Tel (773) 348-3877.

Elán Furs
675 N Michigan Ave.
Map 2 D4.
Tel 640-0707.

Glove Me Tender
900 N Michigan Ave.
Map 2 D3.
Tel 664-4022.

JEWELRY

Harold Burland & Son
5 S Wabash Ave.
suite 712. **Map** 4 D2.
Tel 332-5176.

Tiffany & Co.
730 N Michigan Ave.
Map 2 D4.
Tel 944-7500.

FOOD AND WINE SHOPS

House of Glunz
1206 N Wells St.
Map 1 C2.
Tel 642-3000.

Sam's Wines & Spirits
1720 N Marcey St,
DePaul.
Tel 664-4394.

Spice House
1512 N Wells St.
Map 1C1.
Tel 274-0378.

Treasure Island
1639 N Wells St.
Map 1 C1.
Tel 440-1144.
One of several locations.

Whole Foods
30 W Huron St.
Map 1 A4.
Tel 932-9600.
One of several locations.

MARKETS

Daley Plaza Market
Richard J. Daley Center Plaza, Washington & Dearborn sts.
Map 3 C1.

Evanston Farmers' Market
Tel (847) 866-2936 for market times, location, and further details.

Farmers' Market Information Line
Tel 312-744-3315 for market times, locations, and further details.

Lincoln Park Market
Armitage Ave & Orchard St. **Lincoln Park**.

Near North Market
Division & Dearborn sts.
Map 1 C3.

New Maxwell Street Market
548 W Roosevelt.
Map 3 B4–B5.
Tel 922-3100.

GIFTS AND SOUVENIRS

Chicago Architecture Foundation Shop
See Books, p158.

City of Chicago Store
163 E Pearson St,
Chicago Water Works
Map 2 D4.
Tel 742-8811.

Gallery 37 Store
66 E Randolph St.
Map 4 D2.
Tel 744-7274.

Illinois Artisans Shop
100 W Randolph St.
Map 3 C2.
Tel 814-5321.

Navy Pier Store
600 E Grand Ave, Navy Pier.
Map 2 F5.
Tel 595-5400.

HOME AND GARDEN FURNISHINGS

Jayson Home & Garden
1885 N Clybourn Ave,
DePaul.
Tel (800) 472-1885.

Restoration Hardware
938 W North Ave,
Lincoln Park.
Tel 475-9116.

Smith & Hawken
1780 N Marcey St,
DePaul.
Tel 266-1988.

Williams-Sonoma
900 N Michigan Ave.
Map 2 D3.
Tel 587-8080.
One of many locations.

MEMORABILIA

Yesterday
1143 W Addison St,
Lakeview.
Tel (773) 248-8087.

MUSIC

Best Buy
875 N Michigan Ave.
Map 2 D3.
Tel 312-397-2146.

Dr. Wax Records
5225 S Harper Ave.
Map 8 D2.
Tel (733) 493-8696.
One of three locations.

Jazz Record Mart
27 E Illinois St.
Map 2 D5.
Tel 222-1467.

SPORTING GOODS

Nike Town
669 N Michigan Ave.
Map 2 D4.
Tel 642-6363.

The North Face
875 N Michigan Ave.
Map 2 D3.
Tel 337-7200.

Vertel's Authentic Running & Fitness
24 S Michigan Ave.
Map 4 D2.
Tel 683-9600.

TOYS, GADGETS, AND SPECIALTY SHOPS

American Girl Place
835 N Michigan Ave.
Map 2 D4.
Tel 312-247-5223.

American Science and Surplus
5316 N Milwaukee Ave,
Jefferson Park.
Tel (773) 763-0313.

Chicago Kite/Kite Harbor
5445 N Harlem Ave,
Harwood Heights.
Tel (773) 467-1428.

Sharper Image
835 N Michigan Ave.
Map 2 D4.
Tel 335-1600.

The Disney Store
717 N Michigan Ave.
Map 2 D2.
Tel 654-9208.

Think Small By Rosebud
3209 N Clark St,
Lakeview.
Tel (773) 477-1920.

ENTERTAINMENT IN CHICAGO

Tens of millions of dollars have been spent in recent years by the City of Chicago to rejuvenate old theaters and build cultural attractions. Today, a portion of the money raised through the hotel tax *(see p138)* is channeled directly to the department of culture. And it shows. Chicago's world-class orchestras and opera, intimate jazz ensembles, high-profile musicals, and alternative theater help to attract more than 5 million tourists to Chicago each year. Festivals of all kinds, from music to dance to ethnic, are held in the city's many parks and more than 75 diverse communities *(see pp32–35)*. There are also numerous sports events throughout the year for visitors to Chicago to watch or participate in *(see pp170–71)*.

Silver-painted street performer

Chicago's listings magazine, *Reader*, published weekly

INFORMATION

The city's most complete entertainment listings are in the *Reader*, a free newspaper distributed on Thursdays. *Chicago Magazine*, available at newsstands, is a glossy monthly with listings of the city's major venues. The two daily newspapers, the *Chicago Sun-Times* and the *Chicago Tribune*, publish an entertainment section in their Friday editions, with movie, music, dance, and theater reviews and listings.

Chicago's **Visitor Information Centers** sell tickets as well as providing entertainment information.

Moviefone provides recorded details of movie show times and theater locations, as well as brief descriptions of the movies.

Hot Tix, a ticket agency run by the League of Chicago Theatres, provides half-price tickets to more than 125 Chicago-area theaters on the day of performance.

Most hotels carry a wide selection of entertainment brochures, and hotel staff will help orient you and may arrange for tickets. The **Mayor's Office of Special Events** also provides information on local events, including the numerous neighborhood festivals that take place during summer.

BUYING TICKETS

Tickets for most major entertainment events are sold through **Ticketmaster**. You can buy tickets by phone or at one of its locations. You may be able to buy tickets for sold-out events from a ticket broker (see listings in the yellow pages of the telephone directory), but the price may be astronomical. Be wary of buying tickets from "scalpers" (ticket hawkers) on the street. Some try to sell tickets that are expired or counterfeit.

Many of the major concerts, plays, and musicals in Chicago are reviewed in the national press, which can lead to these shows selling out weeks in advance. It is best to buy tickets for such shows through a ticket agency or the

The Civic Opera House, home to the Lyric Opera of Chicago

venue's box office before arriving in Chicago.

Most people buy movie tickets at the theater. Prices range from $1.50 per ticket for second-run movies to $10 for first-run movies. You can buy tickets using a major credit card through **Moviefone**. This saves standing in line at the theater, but the tickets are nonrefundable and a surcharge of $1 to $2 is added to the price of each.

DISCOUNT TICKETS

Half-price tickets for shows on the day of performance are available from **Hot Tix**. These tickets must be purchased in person and paid for in cash or, at most locations, by credit card.

CityPass Traveler packages admissions to five of the top attractions in Chicago, saving you both time and money. The passes can be purchased through its website or at the participating venues.

TRAVELERS WITH DISABILITIES

Many theaters and concert halls in Chicago are fully wheelchair accessible. Some of the smaller theaters and clubs try hard but are less than adequate when it comes to serving patrons with special needs. Even though a venue has the required seating area for persons in wheelchairs, the building may still be difficult to get around in.

Major theaters and halls provide amplifying headphones for people with hearing impairments.

The **Mayor's Office for People with Disabilities** provides details on which venues are accessible for people with disabilities.

FREE EVENTS

Accomplished young musicians play every Wednesday as part of the Dame Myra Hess series of free noontime recitals at the **Chicago Cultural Center** *(see p52)*. Harold Washington Library Center *(see p82)* also hosts concerts, many free.

The best free seats in the city are in Grant Park and in Millennium Park *(see p53)*. The first-rate Grant Park Orchestra and Chorus give evening concerts, mid-June to mid-August, Wednesday to Sunday, in Millennium Park. (see page 162 for details on other free music events.)

Grant Park is home to many summertime festivals. The Gospel Festival kicks off the season early in June, followed by the renowned Blues Festival. A country-music festival is usually held in July. The season winds down with the Viva! Chicago Latin Music Festival at the end of August, followed by the Jazz and World Music festivals, held in September.

Throughout the summer, dozens of Chicago's neighborhoods block off streets to traffic and hold weekend festivals. Most are free or require a minimal entrance fee. Vendors sell refreshments, artists show arts and crafts, and local bands perform. You can hear great salsa, gritty rock and roll, country music, blues, or jazz – sometimes on

Sidewalk signs in the Loop's theater district

Buddy Guy, one of the world's greatest blues guitar soloists

Concert in Preston Bradley Hall at the Chicago Cultural Center

the same day. These festivals allow visitors to experience Chicago's neighborhoods.

Both **Oprah Winfrey** and **Jerry Springer** tape their TV talk-shows in Chicago. Tickets to the shows are free, but you must reserve them at least one month in advance. Check out the website for the free day schedule: www.msichicago.org /info/admission/prices.html

FREE-ADMISSION DAYS

Monday
Adler Planetarium (Sep–Feb; *pp92–3*).
Chicago History Museum *(p74)*.
Field Museum *(Jan–Feb, Sep–Dec; pp86–9)*.
Museum of Science and Industry *(see pp106–109)*.
Shedd Aquarium (Sep–Feb; *pp96–7*).
Tuesday
Adler Planetarium (Sep–Feb; *pp92–3*).
Art Institute *(pp46–9)*.
Brookfield Zoo *(see p117)*.
Museum of Contemporary Art *(p65)*.
Museum of Science and Industry *(see pp106–109)*.
Shedd Aquarium (Sep–Feb; *pp96–7*).
Thursday
Brookfield Zoo *(see p117)*.
Chicago Children's Museum (5–8pm; *p65*).
Sunday
DuSable Museum of African-American History *(p104)*.

DIRECTORY

USEFUL NUMBERS

Chicago Cultural Center
Tel 744-6630, 346-3278.
www.cityofchicago.org/
culturalaffairs

City Helpline
Tel 311 (event information).

Mayor's Office for People with Disabilities
Tel 744-6673.
www.cityofchicago.org/
disabilities

Mayor's Office of Special Events
744-3315.
www.explorechicago.org/
specialevents

Performance Hotline
Tel 987-1123.

Visitor Information Centers
Tel 744-2400 / 877-244-2246.
163 E Pearson St. **Map** 2 D4.
77 E Randolph St. **Map** 4 D1.
www.cityofchicago.org and
www.explorechicago.org

TICKET AGENCIES

CityPass Traveler
www.citypass.net

Hot Tix
163 E Pearson St. **Map** 2 D4.
72 E Randolph St. **Map** 4 D1.
Tel 312-751-1876.
Mon.
www.hottix.org

Moviefone
444-3456.
www.moviefone.com

Ticketmaster
www.559-1212.
www.ticketmaster.com

TV TALK-SHOWS

Jerry Springer Show
Tel 321-5365.
www.jerryspringertv.com

Oprah Winfrey Show
Tel 591-9222.
www.oprah.com

Performing Arts, Film, and Sports

When it comes to entertainment, Chicago is second to none. The Chicago Symphony and the Lyric Opera are both world-class, while Steppenwolf Theater grew from its beginnings in a basement to become one of the leading theater troupes in the country. Chicago also has its share of art film houses. Many events take place at the city's 552 parks and playgrounds. Ravinia Festival, in Highland Park, showcases music and dance throughout the summer. Spectator sports, especially baseball, are also enormously popular in Chicago, the numerous teams providing year-round entertainment.

MUSIC

The guiding light of classical music in Chicago is the **Chicago Symphony Orchestra**. From September through June, it performs at **Symphony Center**. During the summer, it performs at the **Ravinia Festival**.

The highly acclaimed **Lyric Opera of Chicago** presents lavish productions and brings international stars to **Civic Opera House** during its September-to-March season.

Music of the Baroque is Chicago's leading early-music ensemble. A consortium of Chicago's finest musicians, **Chicago Chamber Musicians** presents a series of free concerts throughout the year at the **Chicago Cultural Center**, held on the first Monday of each month.

Chicago's two world-class string quartets are the venerable **Vermeer String Quartet** and the **Chicago String Quartet**. Both perform frequently at the **DePaul University Concert Hall**.

Mandel Hall at University of Chicago hosts folk, jazz, and classical groups. Northwestern University presents concerts by leading touring ensembles at **Pick-Staiger Concert Hall**.

DANCE

The unique blend of jazz, ballet, and modern dance that **Hubbard Street Dance Chicago** offers will transport you to new places in entertainment. Performances take place at the Music and Dance Theater.

Each season, **Joffrey Ballet of Chicago** presents four performances of classical ballet with a contemporary edge, reflecting the dance company's mandate to present the works of 20th-century American artists.

THEATER

Chicago has a vibrant theater scene. **Goodman Theatre**'s home is located in the Loop's theater district. The troupe presents contemporary plays as well as the classics directed with a fresh approach. Productions often star well-known stage and screen actors.

Nearby is the restored **Ford Center for the Performing Arts Oriental Theater**, which brings Broadway productions to the city. The **Chicago Theater** is a multipurpose venue that presents concerts and theater. The **Auditorium Theatre** (see p44) hosts mainstream musicals such as *Les Miserables* and *Showboat*, as does the **Bank of America Theater**.

Since its inception in a church basement, **Steppenwolf Theater Company** has gained a national reputation for staging avant-garde plays. Although many of the actors who started at Steppenwolf, such as John Malkovich and Laurie Metcalf, have left, they frequently return to perform with the company or direct.

Shakespeare Repertory Company stages three productions a year in **Chicago Shakespeare Theater**, its striking courtyard-style theater at Navy Pier.

Performing Arts Chicago brings in cutting-edge theater, dance, music, and puppetry groups. Performances are held at various venues.

Many notable theaters are located near Lincoln Park and in Lakeview, among them the **Royal George** and the **Victory Gardens Theater**.

SUMMER PERFORMANCES

Chicago's summer home for the performing arts is in idyllic Highland Park, 25 miles (40 km) north of the city, at the internationally celebrated **Ravinia Festival**. Chicago Symphony Orchestra performs here, as do leading jazz ensembles, pop and folk acts, children's performers, and dance troupes, including Hubbard Street Dance and the Joffrey Ballet of Chicago.

The park's sound system is excellent. Reserved seats in the pavilion usually cost from $20 to $60. General admission to the park costs about $10.

Although Highland Park has several good restaurants, most people buy general-admission tickets, bring a picnic dinner (some, lavish spreads with candles, crystal, and fine wine), and sit on the lawn to enjoy the performances.

FILM

Like most cities, Chicago has a cinema multiplex in almost every neighborhood showing first-run movies. There are also several art film houses in the city.

The **Harold Washington Library Center** screens a diverse selection of films. **The Music Box** is a fully restored 1929 movie palace designed to look as though you are outdoors at night. It shows an eclectic mix of foreign, American independent, and classic films. An organist entertains with vintage popular music during intermission on weekend evenings.

The **Gene Siskel Film Center of the Art Institute of Chicago** presents a wide range of standard-setting international cinema. Panel discussion and lectures provide context for the films.

Facets Multimedia has a small screening room where current innovative films from around the world – from South America to Eastern Europe to Africa – are shown. The theater also hosts retrospectives of great directors such as Alfred Hitchcock and Jean-Luc Godard. Facets has the country's largest collection of videos for rent or sale.

SPECTATOR SPORTS

Chicago boasts several professional sports teams, including two baseball teams. The **Chicago White Sox** play for the American League at the **US Cellular Field** on the city's South Side. The much-loved-but-often-disappointing **Chicago Cubs** of the National League play in **Wrigley Field**,

a marvelous inner-city stadium on the north side of Chicago (see p114).

The formerly great **Chicago Bulls** (winners of five world championships in the 1990s) play basketball at the **United Center**, as does Chicago's hockey team, the **Chicago Blackhawks**. The inimitable **Chicago Bears** play football at **Soldier Field**.

DIRECTORY

MUSIC

Chicago Chamber Musicians
Tel 225-5226; 692-9000.

Chicago Cultural Center
78 E Washington St.
Map 4 D1. *Tel 346-3278.*

Chicago String Quartet
Tel 371-4271.

Chicago Symphony Orchestra
See Symphony Center.

Civic Opera House
20 N Wacker Dr. **Map** 3 B1.
Tel 419-0033.

DePaul University Concert Hall
800 W Belden Ave,
Lincoln Park.
Tel 773-722-5463.

Lyric Opera of Chicago
See Civic Opera House.

Mandel Hall
University of Chicago,
1131 E 57th St.
Map 7 C4.
Tel (773) 702-8068.

Music of the Baroque
Tel 551-1415.

Pick-Staiger Concert Hall
Northwestern University,
1977 S Campus Dr,
Evanston.
Tel (847) 491-5441.

Symphony Center
220 S Michigan Ave.
Map 4 D2.
Tel 312-665-1234.

Vermeer String Quartet
www.vermeerqt.com

DANCE

Hubbard Street Dance Chicago
1147 W Jackson Blvd.
Tel 850-9744.

Joffrey Ballet of Chicago
10 E Randolph.
Tel 739-0120.

THEATER

Auditorium Theatre
50 E Congress Pkwy.
Map 4 D3.
Tel 922-2110.

Bank of America Theater
18 W Monroe St.
Map 3 C2.
Tel 977-1700.

Chicago Shakespeare Theater
800 E Grand Ave.
Map 2 F5.
Tel 595-5600.

Chicago Theatre
175 N State St. **Map** 4 D1.
Tel 462-6300.

Ford Center for the Performing Arts Oriental Theater
24 W Randolph St.
Map 3 C1.
Tel 977-1700.

Goodman Theatre
170 N Dearborn St.
Map 3 C1.
Tel 443-3800.

Performing Arts Chicago
Tel (773) 722-5463.

Royal George
1641 N HalstedSt.
Map 1 A1.
Tel 988-9000.

Shakespeare Repertory Company
See Chicago Shakespeare Theater.

Steppenwolf Theatre Company
1650 N Halsted St,
Lincoln Park.
Tel 335-1650.

Victory Gardens
2433 N Lincoln Ave,
Lincoln Park.
Tel (773) 871-3000.

SUMMER PERFORMANCES

Ravinia Festival
Green Bay & Lake Cook
Rds, **Highland Park**.
*Tel (847) 266-5100;
(800) 433-8819.*

FILM

Facets Multimedia
1517 W Fullerton Ave,
DePaul.
Tel (773) 281-9075.

Gene Siskel Film Center of the Art Institute of Chicago
164 N State St. **Map** 3 C1.
Tel 846-2600.

Harold Washington Library Center
400 S State St. **Map** 3 C2.
Tel 747-4300.

The Music Box
3733 N Southport Ave,
Lakeview.
Tel (773) 871-6604.

SPECTATOR SPORTS

Chicago Bears
Halas Hall, 1000 Football
Dr., **Lake Forest**.
Tel 559-1212 (tickets).

Chicago Blackhawks
United Center.
Tel 455-7000 (tickets).

Chicago Bulls
United Center.
*Tel 559-1212 or (800)
462-2849 (tickets).*

Chicago Cubs
*Tel (773) 404-2827;
(800) 843-2827 (tickets).*

Chicago White Sox
Tel 674-1000.

Soldier Field
425 E McFetridge Dr.
Map 4 E5. *Tel 235-7000.*

United Center
1901 W Madison St,
Near West Side.
Tel 455-4500.

US Cellular Field
333 W 35th St. **Map** 5
B5–C5. *Tel 674-1000.*

Wrigley Field
1060 W Addison Ave,
Lakeview.
Tel (773) 404-2827.

Taverns, Nightclubs, and Live Music

Chicagoans have a reputation for working hard and playing hard. Nowhere is the latter more evident than in the city's night life. The blues are a Chicago institution, but jazz, country, folk, and rock music thrive here as well. Acts both big and small play almost nightly, and many music venues are open into the early hours of the morning. Chicago night-life establishments tend to be clustered together. Singles' bars are gathered at the corner of Division and State streets, bars frequented by the college crowd abound on Lincoln Avenue. Clark Street near Wrigley Field, in Chicago's north end, has numerous sports bars. The gay scene is concentrated in the Lakeview neighborhood; Wicker Park offers a variety of alternative-music nightclubs.

BARS AND TAVERNS

Bars and taverns are tucked into every neighborhood of Chicago. Some are rather basic drinking places, but others offer a glimpse into neighborhood life. Most bars in Chicago have limited food choices. Taverns, on the other hand, are serious about food. The American version of European pubs and bistros, taverns are relaxed places where locals go to eat, drink, and socialize.

The most venerable of the downtown taverns was The Berghoff. Now closed, this establishment was the first in Chicago to be issued a liquor license once Prohibition ended. Instead there is the **17 West at the Berghoff**, a casual dining spot featuring some of The Berghoff's signature German dishes and its beers. Two other notable downtown pubs are **Miller's Pub** and **Exchequer Restaurant & Pub**. Both succeed in maintaining a neighborhood atmosphere while catering to a good number of tourists.

Near the Magnificent Mile is **Boston Blackie's**, a dimly lit Art Deco-style sports bar. **Bar Louie**, a handsome bar with good drinks and large menu, is a great place to mingle with the upwardly mobile. **Butch McGuire's** has a major presence on the bar-lined block of Division Street near the Gold Coast. Its atmosphere is pub-like, and the food is good (especially the brunch).

When the city celebrates a sports victory, fans celebrate in the many singles and sports bars near Division, Dearborn, and Rush streets.

Summer in Chicago is a great time to sit outside, enjoy a drink, and people-watch. There are several good beer gardens and patios in Lincoln Park. **John Barleycorn's** and **Charlie's Ale House** are two of the best. Nearby, **Ranalli's** serves good pizza and beer. **Goose Island Brewpub** sells brews made on the premises, some of the finest in town.

NIGHTCLUBS

Chicago offers a variety of nightclubs: there is sure to be one to suit your taste. Expect to pay an admission charge, though some clubs may impose a drink-order minimum instead.

Excalibur is perhaps the most mainstream club in the city. Pool tables and video games fill the first floor; the dance floor is upstairs, where retrospective music is played. If you are into tattoos and body-piercings, visit **Crobar**. With the city's largest dance floor, complete with go-go dancers, it plays a mix of hip-hop, techno, and rock music. **Fulton Lounge**, is set in a converted book bindery in the Fulton Market District, near Greek Town. On offer is acid jazz and the atmosphere invites luxurious lounging on the Art Deco couches until late. The outdoor patio is cool in summer.

JAZZ

Live jazz, from salsa to swing, is played almost every night at the stylish **Green Dolphin Street**. The **Green Mill Cocktail Lounge** may not be impressive from the outside, and its Uptown neighborhood may be slightly run-down, but it is one of the city's coolest jazz clubs.

Jazz Showcase is the best place in Chicago to hear top jazz artists perform. **Andy's** is one of Chicago's most respected clubs and has been going for over 25 years.

BLUES

Major blues acts are presented at the **House of Blues**, a 1,500-seat venue with superb acoustics.

More intimate blues venues include **B.L.U.E.S.**, a small, busy bar with a friendly atmosphere that offers live music every night of the week. **Kingston Mines** also features nightly live blues on its two stages. Both stay open into the early morning hours.

Buddy Guy's Legends brings the big-name acts downtown. Guy himself plays here each January.

FOLK AND COUNTRY MUSIC

The city's leading venue for folk music is the **Old Town School of Folk Music**. The **Abbey Pub** features local and touring groups, favoring Irish bands. It also offers barn dancing every Monday night.

Heartland Cafe is a throwback to the 1960s. It is a healthfood restaurant that also presents poetry readings, storytelling, and live music. **Schubas** is a neighborhood gem showcasing live folk and country music.

Although most of the line-dancing and two-stepping action is in the suburbs, it surprisingly can also be found in the city, at **Charlie's**. A gay bar serious about country music, Charlie's always welcomes straight folks.

ROCK MUSIC

Rock music is alive and well in Chicago. **Empty Bottle** is known for its eclectic calendar of cutting-edge underground acts and experimental jazz, as well as breaking up-and-coming artists.

House of Blues presents big-name rock stars. **Cubby Bear**, across from Wrigley Field *(see p114)*, is a huge sports bar that presents local bands and touring talents, whereas **Metro**, in Wrigleyville

(see p114), is an independent-rock and dancing mecca. Wicker Park's *(see p114)* intimate **Double Door** is an excellent place to see live music. Many famous groups, such as the Smashing Pumpkins and the Rolling Stones, have played here under fictitious names, to the delight of unsuspecting patrons.

The Wild Hare is the city's best venue for live and reggae and African music. National or international acts are presented here nightly.

COMEDY CLUBS

For well-known stand-up comedy acts, visit **Zanies**. Comedians Jerry Seinfeld and Jay Leno have entertained here.

Second City, the celebrated venue that produced many of the comedians who went on to *Saturday Night Live* fame, offers a mix of social-satire sketches and improvisation. Dinner-theater packages are available. Its offshoot, **Second City E.T.C.**, presents comedy revues next door.

DIRECTORY

BARS AND TAVERNS

Bar Louie
226 W Chicago Ave.
Map 1 C4.
Tel 337-3313.
One of six locations.

17 West at The Berghoff
17 W Adams St.
Map 3 C2. *Tel 427-3170.*

Boston Blackie's
164 E Grand Ave.
Map 2 D5.
Tel 938-8700.
One of two locations.

Butch McGuire's
20 W Division St.
Map 1 C3.
Tel 337-9080.

Charlie's Ale House
5308 N Clark St,
Edgewater.
Tel (773) 751-0140.

Exchequer Restaurant & Pub
226 S Wabash Ave.
Map 4 D2.
Tel 939-5633.

Goose Island Brewpub
1800 N Clybourn Ave.
Map 1 A1.
Tel 915-0071.
One of two locations.

John Barleycorn's
658 W Belden Ave,
Lincoln Park.
Tel (773) 348-8899.
One of two locations.

Miller's Pub
134 S Wabash Ave.
Map 4 D2.
Tel 263-4988 or 645-5377.

Ranalli's
2301 N Clark St.
Tel 733-244-2300.
One of several locations.

NIGHTCLUBS

Crobar
1543 N Kingsbury St.
Map 1 A1. *Tel 266-1900.*

Excalibur
632 N Dearborn St.
Map 1 C4. *Tel 266-1944.*

Fulton Lounge
955 W Fulton Market,
West Loop.
Tel 942-9500.

JAZZ

Andy's
11 E Hubbard St,
Map 2 D5. *Tel 642-6805.*

Green Dolphin Street
2200 N Ashland Ave,
Bucktown.
Tel (773) 395-0066.

Green Mill Cocktail Lounge
4802 N Broadway Ave,
Uptown.
Tel (773) 878-5552.

Jazz Showcase
806 S Plymouth Ct.
Map 3 C3.
Tel 312-360-0234.

BLUES

B.L.U.E.S.
2519 N Halsted St,
Lincoln Park.
Tel (773) 528-1012.

Buddy Guy's Legends
754 S Wabash Ave.
Map 4 D3.
Tel 427-0333.

House of Blues
329 N Dearborn St. Map 1 C5. *Tel 527-2583 or 923-2000 (tickets).*

Kingston Mines
2548 N Halsted St,
Lincoln Park.
Tel (773) 477-4646.

FOLK AND COUNTRY MUSIC

Abbey Pub
3420 W Grace St,
Northwest Side.
Tel (773) 478-4408.

Charlie's
3726 N Broadway Ave,
Lakeview.
Tel (773) 871-8887.

Heartland Cafe
7000 N Glenwood Ave,
Rogers Park.
Tel (773) 465-8005.

Old Town School of Folk Music
4544 N Lincoln Ave,
Lincoln Square.
Tel (773) 728-6000.
(tickets and classes).
Also at Lakeview.

Schubas
3159 N Southport Ave,
Lakeview.
Tel (773) 525-2508.

ROCK MUSIC

Cubby Bear
1059 W Addison Ave,
Wrigleyville.
Tel (773) 327-1662.

Double Door
1572 N Milwaukee Ave,
Wicker Park.
Tel (773) 489-3160.

Empty Bottle
10356 N Western Ave,
Ukrainian Village.
Tel (773) 276-3600.

House of Blues
329 N Dearborn St. Map 3 C4. *Tel (312) 527-2583.*

Metro
3730 N Clark St,
Wrigleyville.
Tel (773) 549-4140.

The Wild Hare
3530 N Clark St,
Lakeview.
Tel (773) 327-4273.

COMEDY CLUBS

Second City
1616 N Wells St. Map 1 C2.
Tel 337-3992 or (877) 778-4707.

Second City E.T.C.
1608 N Wells St.
Map 1 C2. *Tel 337-3992 or (877) 778-4707.*

Zanies
1548 N Wells St.
Map 1 C1. *Tel 337-4027.*

SURVIVAL GUIDE

PRACTICAL INFORMATION

Chicago loves visitors. Its Visitor Information Centers are an invaluable source of information, and a stop at one of them should be on every traveler's itinerary. The centers also have details of the many tours available, an excellent way to see the many different faces of Chicago. Getting around the city is both easy and

Newspaper box

safe, if you follow a few guidelines (see pp178–9). The practical information that follows offers a variety of tips, from locating banks (see pp180–81) to making a local phone call (see pp182–3). There is also a section on transit in and around Chicago, as well as details on how to get downtown upon your arrival in Chicago (see pp184–91).

VISITOR INFORMATION

The **Illinois Bureau of Tourism** will mail you information about Illinois hotels, restaurants, and attractions. The **Chicago Convention and Tourism Bureau**'s website will also help you plan your trip. Upon your arrival in Chicago, visit one of the two **Visitor Information Centers** for maps, entertainment and tour brochures, tickets, public transportation passes, and general information.

Visitor Information Center

Sign for one of the city tourist offices

OPENING HOURS

Most businesses are open from 9am to 5pm weekdays and do not close for lunch. Banks are generally open weekdays from 9am to 5pm. Some bank branches open from 9am to early afternoon on Saturdays.

Most major museums are open daily from 9am to 5pm, often with later hours on one weekday night. Smaller museums keep more limited hours; phone for details.

Banks and museums usually close on major holidays.

ETIQUETTE

Smoking is prohibited in public buildings and airports, except in designated areas. Restaurants have been smoke-free since 2006. Since July 2008, smoking has not been permitted in bars, taverns, and restaurants with bars. This ban also applies to stadiums, shopping centers, and taxicabs.

Tipping is integral to Chicago's service industry. For details on restaurant tipping, see page 143. Tip $1 per coat checked; taxi drivers, hairdressers, and bartenders, from 10 to 15 percent. Tip hotel or airport porters up to $1 per bag, valet-parking attendants $1 after they bring you your car. Tip tour drivers between $2 and $3 per group member.

If a concierge was especially helpful, acknowledge it by tipping between $5 and $10.

MUSEUMS

Museums either charge an admission fee or suggest a donation. Expect a separate charge for special exhibits. Smaller museums are often free. Entrance to large museums may be free either once a week or once a month (see p169). Tours are often free.

Museum Campus, a park on the lakefront, is home to the Field Museum (see pp86–9), Shedd Aquarium (see pp96–7), and Adler Planetarium (see pp92–3). Free trolleys run between these museums and public transportation stations. Call the **Museum Campus Information Line** for details.

GUIDED TOURS

Excellent walking, bicycle, bus, and boat tours are offered by the **Chicago Architecture Foundation** (CAF). A fabulous way to discover a few of Chicago's 77 neighborhoods is to take one of the Saturday tours with **Chicago Neighborhood Tours**.

American Sightseeing offers two-hour narrated tours. **Chicago Trolley Company** sells an all-day pass for tours aboard old-fashioned trolleys.

Boat tour season is from April to October. **Wendella Sightseeing** offers evening and lakefront tours. **Mercury, Chicago's Skyline Cruiseline** has narrated 90-minute tours. **Shoreline Sightseeing** offers 30-minute narrated tours on Lake Michigan.

Many companies offer discounts when two or more tours per person are purchased; be sure to ask.

Antique Coach and Carriage will pick you up at your hotel or a restaurant in a horse-drawn buggy.

Italian-style gondola rides on the Chicago River offer a fun experience and a unique view of downtown.

A river cruise tour offered by the Chicago Architecture Foundation

NEWSPAPERS

Chicago has two major dailies: *Chicago Tribune* and *Chicago Sun-Times*. The *Chicago Defender* is published weekdays, primarily for

Special-interest newspapers in Chicago

the city's African-American readership. Business news is found in the weekly *Crain's*. For details on entertainment news, see page 168. Foreign newspapers are available at Europa Books *(see p164)*.

CUSTOMS AND IMMIGRATION

Holders of a valid EU, New Zealand, or Australian passport and a return ticket do not need a visa if staying 90 days or less in the US, but must apply for entry online via the Electronic System for Authorization (ESTA) at least 72 hours before travel (http://esta.cbp.dhs.gov). Canadians need only a valid passport. Foreign visitors may need to prove they have sufficient funds. Strict security checks (taking of photographs and fingerprints) are in place for those arriving in the US.

TRAVELERS WITH DISABILITIES

All facilities operated by the city are wheelchair accessible. Most attractions, buildings (including restaurants), and public transportation are equipped for easy access. However, small entertainment venues may not be. Parking spaces reserved for vehicles with disabled permits are marked by the handicapped symbol either on a sign or painted on the concrete.

Phone the **Mayor's Office for People with Disabilities** for information.

STUDENTS AND SENIORS

Many businesses offer student and senior discounts. For seniors, all that is needed is picture identification with their birthdate on it.

Students will need current student photo ID. An international student ID card is widely accepted. Purchase one at your local youth travel association or

hostel organization. The card can also be purchased from **Council Travel** with proper credentials.

CONVERSION CHART

Imperial to Metric:
1 inch = 2.5 centimeters
1 foot = 30 centimeters
1 mile = 1.6 kilometers
1 ounce = 28 grams
1 pound = 454 grams
1 US pint = 0.5 liter
1 US gallon = 3.8 liters

Metric to Imperial:
1 millimeter = 0.04 inch
1 centimeter = 0.4 inch
1 meter = 3 feet 3 inches
1 kilometer = 0.6 mile
1 gram = 0.04 ounce

Bear in mind that 1 US pint (0.5 liter) is a smaller measure than 1 UK pint (0.6 liter).

ELECTRICITY

All US electric current flows at a standardized 110 to 120 volts AC (alternating current). You may need an adapter plug and voltage converter that fits standard US electrical outlets.

Standard US two-pin plug

US plugs have two flat prongs. Batteries are readily available.

DIRECTORY

Personal Security and Health

Chicago is a friendly city, and most visitors do not encounter any problems. However, it is always best to take common-sense precautions and be aware of your surroundings. If you don't feel safe, you probably aren't. Public transportation is generally safe during the day, but after dark, you may feel more comfortable taking a taxi to your destination. The best source of information is often your hotel concierge. Don't hesitate to ask if your destination or day's itinerary will take you into unsavory neighborhoods. Parks and the paths along the lakefront are populated during the day but are often fairly deserted at night.

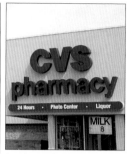

CVS Pharmacy has many branches with 24-hour opening

LAW ENFORCEMENT

The Chicago Police Department has bicycle, motorcycle, car, and foot patrols day and night. There is also a police presence at major community and cultural events. Police officers are usually very helpful if approached, but be mindful: they are not tour guides.

Parking-enforcement and traffic officers make their rounds on foot or in small vehicles. Airports, stores, and hotels have uniformed and plain-clothes staff who also provide security services.

PERSONAL SAFETY

In recent years, violent crime has decreased in Chicago. However, petty crime is still a problem. Your best protection is common sense. Never walk in dark alleys or deserted streets. Don't leave purses or valuables unattended in public places, and don't carry a lot of cash or wear flashy jewelry. Keep one credit card in a concealed secondary

Chicago Fire Department on early-morning firefighting duty

wallet or in the hotel safe. Keep your wallet in an inconspicuous place, and have enough change handy for phone calls and bus fares. Defeat purse snatchers by carrying your bag with the clasp facing toward you and the shoulder strap across your body. Carry your passport separate from your money.

Do not allow anyone other than hotel and airport personnel to carry your belongings. Stow valuables in the room or hotel safe, keeping an inventory of items you deposit. Chicago's homeless sell the newspaper *Streetwise* for $1. Buying the paper is a help to the homeless. Otherwise, do not give money to, or make eye contact with, people asking for spare change.

Much of Chicago's West Side and South Side can be inhospitable. Notable exceptions are Little Italy, Chinatown, Hyde Park, and Pullman. Some safe North Side neighborhoods are next to troubled areas. And, like most US cities, the downtown is primarily a business district: bustling during the day and quieter at night. While the Loop is becoming busier during the evenings, in part because of its theater district, caution should still be exercised.

Chicago parks are safest when crowds are present. Avoid parks after dark, unless you're attending a special event held in one. If you want to go for a jog, ask the concierge at your hotel to map out a safe route.

Finally, be sure you fully understand your hotel's fire-escape procedures.

MEDICAL MATTERS

Many walk-in medical and dental clinics in Chicago are open 24-hours, and are often sufficient for minor injuries and ailments.

Without medical insurance, medical services can be very expensive. Even with insurance, you may have to pay for the services yourself, then claim reimbursement from your insurance company.

Traveler's checks or cash are sometimes the only payment accepted from visitors, though many practitioners take credit cards. Anyone taking a prescription drug should ask their doctor for an extra supply to take with them and a copy of the prescription in case more is needed. Both **Walgreen's** and **CVS Drug** have pharmacies open 24-hours. Call them to find the location nearest you.

EMERGENCIES

Call 911 for emergencies requiring medical, police, or fire services. For non-emergency police situations, such as theft, dial 311, to reach the **City HelpLine**.

Hospital emergency rooms and city hospitals are in the Yellow Pages of the telephone directory. Most Chicago hospitals have 24-hour emergency rooms. Your hotel concierge will know the one closest to the hotel. **Northwestern Memorial Hospital** has an emergency room convenient to both

Police car

Emergency ambulance

Fire boat

downtown and North Side visitors. It also provides a **Physician Referral Service**. The **Bernard A. Mitchell Hospital**, at the University of Chicago, serves the city's South Side.

Private hospitals are listed in the Yellow Pages of the telephone directory. Or, your hotel may be able to arrange for a doctor or dentist to visit you in your room.

For dental emergencies, call the **Chicago Dental Society**, which provides referrals 24 hours a day, every day.

LOST PROPERTY

The chance of recovering stolen property is poor. Nevertheless, you should report all lost or stolen items to the police. Keep a copy of the police report if you plan to make an insurance claim.

The Chicago Police Department has a location at O'Hare Airport; call if you have misplaced something at

the airport other than at a restaurant or on a plane.

Most credit card companies have toll-free numbers to call to report a loss, as do Thomas Cook and American Express *(see p181)* if you lose or have your traveler's checks stolen.

If you lose your passport, contact your embassy or consulate immediately.

TRAVEL INSURANCE

Travel insurance coverage of a minimum of $1 million is strongly recommended, mainly because of the high cost of medical care in the US. Among the most important features the policy should cover are accidental death, dismemberment, emergency medical and dental care, trip cancellation, and lost or stolen baggage coverage. Your travel agent or insurance company should be able to recommend a suitable policy, but it is worth shopping around for the best deal.

Sign outside a Chicago medical center

DIRECTORY

CRISIS INFORMATION

All Emergencies
Tel 911 for police, fire, and medical services.

City HelpLine
Tel 311 for nonemergency police situations and City services.

Illinois Poison Center
Tel (800) 222-1222.

Emergency Rooms
Bernard A. Mitchell Hospital, 5815 S Maryland Ave. **Map** 7 B4.
Tel (773) 702-1000.

Lincoln Park Hospital, 550 Webster Ave.
Tel (773) 883-2000.

Northwestern Memorial Hospital, 251 E Erie St. **Map** 2 D4.
Tel 926-1807.

Medical Referrals
Chicago Dental Society Referrals
Tel (312) 836-7300.

Physician Referral Service at Northwestern Memorial Hospital
Tel 926-8400; (877) 926-4664.

24-Hour Pharmacies
CVS Pharmacy
Tel (800) 746-7287.
Walgreen's Drugstore
Tel (800) 925-4733.

LOST PROPERTY

Midway Airport Police
Tel (773) 838-3003.

O'Hare Airport Police
Tel (773) 686-2385.

Public Transit
Chicago Transit Authority
Tel (888) 968-7282.
www.transitchicago.com
Metra at Union Station
Tel 322-4269.
Metra (general information)
Tel 322-6777.
www.metrarail.com

Lost or Stolen Credit Cards
American Express
Tel (800) 528-4800.
MasterCard
Tel (800) 307-7309.
VISA
Tel (800) 847-2911.

Banking and Local Currency

Most national and international banks have branches in Chicago, and foreign currency exchange is available at the main branches of any large bank. The cheapest exchange, though, may be offered on your credit or debit card, which can be used at most ATMs (automated teller machines). It is a good idea to arrive in Chicago with about $100 cash in US currency, including a few dollars in coins, to cover incidental costs until you are able to exchange your money.

CHASE

Logo of a major Chicago bank

BANKING

Banks are generally open Monday to Friday from 9am to 5pm; 9am to early or mid-afternoon on Saturday.
Many banks charge fees to use a teller for routine matters such as withdrawing money. Always ask if any fees apply before making a transaction with a bank teller.
The major consumer banks in Chicago include **Chase, Bank of America,** and **Harris Bank**. Credit unions will usually serve only their members.

AUTOMATED TELLER MACHINES

There is no need to carry large amounts of cash in Chicago. Hundreds of automated teller machines (ATMs) can be found through-out the city. They are almost always in bank lobbies or on an outside wall near the bank's entrance, as well as in many convenience and grocery stores. Some bars and fast-food outlets also have ATMs on their premises.
US currency, usually in $20 bills, can be electronically withdrawn from your bank or credit-card account through an ATM. Ask your bank at home which American ATM network your card can access in Chicago, and what transaction fees will apply. **Cirrus** and **Plus** are common networks in Chicago. You can also do transactions with some credit cards at ATMs. Always be aware of your surroundings and take care

at ATMs by using them in secure conditions, daylight hours, or when there are plenty of people nearby in order to deter robbers.

CREDIT CARDS

Credit cards allow you to carry minimal cash and may offer merchandise guarantees or other benefits. American Express, Diners Club, MasterCard, and VISA are widely accepted.
Most hotels ask for a credit-card number to guarantee a reservation, taking an imprint of the card when you check in. Car rental agencies insist on a credit-card guarantee even if you are paying for the rental in cash *(see p191)*.
Credit cards are very helpful in emergencies, should you have to fly home on short notice or need medical treatment during your stay. Many hospitals will accept a major credit card as a method of payment.

EXCHANGING MONEY

Exchange rates are printed in the daily newspapers and posted in banks where exchange services are offered, usually at the main branches of large banks. Some banks have designated tellers for foreign exchange.
Foreign exchange brokers in Chicago are few. Among the solidly established is **Travelex. World's Money Exchange** also deals in foreign currency. Two exchanges are located at O'Hare Airport, in terminals 3 and 5 (open

daily); there are no currency exchanges at Midway Airport. Keep in mind, however, that an ATM may provide a better exchange rate and charge a lower transaction fee than a bank or exchange bureau.
Chicago has hundreds of state-regulated "currency exchanges." Most do not exchange foreign currency but instead cash checks, sell money orders, and offer notary services.

CASHING TRAVELER'S CHECKS

Traveler's checks issued by **American Express and Travelex** in US dollars are widely accepted without a fee by most shops, hotels, and restaurants, if accompanied by a recognized form of photographic identification, such as a passport, driver's license, or international student card *(see p177)*.
US-dollar traveler's checks can be cashed at most banks. Remember to inquire about commission fees. Checks in foreign currency can be cashed at a bank branch offering foreign-currency exchange, usually the banks' main locations.
American Express and Travelex will cash their own checks at no fee.

Automated teller machine (ATM)

Coins

American coins (actual size shown) come in 1-, 5-, 10-, and 25-cent, as well as $1, denominations; 50-cent pieces are minted but rarely used. Each value of coin has a popular name: 1-cent coins are known as pennies, 5-cent coins as nickels, 10-cent coins as dimes, 25-cent coins as quarters, and 1-dollar coins (and bills) as bucks.

25-cent coin
(a quarter)

10-cent coin
(a dime)

5-cent coin
(a nickel)

1-cent coin
(a penny)

1-dollar coin
(a buck)

Bank Notes

Units of currency in the US are dollars and cents, with 100 cents to a dollar. Notes, or "bills," come in $1, $2, $5, $10, $20, $50, and $100 denominations. The $2 bills are rarely seen. All bills are the same color so check the amount carefully. New US currency is gradually being introduced. The new $10, $20, and $50 dollar bills with extra security features are now in circulation.

DIRECTORY

BANKS

Chase
605 N Michigan Ave. **Map** 2 D4.
Tel 787-1900.

Harris Bank
111 W Monroe St. **Map** 3 C2.
Tel 461-2121.

Bank of America
500 N Michigan Ave. **Map** 2 D3.
Tel 464-0701.

ATM SYSTEMS

Cirrus
Tel (800) 424-7787.

Plus
Tel (800) 843-7587.

EXCHANGES AND TRAVELER'S CHECKS

American Express
605 N Michigan Ave. **Map** 2 D4.
Tel 943-7840.

Travelex
19 S LaSalle St. **Map** 3 C2.
Tel 807-4941 or (800) 287-7362.

World's Money Exchange
203 N LaSalle St. **Map** 3 C1.
Tel 641-2151.

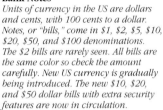

1-dollar bill ($1)

5-dollar bill ($5)

10-dollar bill ($10)

20-dollar bill ($20)

50-dollar bill ($50)

100-dollar bill ($100)

Communications

Chicago's communication systems are, for the most part, both efficient and reasonably priced. Public pay phones are located throughout the city, and at gas stations and tourist centers along the interstates. SBC is the major player in the Chicago telecommunications field. Regular letter service offered by the US postal system is reliable. Express services are offered by post offices and independent courier companies. Visitors will find that Internet, e-mail, and fax services are readily available in Chicago.

Express Mail box

PHONE NUMBERS AND PREFIXES

Most US phone numbers have seven digits. Some emergency and public-service numbers have only three. US prefixes (area codes) are always three digits.

Chicago and its environs use six prefixes: 312 (Downtown Core), 773 (surrounding downtown), 847 and 224 (north and northwestern suburbs; note that even local calls made in this area require dialling 1 and the area code, such 11-digit dialling for local calls will eventually apply to all areas), 708 (near western and southern suburbs), and 630 (far western suburbs).

PUBLIC PAY PHONES

Chicago's pay phones are found throughout the city, particularly in restaurants, gas stations, and department stores. Most are coin operated, though you can use a calling-card number to charge calls to your account. Some also accept credit cards.

Most pay phones are operated by AT & T. Some may belong to a company other than AT & T, though the phones often look similar. Phone companies set their own rates, so prices vary. Use only public phones that have details of the charges posted.

PAY PHONE CHARGES

Calling a number with the same prefix as the one from which you are calling is considered a local call. The minimum charge for a local call made from a pay phone is 50 cents and will buy from three to five minutes. When it is time to insert more money, a recording will interrupt to tell you how much to deposit.

When calling within the same area code, simply dial the phone number. When calling another area code, first dial 1 and the prefix.

Phone books are now rare at pay phones. Dial 411 to connect to national directory assistance. The minimum charge is 50 cents.

Rates for long-distance calls vary, depending on the time of day, the distance called, and the long-distance carrier. Be sure to have plenty of coins or a calling card before placing the call from a pay phone. If billing the call to a calling-card number, follow the instructions on the card or those on the phone. Dialing instructions are in the white pages of the phone directory.

Long-distance calls are less expensive when dialed without the help of an operator. Savings on calls within the US are available during the night and weekends. Discounts for calls to locations outside the US vary; ask the international operator for details. A list of country codes is in the Yellow Pages of the phone directory.

USING A COIN-OPERATED PHONE

1 Lift the receiver and listen for the tone.

3 Press the number.

Coins
Make sure you have the correct coins available before you dial and a sufficient quantity of them.

25 cents

5 cents   10 cents

2 Insert the required coin or coins. The coin drops as soon as you insert it.

4 If you do not want to complete your call or the call does not connect, press the coin-release lever and take the coins from the coin return located at the bottom left-hand corner of the phone.

5 If the call is answered and you talk longer than the allotted time, a recorded message will interrupt and tell you how much more money to deposit. Pay phones do not give change but will return unused coins to the coin return.

CELL PHONES

It is possible to rent a cell phone in Chicago. **International Sound** offers free downtown delivery. AT&T, Nextel, and Sprint are the largest mobile service providers. Chicago's cell phone network is not GSM-compatible. Check with your carrier whether you will be able to tune your own phone to local Chicago networks.

TV AND RADIO

Six major TV networks are broadcast in Chicago: CBS on channel 2, NBC on channel 5, ABC on channel 7, WGN on channel 9, PBS on channel 11, and FOX on channel 32.

AM radio stations include WBBM news (780Hz) and WGN talk/sports (720Hz). FM radio stations include WBEZ news and jazz (91.5M).

See pages 176–7 for details on Chicago newspapers.

USEFUL DIALING CODES

- Long-distance direct-dial call outside your local area code, but within the US and Canada: dial **1**.
- International direct-dial call: dial **011**, followed by country code (UK: 44; Australia: 61; New Zealand: 64;; Ireland: 353), then the city or area code, then the local telephone number.
- International call via the operator: dial **01**, the country code, the city code (minus the first 0), then the local telephone number.
- International directory inquiries: dial **00**.
- International operator assistance: dial **01**.
- An **800, 866, 877**, or **888** prefix indicates that the call is toll-free. Dial **1** before the prefix.
- Directory assistance for toll-free numbers: dial **1-800-555-1212**.
- Directory assistance for outside local area: dial **1-AREACODE-555-1212**.
- Local operator assistance: dial 0.
- General directory inquiries: dial **411**.

Entrance to Oak Park's post office

POSTAL SERVICES

Apart from post offices, letters can be mailed at most hotel concierge desks (which usually also sell stamps); at letter slots in the lobbies of office buildings; at air, rail, and bus terminals; and at a street mailbox, though these can be few and far between. Collection times are printed on the inside of the pull-down door of each mailbox, which are always painted blue, or red, white, and blue. Stamps can be bought at the **Chicago Main Post Office** or branch offices located throughout the city.

All letters are delivered on first-class service. The delivery time can sometimes be as long as five business days.

The US Postal Service offers two special delivery services. **Priority Mail** guarantees the delivery in two to three business days; **Express Mail** guarantees delivery on the next business day. If using either Express Mail or Priority Mail, first weigh your letters at a post office to determine the postage required.

Two other companies offer mail services. **FedEx** offers a variety of overnight mail services. **UPS** delivers parcels and packages. FedEx and UPS services are usually available through mailing businesses such as **Mail Boxes Etc**.

Letters and parcels will be held for 30 days for collection at the Main Post Office. Address mail with: Name, General Delivery, Chicago Main Post Office, 433 West Harrison Street, Chicago, IL 60607. You will need to show photo ID to collect mail.

E-MAIL AND FAXES

Visitors to Chicago can use e-mail and the Internet, as well as fax machines, in the larger hotels and those with business facilities, or at one of the Internet cafés now beginning to dot the Loop and North Side. However, these businesses tend to close down as quickly as they open, so it is best to ask your hotel concierge or at a visitor center about current businesses. One popular Internet café in Chicago is **Screenz**, part of a national chain.

Online time at cafés may be charged by the minute (from 8 cents to 20 cents) or by the hour (from $4 to $10).

Mail Boxes Etc., a national mailbox-service business

GETTING TO CHICAGO

Chicago is one of the US's most important transportation hubs. All major airlines fly into one of its two airports: O'Hare or Midway. The major carriers often have similar fares, though you can sometimes find savings by flying into Midway. Discount ticket services, travel companies on the Internet, and charter airlines may also offer very substantial savings. Amtrak trains from across the US and from Canada arrive in Chicago daily, and several interstate highways run through Chicago *(see pp190–91)*, making the city easily accessible by train, car, or bus. Long-distance bus travel is generally both comfortable and convenient.

Star Alliance passenger jet

ARRIVING BY AIR

Aside from driving into the city, the easiest way to get to Chicago is by air. Flights from the East Coast of the US take about two hours; from the West Coast about four hours.

All major airlines fly into Chicago, among them Air Canada, Continental, British Airways, Lufthansa, American Airlines, and United Airlines.

Chicago is served by two airports. The largest and busiest is O'Hare, located 17 miles (27 km) northwest of the city. Midway Airport is much smaller and located about 8 miles (13 km) southwest of downtown.

AIR FARES

It pays to shop around for fares, especially if you are booking a departure flight less than 14 days in advance. Many major airlines offer discounts for tickets purchased at least 14 days before departure. These tickets usually carry restrictions and penalties for changes to your itinerary; ask before paying.

Investigate smaller carriers, especially if you are making last-minute plans; their fares are often less than half those of the major airlines. You may also find flights into Midway Airport to be less expensive than those into O'Hare.

For inexpensive consolidated tickets (those bought from a travel agent), contact **Cheap Tickets or Priceline.com** online. An extensive list of consolidators can be ordered from **Intrepid Traveler**.

When booking a flight, bear in mind that "direct" means that the plane may make one or two stops along the way, but you won't need to change planes. "Nonstop" means you fly directly to your destination.

O'HARE AIRPORT (ORD)

Chicago's O'Hare Airport is one of the world's busiest airports, servicing up to 70 million passengers each year. Three terminals are used for domestic flights, one for international flights.

O'Hare has been extensively remodeled in recent years. Today it is clean and spacious. The food at most of its restaurants is good, prices aren't grossly inflated, and the atmosphere is pleasing. There are also many upscale stores and kiosks throughout the airport. A branch of the Chicago Children's Museum *(see p65)* is in Terminal 2.

Rental carts are available for use within the airport. Skycaps (porters) will also transport your luggage to a taxi or shuttle; they should be tipped from 50 cents to $1 per bag.

Terminal 1 is dominated by United Express, United Airlines (departures), Ryan International (departures), and Lufthansa (departures). Terminal 2 serves Continental, Air Canada, Northwest Airlines, America West, United/United Express, and US Airways. Terminal 3 serves Alaska Airlines, American, American Eagle, Delta, Iberia, and Spirit. Terminal 5 is for international flights. There is no Terminal 4.

To get between domestic terminals, the international terminal, and the long-term parking lot, take the free Automated Train System (ATS). There is also free shuttle service between parking lot F and the ATS terminal at parking lot E.

O'Hare has several Airport Information counters on the lower level of each domestic terminal, and on the lower and upper levels of the international terminal. The counters are open daily from 6:30am to 10pm. Multilingual specialists are on hand to provide directions and translation assistance.

Teletext phones for the hearing impaired are located next to the airport information booths as well as at phone banks throughout the airport.

Automatic bank teller machines are located on the upper levels of all terminals.

AIRPORT	INFORMATION	DISTANCE TO CHICAGO	TAXI FARE (OFF-PEAK HOURS)	CONTINENTAL EXPRESS TO DOWNTOWN	OMEGA SHUTTLE TO SOUTH SIDE
O'Hare	(773) 686-2200	17 miles (27 km)	$30–$35	$25	$30
Midway	(773) 838-0608	8 miles (13 km)	$20–$25	$25	$17

MIDWAY AIRPORT (MDW)

Midway airport is located just 10 miles (16 km) from downtown Chicago and is one of the fastest growing airports in the US. A $761-million six-year development project (completed in 2004) has transformed this once small, single-storey building into a user-friendly 21st-century facility. Services include a food, retail and beverage area called Midway Boulevard as well as a six-storey parking garage. A two-level terminal system now separates arrivals and departures with the ticketing area above and baggage pick-up below. Road links to the airport have also been improved and the concourse has expanded from 29 to 43 gates.

International services are available from this airport.

GETTING INTO THE CITY

A convenient, inexpensive way to get into the city from either airport is via CTA train *(see p188)*.

Blue-line trains run directly to and from O'Hare Airport, 24 hours a day. The ride to

the downtown Dearborn Street station takes about 45 minutes. Orange-line trains run between Midway Airport and downtown, stopping at all orange-line Loop stations, from 4am to midnight. Allow 35 minutes for the ride. Trains on both lines depart frequently. One-way train fare is $1.75.

Continental Airport Express operates a shuttle service between each airport and downtown Chicago. Shuttles operate daily, beginning at 6am. Airport Express also provides service between both airports and McCormick Place Convention Center.

Omega Airport Shuttle operates shuttle service between O'Hare and Midway airports between 7am and 10pm daily. Omega also offers shuttle service to Hyde Park on Chicago's South Side.

It is possible to share a taxi ride from either airport to downtown. Airport curbside dispatchers will help get you a taxi or put you with other persons going to the same area; it will cost you about

Sign for CTA blue-line trains

Concourse of the international terminal at O'Hare Airport

$20 for the shared taxi ride. Information counters of limousine and rental car agencies *(see p191)* are in the baggage claim areas of both Midway and O'Hare airports.

Driving time from O'Hare International Airport to downtown Chicago is about 45 minutes, and 30 minutes from Midway, but allow up to twice this time during rush hour (from 6am to 9am; 3pm to 7pm). Taxis are not immune to traffic jams. During rush hour, it is much faster to use public transportation to and from either of the airports.

DIRECTORY

AIRPORTS

Midway Airport
Tel (773) 838-0608.
www.flychicago.com

O'Hare International Airport
Tel (773) 686-2200 or (800) 832-6352.
www.flychicago.com

AIRLINE NUMBERS

Air Canada
Tel (888) 247-2262.

American Airlines
Tel (800) 443-7300.

British Airways
Tel (800) 247-9297.

British Midland
Tel (800) 788-0555.

Continental Airlines
Tel (800) 525-0280.

Lufthansa
Tel (800) 645-3880.

United Airlines
Tel (800) 241-6522.

AIR FARES

Cheap Tickets
www.cheaptickets.com

Intrepid Travel
Tel (866) 847-8192.
www.intrepidtravel.com

Priceline.com
www.priceline.com

AIRPORT SHUTTLES

Continental Airport Express
Tel (773) 247-1200, or (888) 284-3286.
www.airportexpress.com

Omega Airport Shuttle
Tel (773) 483-6634.
www.omegashuttle.com

AIRPORT HOTELS

At O'Hare Airport
Hilton O'Hare, PO Box 66414, Chicago, IL.
Tel (773) 686-8000.

Crowne Plaza O'Hare, 5440 N River Rd, Rosemont, IL.
Tel (847) 671-6350.

Hyatt Regency O'Hare, 9300 W Bryn Mawr Ave, Rosemont, IL.
Tel (847) 696-1234.

Embassy Suites Hotel O'Hare 5500 N River Rd, Rosemont, IL.
Tel (847) 678-4000.

Westin O'Hare 6100 N River Rd, Rosemont, IL.
Tel (847) 698-6000.

At Midway Airport
Holiday Inn Express Hotel & Suites 6500 S Cicero Ave.
Tel (877) 863-4780.

Courtyard by Marriot 6610 S Cicero Ave.
Tel (708) 563-0200.

ARRIVING BY CAR

If you arrive in Chicago from the southwest, on I-55 (Stevenson Expressway), follow the freeway to its end, to Lake Shore Drive, then follow Lake Shore Drive north. Shortly you will pass the city center, and have one of the best views of Chicago's skyline. Several exits lead off Lake Shore Drive into downtown or the North Side, including the Wacker Drive exit. Taking Lake Shore Drive is a good way to traverse the city.

Historic Route 66 running from Los Angeles joins I-55 on the outskirts of Chicago.

I-90 East (Northwest Tollway to Kennedy Expressway) running from the northwest, from O'Hare Airport, will bring you into the city. Take the Ohio Street exit for downtown.

Arriving by car from the west, I-290 East (Eisenhower Expressway) will become Congress Parkway at the southwest edge of Chicago's downtown Loop. From the parkway, drive north for destinations downtown or beyond.

From the south, I-57 leads into the Dan Ryan Expressway and to I-90 and I-94, which converge in the city. For destinations in the Loop, there are a number of options. The Washington Street or Monroe Street exits will put you on one-way streets that run into the Loop. For destinations just north of the Loop, such as the Magnificent Mile, take the Ohio Street exit east.

The **Illinois Department of Transportation** has a useful website, which details driving directions to Chicago and throughout Illinois, as well as information about weather and road conditions. See pages 182–3 for more details on driving in Illinois.

ARRIVING BY LONG-DISTANCE BUS

The main terminal in Chicago for **Greyhound Bus Line**, the bus line that services almost all parts of the US, is in the Downtown Core. However, it is not within easy walking distance to hotels in the Loop, so plan on taking a taxi or public transportation to your final destination.

Greyhound also stops near O'Hare Airport at the CTA Cumberland station and on the city's South Side at 95th and Dan Ryan Expressway.

Greyhound buses are clean and modern. Ask when purchasing tickets about any discounts. They are usually offered to children, seniors, students, members of the military, and US veterans. Ask also about any promotional packages that may be available.

Greyhound's Ameripass allows up to 60 consecutive days of unlimited travel anywhere in the continental US. Tickets may be less expensive if you buy them in advance, though walk-up, or unrestricted, fares are also readily available.

Greyhound provides assistance to travelers with disabilities with 48 hours' notice, including priority seating. In some cases, a personal care assistant may travel for free. Call the Greyhound **ADA Assist Line** for details.

Sign for historic Route 66

Amtrak train in train yard near Union Station

ARRIVING BY TRAIN

Chicago is the national rail hub of **Amtrak**, the US's passenger rail line. Fifty trains linking to hundreds of US destinations, as well as those from Canada, arrive at or depart from Chicago's **Union Station** daily. Amtrak also services 34 destinations in Illinois, either through trains or connecting buses.

Its commuter trains have refreshment cars. Long-distance routes have both dining cars and sleeping cars.

Amtrak offers discounts to travelers with disabilities, students, seniors, and children. There are also group and convention rates. Ask too about any promotional discounts or package deals.

Reservations are necessary on many Amtrak routes and advised for all travel during peak periods: the summer months and major holidays.

The 1925 building housing Union Station was renovated in the early 1990s. Ticket agents, a food court, lounge, 10-story waiting area, storage lockers, and Metra commuter train station (see pp190–91) are all to be found within the building, which is wheelchair accessible. "Red cap" Amtrak porters are available to help you with your luggage.

Although Union Station is just west of the Loop and close to downtown Chicago, it is not an easy walk to hotels or CTA trains when you are carrying luggage. If arriving in Chicago by train, it is best to plan on taking a taxi to your hotel.

Long-distance Greyhound bus

A typical Chicago taxi cab

GETTING TO McCORMICK PLACE

Located one mile (1.5 km) south of downtown Chicago, McCormick Place Convention Center is the largest exhibition and meeting facility in North America. Even though it is close to the Loop, the walk is not a practical one. A taxi ride from the Loop to McCormick Place will cost about $6. Large conventions often provide shuttle bus services from major downtown hotels, and sometimes, from the airports. The McCormick Place Busway has improved travelling times from downtown to the Center.

The Metra Electric line *(see pp190–91)* services the 23rd Street/McCormick Place station. Trains depart from the Randolph Street and Van Buren Street stations.

If you are arriving in Chicago at Union Station, take the No. 1, 7, or 126 eastbound CTA bus to Michigan Avenue. Transfer to either southbound bus No. 3 or 4; both will take you to the 23rd Street bus stop outside the convention center.

If driving to McCormick Place from O'Hare Airport, take I-90 (Northwest Tollway) east to I-94 (Kennedy/Dan Ryan Expressway), exiting to I-55 north (Stevenson Expressway). Follow the signs to Lake Shore Drive South (31st Street exit) and to McCormick Place.

From Midway Airport, take Cicero Avenue north to the I-55 (Stevenson Expressway), then continue north to Lake Shore Drive South, following the signs to McCormick Place.

The convention center can be reached via public transportation from O'Hare and Midway airports. However, you may find it more convenient to take a taxi or, if available, a shuttle bus, as there is no direct transit route: you will need to transfer to a CTA bus once downtown.

If using public transportation from O'Hare Airport, take the blue-line CTA train *(see p185)* downtown, transferring to the green, orange, or purple line to reach Adams station. Then take the southbound CTA bus No. 3 or 4 from Michigan Avenue to 23rd Street.

From Midway Airport, take the orange-line CTA train *(see p185)* to Roosevelt Street station, then southbound CTA bus No. 3 or 4 to 23rd Street.

The **Chicago Convention and Tourism Bureau** provides information on meeting services, convention planning, and accommodations.

DIRECTORY

LONG-DISTANCE BUS SERVICES

Greyhound Bus Line
630 W Harrison St. **Map** 3 A3.
Tel 408-5800 *or*
(800) 231-2222.
or
14 W 95th St.
Tel 928-8606.
www.greyhound.com

Greyhound ADA Assist Line
Tel (800) 752-4841.

TRAIN INFORMATION

Amtrak at Union Station
Tel (800) 872-7245.
www.amtrak.com

Union Station
225 S Canal St.
Map 3 B2.
Tel 756-0934.

PUBLIC TRANSIT

Metra Passenger Information
Tel 322-6777.
www.metrarail.com

Regional Transit Authority (RTA)
Tel 836-7000 *or (888) 968-7282.*
www.transitchicago.com

USEFUL NUMBERS AND ADDRESSES

Chicago Convention and Tourism Bureau
2301 S Lake Shore Dr,
Chicago, IL 60616.
Tel 567-8500.
www.choosechicago.com

Illinois Department of Transportation
Map Sales, Room 128W, 2300 S Dirksen Pkwy, Springfield, IL 62764. *Tel* (217) 782-0834.
www.dot.state.il.us

McCormick Place
2301 S Lake Shore Dr,
Chicago, IL 60616.
Tel 791-7000.
www.mccormickplace.com

Trade show in Hall B, North Building, McCormick Place

Getting Around Chicago

No parking from 11pm to 6am

Although Chicago is a sprawling Midwestern metropolis, many of the city's sights and main cultural centers are located downtown, making the city a walker's dream. The city's public transportation is inexpensive and efficient. The train system, known as the "L" for "elevated," is the easiest way to get around. Buses crisscross the city, but the system is complicated and best left to regular commuters. Taxis are affordable, convenient, and readily available.

Cyclist taking advantage of a quiet spell on Chicago's lakefront path

PLANNING YOUR JOURNEY

Public transit in Chicago is extremely busy during the rush hours, which are weekdays from 6am to 9am and 3pm to 7pm. You may wish to avoid it at these peak times. Ask your hotel concierge and check a calendar of events to avoid getting caught in the middle of a particular celebration, of which there are many (see pp32–35).

STREET LAYOUT AND NUMBERING

Chicago streets are laid out on a grid system. Most streets run north and south or east and west, though some run on the diagonal.

The zero point in the city is at Madison and State Streets, in the Loop. Street numbers ascend by 50 or 100 numbers in each block as they radiate out from Madison and State. Most streets in the Loop are one-way streets.

Typical pedestrian and vehicular traffic on busy State Street

TRAFFIC SIGNS

All traffic signs, including those denoting speed limits, are black and white. Informational signs, such as those indicating highway exits, are green and white. Most intersections are also marked with green-and-white signs bearing the name of the streets. These signs are posted high on utility poles.

"Caution" and "Yield" signs are yellow and black. White-and-brown signs indicate the major city sights and landmarks.

Pedway

WALKING

Walkway sign

The best way to explore downtown Chicago is on foot. Many of the major sights and shopping areas are only a short walk from each other. Streets are relatively flat, so you will not have to tackle hills during your outings.

Traffic lights signal drivers to stop (red), go (green), and proceed with caution (yellow). For pedestrians, electronic "Walk" signs show an illuminated human figure. A red hand indicates that pedestrians should not cross the street. Never rely solely on the traffic lights; look both ways before crossing the street, and watch for cars making right turns or racing through yellow lights.

In the Loop, an extensive system of pubic underground pedestrian walkways, or pedways, links train stations with major buildings.

BICYCLING

Chicago is currently developing a number of pro-cycling initiatives including an expanding network of cycle lanes. However, cyclists on the streets must still use extreme caution, obey traffic laws, and wear a safety helmet.

The lakefront, however, offers miles of scenic path for recreational riding, although it can be busy. **Bike Chicago** rents bicycles and in-line skates; **Bobby's Bike Hire** also rents bicycles and leads neighborhood tours. Informal rules-of-the-road exist on the path, but it is often difficult for walkers, cyclists, and in-line skaters to coexist on it. The best time to enjoy it is during business hours when traffic is quieter.

TAXIS

Most Chicago taxi drivers are good drivers. But, as in any city, there are exceptions. For a serious complaint, note the name of the taxi company and the car number (on the side of the taxi) and call **Consumer Services**.

You likely will be able to flag a vacant taxi on a busy street, or find one waiting outside a hotel. If the taxi's roof light is lit, it is available. To be picked up at a specific time, phone to reserve at least one hour in advance.

Taxis charge a base fare of about $2.25, plus $1 for a second passenger. A $1 surcharge is added to all airport trips. Fare information is posted inside each taxi.

DRIVING

Vehicles are driven on the right-hand side of the road in the US, except on one-way streets. The Illinois speed limit is 30 mph (48 km/h) on city and residential roads, 55 mph (88 km/h) on metro highways. You must wear a seatbelt.

A right turn on a red light is permitted unless a sign prohibits it. Left turns are not allowed at some intersections during peak times, or are allowed only when the green arrow signal is illuminated.

See pages 190–91 for details on interstates and renting a car.

PARKING

Street parking in Chicago falls into three categories: free, metered, and restricted. Free street parking is scarce. Metered street parking is most readily available. The parking meters usually take quarters only. Depending on the area, 25 cents will buy from five minutes to one hour parking time. The vehicle may be ticketed once the time runs out. Parking is free in some metered areas in the evenings and on Sundays.

Residential areas often have permit-only parking at night; restrictions are noted on signs. Parking tickets are expensive and tickets for a rental car will follow you home. Never park in front of a fire hydrant or driveway; your car will likely be towed.

The city operates a few parking lots that have low rates. Commercial lots abound; the closer the lot is to downtown, the more expensive. Some businesses offer customers validated parking (discounted or free parking if you have your ticket stamped in the store).

Parking meter for street parking

PENALTIES

If your car is towed off a downtown city street, call **City Services** to locate it. If it is towed from a privately managed parking lot, call the telephone number on the sign posted nearby.

Expect to pay at least $100 to retrieve your car. If it is a rental car, be prepared to show your rental contract.

Parking tickets and minor traffic violations may be paid by money order or credit card. For moving violations, your ticket will have information about where and how to pay or contest the ticket.

TRAVELING BY PUBLIC TRAINS AND BUSES

The **Chicago Transit Authority** (CTA) operates an extensive system of trains and buses. The train system is called the "L," for "elevated" – even when the lines run underground. There are eight train lines: blue, brown, red, green, yellow, orange, pink, and purple. Free CTA system maps *(see inside back cover)* are available at the stations. Many CTA train stations are wheelchair accessible. Buses stop about every two blocks at posted CTA signs that indicate the number and name of the route, but not the direction. Some buses do not travel the entire route; check the destination sign on the bus. To board a bus, hail the driver and remain on the curb until the bus has come to a stop.

Adult fare is about $2; child fare about $1. Transferring between routes costs 25 cents. Change is not provided on CTA buses.

Machines in the stations will dispense cards that can be used on both CTA trains and buses. Passes for unlimited travel are available at the CTA website, Visitor Information Centers, and other locations.

Trolleys and shuttle buses provide free service to several

CTA transit card

A Chicago Transit Authority elevated train in the Loop

city sights. Visit the **Department of Transportation** website or a Visitor Center *(see pp176–7)* for details.

DIRECTORY

BICYCLE RENTALS

Bike Chicago
at Navy Pier. **Map** 2 F5.
Tel (888) 245-3929.
www.bikechicago.com

Bobby's Bike Hire
Tel (312) 915-0995.
www.bobbysbikehire.com

TAXI NUMBERS

American-United Cab
Tel (773) 248-7600.

Checker Taxi
Tel 243-2537.

Flash Cab
Tel (773) 561-1444.

Yellow Cab
Tel 829-4222.

USEFUL NUMBERS

Chicago Transit Authority (CTA)
Tel (888) 968-7282.
www.transitchicago.com

City Services
Tel 744-7275 to pay tickets by credit card.

Consumer Services
www 744-4006.

Department of Transportation
Tel (312) 744-3600.
www.cityofchicago.org/transportation

Traveling Outside Chicago

Traveling outside Chicago is most convenient by car, though there is also an inexpensive and extensive public transportation system to the many suburbs and beyond. Rush hours are the only real obstacle to smooth traveling. The so-called reverse commute has vanished. At peak times during the day, city dwellers are going to work at industry headquarters located in the suburbs; at the same time, suburbanites are heading into the city for office jobs. Rush hour can start as early as 5:30am and last until 9am. The afternoon rush begins as early as 3pm and often lasts until past 7pm.

METRA

A network of 11 commuter train lines that begin in the city center and stretch out like tentacles to the suburbs is operated by **Metra**. The 495-mile (795-km) system has 230 stations in the Illinois counties of Cook, Du Page, Lake, Will, McHenry, and Kane. It also services some cities in Indiana and Wisconsin. Trains run on a published schedule, frequently during rush hour and every one to three hours at other times. The trains are more comfortable than CTA trains (see p189). They do not have baggage check.

On weekends and holidays, youngsters ages 12 to 17 ride for half fare. Kids under 12 may ride free when accompanied by a fare-paying adult. Weekend passes are also available for unlimited travel on all Metra lines.

Metra trains depart from five stations surrounding the Loop: Union Station, Ogilvie Transportation Center, Randolph Street Station, Van Buren Street Station, and LaSalle Street Station.

Union Station, at Adams and Canal streets, is the main Metra station. The Electric Line, which runs to McCormick Place, stops at three stations along Michigan Avenue: at Randolph and Van Buren Streets and at Roosevelt Road. The Union Pacific North Line runs to Highland Park, stopping just outside the Ravinia Festival gate.

Metra has wheelchair-accessible cars; phone for details or visit the **Metra Passenger Services** center.

PACE

The suburban bus system, **Pace**, is a division of the Regional Transportation Authority (RTA), which also oversees Metra and the CTA. Pace provides fixed bus routes, Dial-a-Ride services for travelers with disabilities, vanpools, and special-event buses throughout Chicago's six-county suburban region. Pace buses also provide good connections between Metra stations and shopping malls.

Much of the Pace system is wheelchair accessible; phone for details, or visit the **RTA Customer Service Center** for information, along with free maps and timetables.

INTERSTATES

The several highways running through and around Chicago are of two types: freeways and tollways. Freeways are tollfree public highways. The charge for driving on a state tollway ranges from 15 cents to $2, which will be collected at a tollbooth. Generally, lanes at the tollbooths are designated as exact change (automatic), needing change (manual), and I-Pass (an electronic system that allows specially equipped cars to drive through, automatically deducting the toll from the vehicle's account). Getting on or off a tollway usually also involves a fee, and because those booths are unattended, exact change is necessary.

Interstates are divided multilane highways and are the main routes between cities. Most swell to six or more lanes as they near large cities. Interstate numbers are posted on red, white, and blue shield-shaped signs.

Main interstate routes have two-digit numbers, with those with even numbers generally running east-west and those with odd numbers generally running north-south. There are exceptions, however. While I-94 runs east-west across the US, it runs north-south in Illinois.

Interstates with three digits are loops (if the first digit is 2, 4, 6, or 8) or spurs (first digit

CTA bus No. 56, which terminates at Jefferson Park

Stairs to main concourse at Chicago's historic Union Station

View from scenic US Route 20, running northwest through Illinois

of 1, 3, 5, 7, or 9) of the main interstate route.

I-55 (Stevenson Express-way) runs from US-41 (Lake Shore Drive) in Chicago to St. Louis, then to New Orleans via Memphis.

I-90 runs from Boston to Seattle, and in Illinois from the Indiana line on the Chicago Skyway through Chicago on the Dan Ryan and Kennedy Expressways, and to Rockford and the WI line on the Northwest Tollway. The Chicago Skyway, however is no longer designated as I-90, but rather, as TO I-90.

I-190 is the spur from I-90 to O'Hare Airport.

I-94 runs from Montana to Michigan. In Illinois, it is called Edens Expressway and merges with I-90, the main highway through Chicago.

NAMED HIGHWAYS

Many Illinois highways are commonly referred to by name rather than by number. The stretch of I-90/94 that runs from the city center south to 95th Street is called the Dan Ryan Expressway.

The stretch that runs from the city center northwest to O'Hare Airport is known as the Kennedy Expressway.

I-290 is also known as the Eisenhower Expressway, and as Congress Parkway within the city center. I-55 is called the Stevenson Expressway.

SPEED LIMITS AND FINES

The speed limit for cars on Illinois' open highways is 65 mph (105 km/h) and 55 mph (88 km/h) on metro highways. Speeding tickets

carry heavy fines. A minimum speed regulation in Illinois means you also could be ticketed for driving so slowly that you impede traffic.

Speed limit (in mph)

Rest area, indicated off an interstate

Roadside tests and fines for drinking and driving are increasingly common.

RENTAL CARS

To rent a car, you must be at least 25 years old, with a valid driver's license (for foreign visitors, an international driver's license) and a major credit card in your name.

Before leaving home, check your insurance policy to see if you are covered in a rental car. If not, you should buy damage and liability insurance when renting the car.

Most agencies offer a range of vehicles, from "economy" models to convertibles. All rental cars are automatic and have power steering.

Refill the car with gasoline before returning it or you will pay a service charge.

Two car rental agencies in Chicago

STREET FINDER

Map references given in this guide for sights, hotels, restaurants, shops, and entertainment venues refer to the Street Finder maps on the following pages (*see* How the Map References Work *below*). A complete index of the street names and places of interest marked on the maps can also be found on the pages that follow. The map opposite shows the area of Chicago the eight *Street Finder* maps cover. This includes the sightseeing areas (which are color-coded) as well as the whole of central Chicago. The symbols used to represent sights and useful information on the *Street Finder* maps are listed below in the key.

HOW THE MAP REFERENCES WORK

The first figure tells you which *Street Finder* map to turn to.

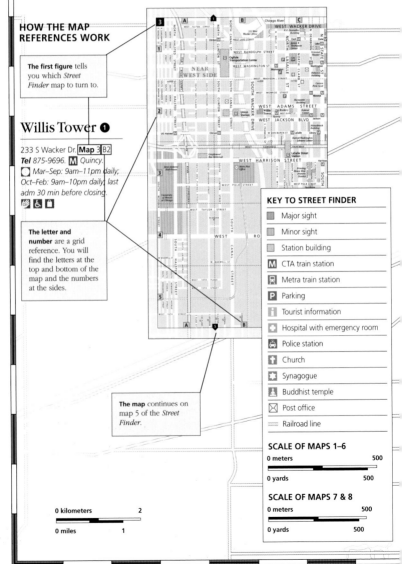

Willis Tower ❶

233 S Wacker Dr. **Map** 3 B2
Tel 875-9696. **M** Quincy.
◯ Mar–Sep: 9am–11pm daily;
Oct–Feb: 9am–10pm daily, last
adm 30 min before closing.

The letter and number are a grid reference. You will find the letters at the top and bottom of the map and the numbers at the sides.

The map continues on map 5 of the *Street Finder*.

KEY TO STREET FINDER

■	Major sight
■	Minor sight
■	Station building
M	CTA train station
■	Metra train station
P	Parking
i	Tourist information
✚	Hospital with emergency room
■	Police station
✝	Church
✡	Synagogue
■	Buddhist temple
⊠	Post office
≡	Railroad line

SCALE OF MAPS 1–6
0 meters	500
0 yards	500

SCALE OF MAPS 7 & 8
0 meters	500
0 yards	500

0 kilometers	2
0 miles	1

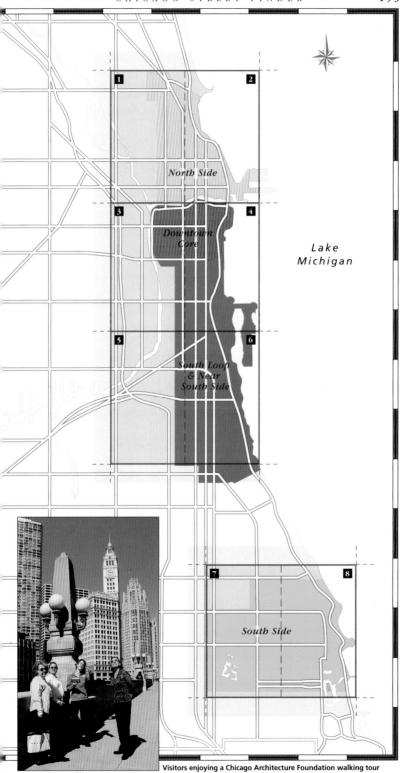

1

2

North Side

3

4

Downtown Core

Lake Michigan

5

6

South Loop & Near South Side

7

8

South Side

Visitors enjoying a Chicago Architecture Foundation walking tour

Street Finder Index

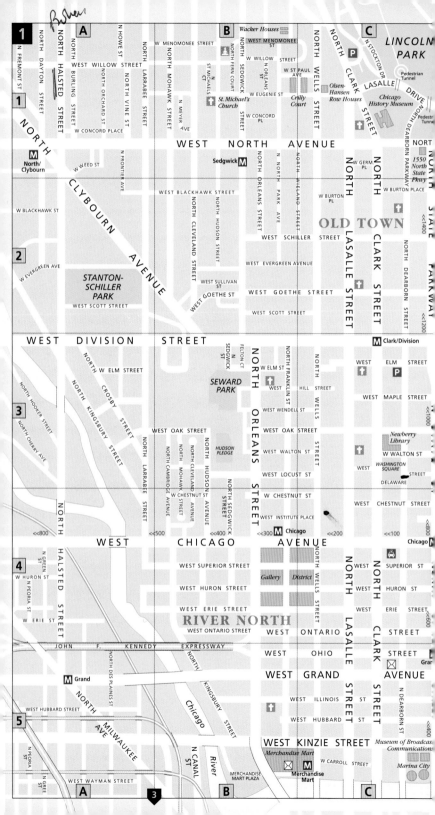

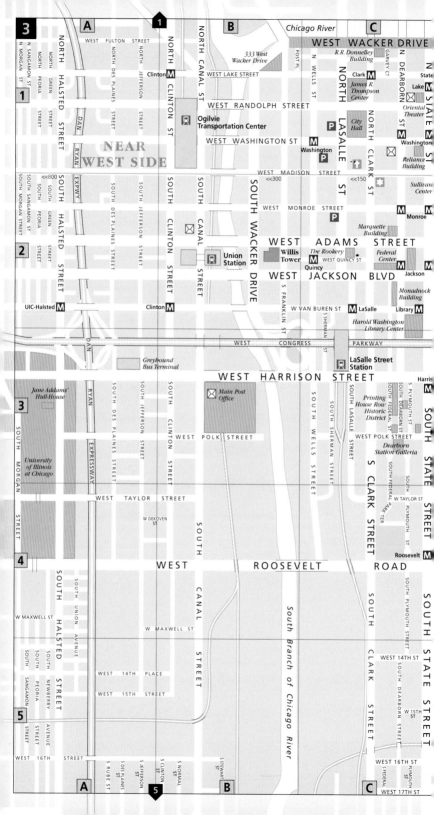

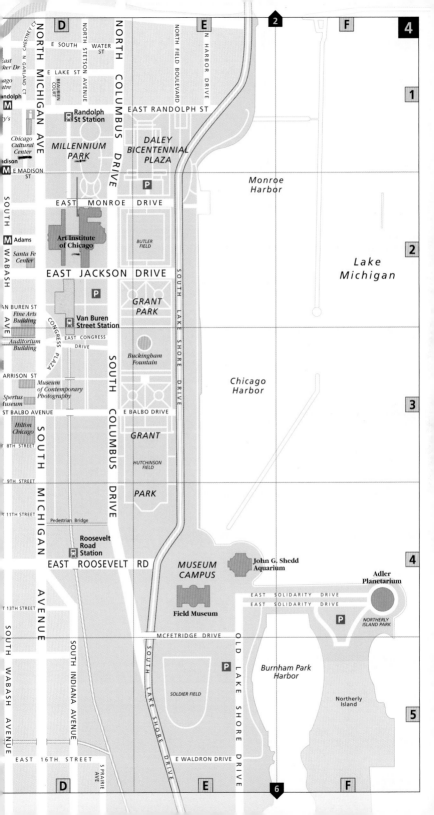

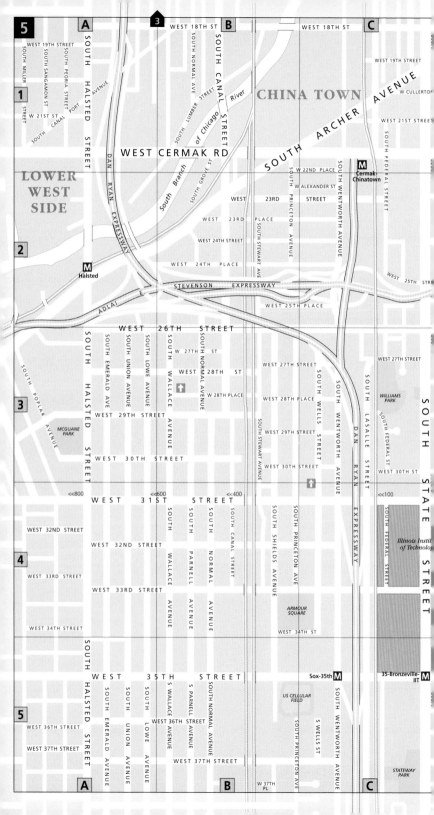

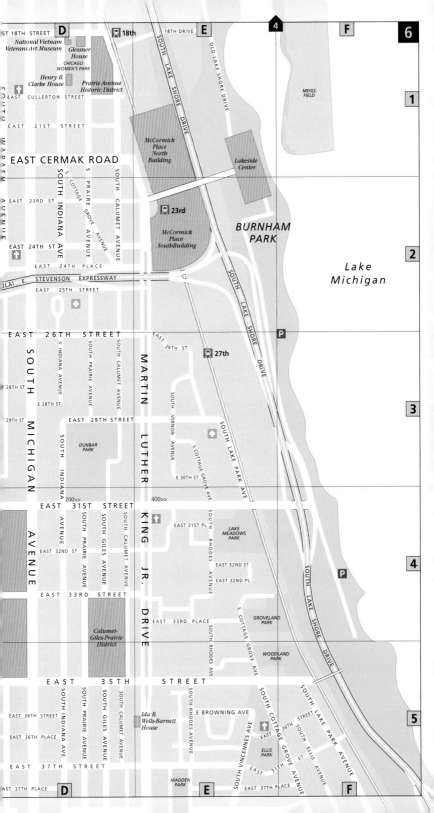

47th

AST 47TH STREET

S KENWOOD

E 47TH PL

SOUTH KIMBARK AVENUE

SOUTH KENWOOD AVENUE

SOUTH DORCHESTER AVENUE

SOUTH LAKE PARK AVENUE

SOUTH CORNELL AVENUE

SOUTH LAKE SHORE DRIVE

Lake Michigan **1**

AST 48TH STREET

CHICAGO BEACH DRIVE

EAST 49TH ST

KENWOOD PARK

CORNELL AVE

AST 50TH STREET

EAST 50TH STREET

E END AVE

T MADISON PARK AVE

E 50TH PL

1400>>

EAST HYDE PARK BOULEVARD **2**

BURNHAM PARK

SOUTH KENWOOD AVE

SOUTH DORCHESTER AVENUE

SOUTH BLACKSTONE AVE

SOUTH HARPER

SOUTH LAKE PARK AVENUE

SOUTH

LM LAYLOT ARK

EAST 52ND STREET

ST 53RD STREET

53rd EAST 53RD STREET

NICHOLS PARK

SPRUCE PLAYLOT PARK

AVENUE

SOUTH CORNELL AVENUE

HYDE PARK BOULEVARD

SOUTH SHORE DRIVE

SOUTH EVERETT AVENUE **3**

EAST 55TH PL

EAST 55TH STREET

HYDE PARK

SOUTH LAKE PARK AVENUE

P

EAST 56TH STREET

55th-56th-57th

SOUTH KIMBARK AVE

EAST 57TH STREET

EAST 57TH DRIVE

P

Museum of Science and Industry

SOUTH KENWOOD AVENUE

SOUTH DORCHESTER AVENUE

SOUTH BLACKSTONE AVENUE

SOUTH HARPER AVENUE

SOUTH STONY ISLAND AVENUE

P **P**

SOUTH LAKE SHORE DRIVE **4**

bie ouse

P

EAST 59TH STREET **59th**

EAST 60TH STREET

SOUTH DORCHESTER AVE

SOUTH HARPER AVE

S STONY ISLAND AVE

SOUTH CORNELL DRIVE

West Lagoon

JACKSON PARK **5**

S KENWOOD AVE

S KIMBARK

EAST 61ST ST

East Lagoon

General Index

Acknowledgments

Dorling Kindersley and International Book
Productions would like to thank the following
people whose contributions and assistance have
made the book possible:

At Dorling Kindersley:
Managing Art Editor: Jane Ewart
Managing Editor: Helen Townsend
Senior Publishing Manager: Louise Lang
Production Controllers: Marie Ingledew,
Michelle Thomas
Cartographers: Casper Morris, Dave Pugh

Main Contributors
Lorraine Johnson is a freelance writer living
in Toronto who has a lifelong fascination with
Chicago. She is the author of six books and
contributes articles and book reviews regularly to
magazines and newspapers.

John Ryan lives in Chicago. A professional musician
and former chef, he manages the Elgin Symphony
Orchestra in addition to writing regular food columns
for America Online.

Additional Contributors
J.P. Anderson, Penney Kome

Special Research
Dana Joy Altman
Deanna Cates

Proofreader
Maraya Raduha

Indexer
Barbara Sale Schon

Cartography
Visutronx, Ajax, Ontario, Canada

Design and Editorial Assistance
Emma Anacootee, Sherry Collins, Conrad van Dyk,
Karen Fitzpatrick, Jacky Jackson, Laura Jones,
Sam Merrell, Catherine Palmi, Rada Radojicic,
Brett Steel, Lauren Viera, Ros Walford.

Additional Picture Research
Rachel Barber, Rhiannon Furbear, Ellen Root

Special Assistance
Particular thanks go to Vanetta Anderson, Chicago
Office of Tourism; Norah Zboril, City of Chicago,
Mayor's Office, Special Events; Daniel J. Curtin, City of
Chicago, Department of Aviation; Jeff Stern, Chicago
Transit Authority; Diana Holic and Dawn Kappel,
Adler Planetarium and Astronomy Museum; Brigid
Murphy, Newberry Library; Mily Anzo, Museum of
Science and Industry; Patricia Kremer, Field Museum;
Corey Tovian and Gwen Biassi, John G. Shedd
Aquarium; Rosemary Haack, City of Lake Forest;
Janice Klein, Mitchell Museum of the American
Indian; Ms. Chase Ruppert, McCormick Place
Convention Center; Stephen Majsak, Chicago
Architectural Foundation; Lois Berger, Chicago Public
Library, Harold Washington Library Center; Jennifer
Swanson, Lincoln Park Zoo; Adam Davies, Chicago
Place; Angela Sweeney, Water Tower Place; Kelly
Boggs and Michael Rilley, Chicago Theatre; Sarah
Hamilton Hadley, Terra Museum of American Art;

Karen Irvine, Museum of Contemporary Photography;
Zarine Weil, Robie House; Ken Price, Palmer House
Hilton Hotel; Michilla Johnson, Buddy Guy's Legends
Jennifer Kocolowski, Goose Island Beer Co.;
Jan Berghoff, 17/West; Janet Femarek and David
Caruso, Ed Debevic's Restaurant

Photography Permission
Dorling Kindersley and International Book
Productions would like to thank everyone for
their assistance and kind permission to photograph
at their establishments.

Picture Credits
KEY: t=top; tl=top left; tlc-top left center; tc=top
center; trc=top right center; tr=top right; cla=center
left above; ca=center above; cra=center right above;
cl=center left; c=center; cr=center right; clb=center
left below; cb=center below; crb=center right below;
bl=bottom left; b=bottom; br=bottom right;
bcl=bottom center left; bc=bottom center;
bcr=bottom center right.

Works of art have been reproduced with the
permission of the following copyright holders:

© ADAGP, Paris and DACS, London 2006: 124bl,
© ARS, NY and DACS, London 2006: 85cl; ©
Succession Miro/ADAGP, Paris and DACS, London
2006: 124tr; The work illustrated on page 2–3 has
been reproduced by permission of the Henry Moore
Foundation *Sundial Sculpture* 1965-6 Henry Moore
2–3 and on page 103 *Nuclear Energy* Henry Moore
103tc; © Sucession Picasso/DACS, London: 39tc; ©
Estate of Grant Wood/DACS, London/VAGA, New
York 2006: 47ca.

Every effort has been made to trace the copyright
holders. Dorling Kindersley apologizes for any
unintentional omissions and would be pleased, in
such cases, to add an acknowledgment in future
editions.

The Publishers are grateful to the following
museums, companies, and picture libraries for
permission to reproduce their photographs:

© ADLER PLANETARIUM AND ASTRONOMY MUSEUM: 21bl,
92tr, 93tc, 93cr; Craig Stillwell 11br.
ALAMY IMAGES: Edward Hattersley 19crb; John
Henshall 10cl; Andre Jenny 121tl; Kim Karpeles 10tc,
11tc, 122cl, 123crb; Linda Matlow 11cl, 122tr.
THE ART INSTITUTE OF CHICAGO: All rights reserved –
Mary Cassatt, American, 1844–1926, *The Child's
Bath*, oil on canvas, 1893, 39 1/2 x 26 inches, Robert
A. Waller Fund, 1910.2 – 47tl; India, Andhra Pradesh,
Madanapalle. *The Divine General Karttikeya/
Shanmukha*, Ganga Period, 12th century. Granite.
Restricted Gift of Mr. and Mrs. Sylvain S. Wyler
1962.203 46 tr ; Nepal, Kathmandu Valley, *God Indra*,
16th century, Gilt bronze with gemstones. The James
W. and Marilynn Alsdorf Collection 173.1997 46cb;
Rembrandt Harmenszoon van Rijn, Dutch, 1606–1669,
Old Man with a Gold Chain, oil on panel, c.1631,
83.1 x 75.7 cm, Mr. and Mrs. W.W. Kimball
Collection, 1922.4467 – 47bc; Charles Percier and
Alexandre Theodore Brogniart Londonderry Vase,
Sevres Manufacture, 1813, hard-paste porcelain with
polychrome enamel decoration gilding and ormolu

mounts, height: 137 cm, Harry and Maribel Blum Foundation Fund and the Harold L. Stewart Fund, 1987 49cl.

THE CANADIAN PRESS/ASSOCIATED PRESS AP: 31ca; AP/Wide World Photos Inc. Charles Bennett 178bl. CHICAGO ARCHITECTURE FOUNDATION: Bill Richert 176br, 185bl. CHICAGO HISTORICAL MUSEUM: 74bl; ICHi-2212 – 8–9; ICHi-08732 – 15bl; ICHi-30084 – 17cb; ICHi-31412 – 19tl; ICHi-31413 – 31tr; ICHi-31411 – 71br; ICHi-09440 – 72cla; ICHi-31414 – 72c; ICHi-14063 Currier & Ives 14crb; ICHi-05630 Inger & Bodtker 175 (inset); ICHi-10889 Edward Kemeys 15c; ICHi-05769 Louis Kurz 9 (inset), 37 (inset); ICHi-05836 Leslie's Weekly 17bc; ICHi-06291 Scribner's Magazine 137 (inset); ICHi-13946 US Treasury Department 127 (inset); ICHi-27363 Paris Raoul Varin 15bc. CHICAGO PARK DISTRICT: Brook Collins 122bl CHICAGO PUBLIC LIBRARY, HAROLD WASHINGTON LIBRARY CENTER: 82tl; *Events in the Life of Harold Washington* ceramic tile mosaic by Jacob Lawrence 24br; *Sleeping Beauty* sculpture by Alison Saar 80tr. CHICAGO READER: 168cla. CHICAGO TRANSIT AUTHORITY: 190c. CITY OF CHICAGO, DEPARTMENT OF AVIATION: 18cb, 185tr. CITY OF CHICAGO, OFFICE OF TOURISM: © Willy Schmidt 35bl, 60bc; © Peter J. Schultz 21tr, 33br, 180bl; Chicago Air and Water Show 33cr. COLUMBUS ASSOCIATION FOR THE PERFORMING ARTS: 54b. CORBIS: © Corbis 18cra, 109cra; © Sandy Felsenthal 28cl, 32cl; © Mitchell Gerber 30br; © Robert Holmes 48br; © Layne Kennedy 48cl; © Francis G. Mayer, *The Basket of Apples* by Paul Cézanne 49tr, *On the Seine at Bennecourt* by Claude Monet 49br; © Derick A. Thomas, Dat's Jazz 30tr; © AFP/Corbis 31clb; © Bettmann/Corbis 17tl, 29cla, 30cl, 31bc, *A Sunday on La Grande Jatte* by Georges Seurat 47cr, *American Gothic* by Grant Wood, Friends of the American Art Collection. All rights reserved by the Art Institue of Chicago 47tr, 77br; © Hulton-Deutsch Collection/ Corbis 18tl; © UPI/Corbis-Bettmann 18bc. COURTESY OF CHICAGO DEPARTMENT OF CULTURAL AFFAIRS: Chicago Photographic Department 22cr, 41br. CRAIN'S CHICAGO BUSINESS: 177tl.

THE DAVID AND ALFRED SMART MUSEUM OF ART, THE UNIVERSITY OF CHICAGO: reproduced with permission 101tc; University Transfer – Dining Table and Six Side Chairs, Frank Lloyd Wright 102cr. JOEFF DAVIS: 28bc, 120tc, 121tr, 123tc, 187bl; Mathew Cassel 178tr

FIELD MUSEUM: Courtesy of the Field Museum, 86cl, 87t, 87cb, 89bl; John Weinstein © 1998 – 23ca; George Papadakis © 1998 – 86tr; 87ca, 87crb. FLICKR.COM: www.flickr.com/photos/solarwind-chicago/3605736668/ 77cr.

GOOSE ISLAND BEER COMPANY: © Daniel J. Wigg 151br. THE GRANGER COLLECTION, NEW YORK: 14. COURTESY OF HERSHEY'S CHICAGO: 63tl.

INTERNATIONAL MUSEUM OF SURGICAL SCIENCE, CHICAGO: 22clb; *Hope and Help* sculpture by Edouard Chaissing reproduced with permission 75c.

JANE ADDAMS' HULL-HOUSE: Jane Addams' Hull-House Museum, University of Illinois at Chicago 116tl. JOHN G. SHEDD AQUARIUM: 97c; © Edward G. Lines 96tr, 96cl, 96bc, 97tl, 97b, 97cb, 97tc. JP MORGAN CHASE & CO: 180cla.

KIMPTON GROUP: 138cl, 139tl, 139bc; LINCOLN PARK ZOO, CHICAGO: 113t, 113cb; © Grant Kessler 21crb; Greg Neise 120bl.

MCCORMICK PLACE CONVENTION CENTER: 187bl. MILLENNIUM PARK PROJECT: Skidmore, Owings & Merrill LLP 53t. MITCHELL MUSEUM OF THE AMERICAN INDIAN: 131tl. MUSEUM OF CONTEMPORARY PHOTOGRAPHY, COLUMBIA COLLEGE CHICAGO: Tom Nowak 81tl, 84tr. MUSEUM OF SCIENCE AND INDUSTRY: 106tr; © 2000 Dirk Fletcher 23br, 107tl, 108bl, 109tl; J.B. Spector 106cl, 107cb.

THE NEWBERRY LIBRARY: 67br.

PALMER HOUSE HILTON HOTEL: 5tr, 138br. PHOTOSHOT/WORLD PICTURES: 121bl. PICTURES COLOUR LIBRARY: Clive Sawyer 10br.

SPERTUS MUSEUM (SPERTUS INSTITUTE OF JEWISH STUDIES): 22br; *Eternal Light* by Fredrich Adler 84cl; *Flame of Hope* by Leonardo Nierman, 1995. Collection of Spertus Museum 81tc. STREETWISE: 177tc.

COURTESY OF WATER TOWER PLACE: 163tl; Solari Photography 61t. FRANK LLOYD WRIGHT HOME AND STUDIO FOUNDATION: Courtesy of Henrich Blessing and the Frank Lloyd Wright Home and Studio Foundation, 25br. WRIGLEY BUILDING: The Wrigley Building and design are registered trademarks of the Wm. Wrigley Jr. Company, used by permission 60br, 62tl.

VENUS RESTAURANT: 151tl.

JACKET Front – DK IMAGES: Andrew Leyerle clb; PHOTOLIBRARY: Index Stock Imagery/Alyx Kellington. Back – DK IMAGES: Andrew Leyerle bl, cla, clb, tl. Spine – DK IMAGES: Andrew Leyerle b; Photolibrary: Alyx Kellington t.

All other images © Dorling Kindersley. See www.DKimages.com for more information.

SPECIAL EDITIONS OF DK TRAVEL GUIDES

DK Travel Guides can be purchased in bulk quantities at discounted prices for use in promotions or as premiums. We are also able to offer special editions and personalized jackets, corporate imprints, and excerpts from all of our books, tailored specifically to meet your own needs.

To find out more, please contact: (in the United States) **SpecialSales@dk.com** (in the UK) **TravelSpecialSales@uk.dk.com** (in Canada) DK Special Sales at **general@tourmaline.ca** (in Australia) **business.development@pearson.com.au**

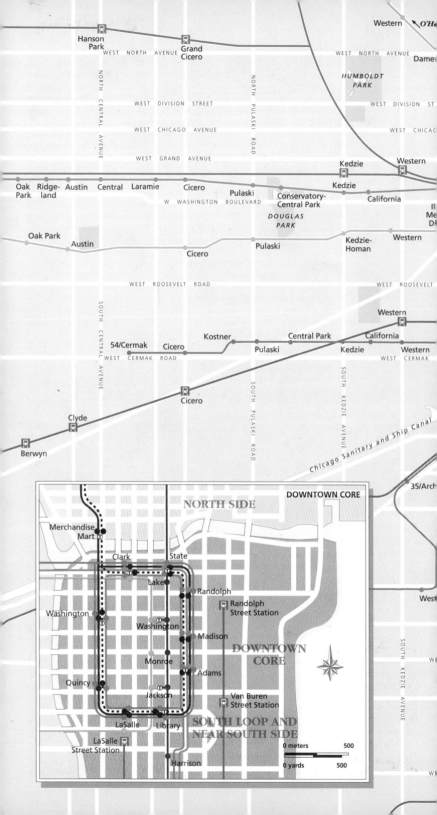